Him Off The Viz

This book is dedicated to my Mum and Dad
Also to my dear brother Steve
It breaks my heart that they aren't here to read it
RIP

Him Off The Viz

Simon Donald

tontobooks

www.tontobooks.co.uk

First published in 20010 by Tonto Books Limited
Copyright © Simon Donald 2010

1

ISBN-13:
9781907183119

British Library Cataloguing in Publication Data:
A catalogue record for this book is available from the British
Library

Cover design and photo section by Simon Donald

Printed & bound in Great Britain
by CPI Mackays

Tonto Books Ltd
Produced Up North
United Kingdom

www.tontobooks.co.uk

Contents

Foreword

In the north east of England football, in particular, has been the entertainment and sport of the masses for the past century and a half.

Arriving in the early 1970s as Newcastle United's new, and rather expensive, centre forward, I was quickly taken to the hearts of the warm Geordie people of Tyneside. I would arrive at St James' Park a little over an hour before kick-off and, as my car pulled into the parking space, a mêlée of kids would engulf me, thrusting scraps of paper or bus tickets at me and demanding my autograph.

One of those kids stood out. He was one with an autograph book, open to a specific page, and held at a particular angle so my signature was just so. He was the one that was organised, who knew just how to get things done, and the next time I met him he was all grown up. It was in the green room at Tyne Tees Television, where I was a panel guest on his show *The Regionnaires*.

In between these two meetings, each of us had experienced a complete career or three, notwithstanding my football management and, of course, *Viz*, the adult comic that transformed comic thinking throughout the world of entertainment and, indeed, the entertainment of the world.

It was my sixtieth birthday in January 2010 and the radio station for which I broadcast daily put on a wonderful bash, inviting lots of people I have known down the years. Simon was there and stood and spoke so kindly of his fond childhood memories of me, which made my mind drift back to St James' Park in the bleak 1970s.

So, the moral of this foreword is, be kind to those brats with autograph books. You never know when they'll be invited to speak about you!

Malcolm MacDonald
September 2010

Introduction

I've never been good with formal introductions, but here goes. Reader, meet my book. Book, meet my reader.

As I write I sit in my rather unimpressive accommodation at the Edinburgh Fringe 2010, the weather is grim, the view from my window is grey, but I find myself in a strangely satisfying situation.

I've spent the last two years or so writing the story of my life so far. My original plan was to release my autobiography to coincide with the thirtieth anniversary of *Viz* comic, in December 2009. I could never have predicted that during the time I've spent on the book I would face not one but three life-changing situations. This combination of tragic and challenging events delayed the book by over a year and became an integral part of its contents.

I had feared that to catalogue my entire life to date would be a challenging process in itself, as in it, as you will read, I've had my fair share of hurdles to get over. When reflecting initially on my past I envisaged difficulties in the writing process caused by problems now long since resolved, yet still prominent, dark and potentially depressing in my memory. However, I was to find the writing process actually revealed to me the extent to which my life has been a success, and opened my eyes to all of the positives on which I had never previously focused enough attention. This book's creation has most definitely changed the way I see my life for the better, although, as you will find, at the moment I learned to see how good my life is, the shit really hit the fan.

My greatest worry presenting this work to the reader is not that my life may not be of interest. On the contrary, there's plenty that I hope will appeal to the autobiography lover: genuine highs and lows, tragedy, love and loss and a backbone of anecdotes that need no exaggeration or embellishment to entertain.

My underlying worry is that I am exposing myself as a writer of limited education with almost no experience of reading books, let alone authoring one. At primary school I was one of the brighter children, although my reports always reflected slow progress with written work. By the time I reached secondary school I had achieved seven As in my first report. However, within one year I had become disruptive through frustration, my reports now cataloguing a drastic fall from grace centring on my 'laziness' around reading and writing. I achieved only two O levels and left school at sixteen.

At the age of forty, on my own initiative, I sat a series of tests for dyslexia. The results stunned me: a writing speed two thirds that of an eighteen year old and a reading speed so slow that in the comprehension test the allotted time lapsed and I had to complete the work on honesty basis at home. The comprehension results put me in the lowest bracket for time to complete the test but in the highest for understanding written English.

Although this explained to me so many of the problems I've faced over the years with reading and writing, most notably in school, the true benefit of these tests came when I was given a visual test involving reading through coloured filters. When an orange overlay was placed over a block of text, next to an identical block that wasn't covered, I nearly fell off my seat. The text instantly lay down flat and square. If you don't suffer from this particular visual condition it must be very difficult to understand that I had never previously seen text in the same way that other people do. My brain fails to make an accurate picture, which I've heard equated to 'undulation' or 'movement' of the text. Although I don't think this is a particularly accurate description, I am at a loss to provide one myself, suffice to say if I look through an orange filter it's a hell of a lot easier for me to read.

I was prescribed with special spectacles that come with a card declaring that the user suffers from 'specific learning difficulties' and should be allowed to wear them at all times. I'm not at liberty to describe myself as dyslexic, as I haven't yet taken the second part of the test, which requires seeing a psychologist. I don't really know if there would be any specific benefits to this, as I've already got a lot of benefits simply from realising that my brain works differently when it comes to reading and writing and that things hadn't been figments of my imagination.

Even with my special glasses reading is still something for which I have no time. It's difficult and unpleasant for me. However, since the tests I have confidence that I'm not lazy, a stigma I'd carried ever since school.

I've taken to buying audio books, and I absolutely love them, and whilst writing this book I've listened to many autobiographies, the cream of which I have found inspirational.

'So how have you written this book, then, you big daft knacker?' I hear some of you ask. Well, I've done that using twenty-first-century magic: audio recognition software. What you are reading is what I have spoken into a microphone, my computer then writing it out before my eyes. It really is quite amazing. It is not flawless, and some of the mistakes it can make can be quite embarrassing.

I wrote a piece for my blog on my website in which I said to the machine, 'Richard Herring's material on racism was some of the best and most thought provoking I've heard in thirty years.'

Unfortunately the software interpreted this as, 'Richard Herring's material *and* racism was some of the best and most thought provoking I've heard in thirty years.'

I published it on my site, only to spot the error myself minutes later.

About half of the book has been written using the MacSpeech Dictate programme; the rest I have keyed in by hand, something at which I have got much better since devoting so much time to the project.

Some people are absolutely fascinated at the idea that I have never really read any books. I am commonly asked how I can have accumulated knowledge without reading. I invariably find myself explaining that there are many other sources of knowledge, in particular for me, television. Educated people are often taken aback at the idea that I could have learned almost everything I know from television; however, I assure them, as I assure you now, if you watch the right programmes you can learn an awful lot. The other side of that coin is, of course, that if you choose the wrong programmes you could well lose the will to live.

My Dad too, despite being a historian of some renown, was limited in his writing ability. He read constantly, but rarely attempted joined-up handwriting, mainly scribbling notes in untidy block capitals. I'm sure his lack of confidence in his writing may have resulted in him not committing more of his knowledge to paper. However, his photographic work led to a series of books on the history of Newcastle upon Tyne.

My book was originally to be called *Are You My Neighbour's Milk Man?* The idea behind this comes from my many appearances as a pundit, or 'talking head', on the list programmes started by the BBC's *I Love the 1970s* series, a format later hijacked by all the other stations and completely done to death in recent years. The net result of my appearing on so many of these shows is that people often know my face but don't know where they've seen it. Many people think they know me as a friend of a friend. Only last night I was asked by a musician which band I play in. The funniest incident of this type I remember was a lady asking me, 'Are you my neighbour's milkman?'

I replied politely, 'I'm not, no. I get this a lot: my face is on TV as a pundit, but rarely talking about my own work. Do you think that's it? Perhaps you've seen me on TV?'

'No, that's not it. It's definitely not TV. Where do I know you from?'

'I guess I am your neighbour's milkman, then.'

She walked away, satisfied.

I think this is a vaguely amusing story, but the trouble with using it as a book title is that it requires lengthy explanation, so I went with the most common thing that's said to me when people finally realise where they know my face from: 'Eeee! It's him off the *Viz*!'

This also pays homage to the turns of phrase we always used in the comic, such as 'Mick Hucknall out of Simply Red' and 'John Craven off John Craven's *Newsround*'.

Reflecting on what I've written, I think my life story deserves more about my relationships, but sadly due to the prolonged deterioration and final collapse of the longest relationship I've had in my life, which took place during the writing of the book, I really steered away from discussing such personal matters. I feel this is a shame, as the good times are not really given the coverage they deserve.

Likewise, music gets far less coverage than it really should, as it's always been a great love of mine. My intention was initially to write sections on different subjects rather than to run through my life chronologically. The section on music was never fully developed. Parts of it appear, but much remains as unfinished notes telling some lovely stories. Maybe there's another book in all that somewhere down the line.

To sum up my reflections on this project, I've seen my life in a better light, and I've been quite humbled by the people who've stepped up to pay compliments about my work. I really struggle to express how much it means to me to have the likes of Stewart Lee, Vic Reeves and Michael Palin say such kind words, Michael in particular. As I sit here and write I can see myself in my mind's eye as a young boy, absorbing *Monty Python* like a sponge, idolising its creators. I made *him* laugh. That means so much.

Terry Jones was kind enough to write a foreword to *Viz*'s *Profanisaurus*, so I've possibly impressed more than one Python. I also saw Terry Gilliam on Highgate High Street once, but maybe that doesn't count.

I read a lot of nice words written around the time of *Viz*'s thirtieth anniversary, and remember in particular a piece in the brochure for the anniversary exhibition in London. I sat on the tube home reading it and saw a quote that woke me from the slumber of nonchalance I'd slipped into at some point in the late 1980s, when the sales figures and compliments were bombarding us at a numbing pace. It said, '*Viz* re-invented the Great British sense of humour.'

I don't know if that's true or not, but just the fact that someone said it is significant. It feels nice to have been involved in something so noteworthy.

I think as a marker of my own achievement I would single out one very special moment in my life. When Spike Milligan died, Channel 4 News spoke live to two people about his impact on British comedy: Nicholas Parsons and me. It's simply too much to contemplate, looking back at the creation of our little comic in the bedroom where we used to play with our train set and Matchbox cars, thinking that we made something there so big that it led to me representing the world of modern comedy when the man who introduced me to silliness passed away. It was an honour to say a few words.

Parsons, his face alongside mine on a split screen, as we were in different cities, tried to address the innocence of Spike's humour: 'You know, Spike loved to touch children.'

I failed to contain a childish splutter, but I knew Spike was looking down and laughing.

So, dear reader, I hope you enjoy my story. It's bound to have inaccuracies, omissions and some boring bits that are only of interest to the sort of people who like that kind of thing. If you don't like this book, refunds are not available.

As well as the three dedications I've made to my family, this book is for all the people who feature in its pages but who are no longer with us.

Simon Donald
Edinburgh, August 2010

I

Congratulations!
A Bouncing Baby Foulmouth

The trouble with telling my life story in a comedy-knockabout fashion is that it gets off to a pretty unfunny start. It doesn't really matter how I look at the events of my arrival – I just can't dress it up for humour. I guess the old adage 'you just can't polish a turd' fits.

I was born on 19 March 1964 in the back bedroom of 20 Sunbury Avenue, a red-brick terraced house in Newcastle upon Tyne. It was a tidy Victorian street with a cinema, a pub and a commuter railway station at one end and a library at the other. It was very English, very suburban.

Sadly, my advent was to have awful consequences for the happy family into which I arrived that night. My birth appears to have caused my mother to suffer an episode of what was later diagnosed as multiple sclerosis, from which she would never fully recover. She never walked unaided again; she was never able to carry me; she was never able to take me out anywhere without the help of others. The condition is incurable and her health was to worsen steadily from that day on.

Many people with tough lives have had a moment that changed their lives for the worse. I didn't have a moment that changed *my* life for the worse so much as the beginning of my life changed everyone else's for the worse. That's been quite a lot to deal with.

Heavy? Don't worry. Plenty of toilet jokes later on.

The Donald family comprised of, firstly, Mum, born Kathleen Evelyn Rickard, known as Kay. One of four sisters from Jesmond, the neighbourhood where we lived, she had grown up only a few streets away. Her parents still lived in the family house on Lily Crescent, which would later play a great role in my life story. Mum had been a display artist for Fenwick of Newcastle – a large department store – a job of which she was rightly proud. She'd given up work to start our family, but continued to utilise her artistic skills by making wooden and soft toys. She walked with the aid of two sticks and drove a Thundersley Invacar, a three-wheel invalid carriage provided by the government to those with disabilities in the 1960s.

Dad, Hugh Ernest James, known as Ernie when he was younger, later as Jimmy, was older than his two sisters and came from Shieldfield in Newcastle. He had worked as a salesman for Ever Ready batteries, but was now selling heating oils, notably Esso Blue paraffin, famed for its 'Boom-boom-boom-boom, Esso Blue!' advertising campaigns. His first job was as a horse-drawn milkman, and as his name was Ernie at the time I was later to enjoy greatly Benny Hill's hit single 'Ernie, the Fastest Milkman in the West', although I was disappointed to hear Dad's horse wasn't called Trigger. Dad's real love in life was local history and he would go on to be one of the leading authorities on the history of Newcastle. He drove a company car, a Tweed Grey Morris 1100 with red vinyl seats.

My eldest brother, Stephen James, later known as Steve, was six years my senior and was an exceptional child. His behaviour was often difficult, but he was extremely intelligent and very imaginative. The middle child was Christopher Mark, known as Chris, four years my senior: he was a very shy boy.

Jesmond is a leafy, well-to-do, cosmopolitan suburb. It has a range of housing from the terraced Victorian 'Tyneside' flats to mansions you'd need a mortgage just to look at. It's a lovely place. When I was small it was the haunt of not only old-school middle-class and upper-middle-class families, but the more modest streets where we first lived were populated by the aspirational working class and the poorer middle class. Those streets where I grew up are nowadays sadly predominantly occupied by loudmouthed middle-class student arseholes.

My Dad was one of the aspirational working class, but he probably considered himself a cut above those in the surrounding streets, as Sunbury Avenue was the only terrace in West Jesmond in which the properties were houses as opposed to flats. Plus he'd bagged himself the ultimate goal for a working-class social climber – a middle-class wife.

My mother wasn't just beautiful and from a good family, but she was also a very talented woman. Not a bad result when you've grown up in a tenement, later demolished as a slum, with four families sharing a communal standpipe for water.

Andy Pandy, Dickie Donald and the man on the moon

My early memories are all quite happy. My first recollection is sitting listening to The Beatles' 'Yellow Submarine' on the radio as I sat on the mat in the back kitchen while Mum cooked flapjacks. The room was a traditional cooking-and-eating space with an open fire, in front of which was a woven plastic mat in black, yellow and red. My Mum's nutty flapjacks were my favourite thing in the world. Mysteriously, they didn't contain any nuts. I later sat on the same mat feeling ill whilst my brothers watched the last-ever episode of *Bleep and Booster* on *Blue Peter* in the front room, and I was very upset about missing it. This happened during one of the rare periods in my early life when we had a TV set.

After Mum took ill Dad had taken a job that didn't pay as well as his previous one in order that he could be at home every night. The result was that we lived a little bit beyond our means, in a nice neighbourhood, but leading a comparatively frugal existence.

In order to see the essential 1960s children's daytime slot *Watch with Mother* I would be taken across the street to number 27. I would sit on the floor with Claire and Andy Storey and watch *Andy Pandy*, *The Woodentops* and *Bill and Ben*. Dad later told me that at around the same time I watched the 1966 World Cup final in a TV shop window in the Grainger Market from my pushchair. I have no recollection of this, but it does make a great story. Unfortunately, I can never tell it without coming clean about not remembering it at all.

3

A less happy memory is riding my metal Tri-ang tricycle on the cobbles in the back lane. The cobbles were about to be covered over with tarmac and huge piles of gravel had been dumped. Owain Harris, our next-door neighbour, who was a couple of years older than me, decided to give me a push. He pushed very hard and the trike started going faster than I was happy with ... I was heading straight for a mountain of dark grey gravel. Owain, oblivious, continued to push me as fast as he could. The front wheel piled straight into the gravel and I went over the handlebars. My face was plunged into the pile of sharp little stones.

Once I'd run screaming into the house, in fine 1960s fashion all the medical attention I would receive was given to me in the back kitchen by Mum and Dad. The gravel was picked out of my wounds with tweezers, I was dabbed with surgical spirit and returned outside to play. I still see the scars on my forehead and under my eyebrow every time I look in the mirror.

Owain's granddad was the bloke who used to flip the pancakes on *Blue Peter* on Shrove Tuesday, although this fact is not relevant to the trike incident.

Steve stayed up all night to watch the moon landing. Chris and I were woken by our parents to see the monumental moment. All I really remember about it was the seemingly endless footage of craters passing by as the astronauts looked for somewhere to land the craft. During a later moon mission I tried looking at the moon to see if I could see the men on it, but alas I couldn't.

Mum had a budgie called Dickie who lived in the back room. He could say his own name and address: 'Dickie Donald. Dickie Donald ... 20 Sunbury Avenue.'

He could also repeat anything he heard regularly enough, so took to saying 'Hurry up, Stephen ... Hurry up, Stephen ...'

One day I came downstairs and Dickie wasn't in his cage. Dad told me that he'd gone to live in Pets' Corner in Jesmond Dene. From then on, every Sunday we would take our usual walk in the Dene and stop at the aviary. I would look hard and long for Dickie but could never see him amongst the dozens of colourful birds buzzing around inside. My Dad could always find him and would quickly point him out. However, I could never follow his finger in time and the elusive Dickie was gone before I could see him.

I was telling this story to some friends a couple of years ago and they all began to laugh at me. Forty years on, the penny dropped. Dickie hadn't gone to the Dene at all. He'd gone to Budgie Heaven.

I don't remember the house at Sunbury Avenue too well beyond these few stories, although the smell of the cast-iron paraffin heater, the only source of heat in the bathroom, will live with me forever.

Like Steve and Chris, I attended Mrs Glover's nursery school on Sanderson Road, in the downstairs back room of Mr and Mrs Glover's house. In the garden one sunny day there was a terrifying sudden white explosion on my arm. Traumatised, I cried my eyes out. Mrs Glover wiped the mess from my arm with a handkerchief, saying, 'It's just a bird's bibbit, dear.'

I was also traumatised at Mrs Glover's when we had a 'show and tell'. I was allowed to take in Chris's snow globe, his pride and joy, to show everyone. The big moment came and Mrs Glover shook the globe in order to agitate the snow. As she did so, it slipped from her hand and smashed into pieces on the floor. Once again, I was inconsolable, convinced I was somehow to blame and terrified of the consequences. When Dad arrived to collect me, to my complete surprise, Mrs Glover came clean and to my great relief I was in the clear.

At a certain point during the day at Mrs Glover's we would have milk. This was a treat at the time, but was superseded when we took part in some research at Newcastle University. All of the day's nursery attendees crammed into her Old English White Morris 1100 with black vinyl seats for the mile or so drive. Quite what we had to do I don't remember, but it involved drawing on the back of 'computer paper', scrap paper produced by print-outs from the university's cathedral-sized computers. At break time we were given orange juice and Digestives. This was luxury beyond belief. I'd never had either of these things before and they were both *amazing*.

Dad would take us to Jesmond Pool on Saturday mornings. The pool was on the next street to us, in a red-brick building with tall frosted windows, standing between streets of terraced flats. I was content to sit in the footbath and splash around while Dad taught my brothers to swim. Soon a brand-new pool opened in Gosforth and Saturday mornings got a lot more exciting. Now a short car journey would take us to Gosforth Baths, which had a special shallow pool for small children. I was soon learning to swim. This new facility had the state-of-the-art coloured changing basket system, with corresponding wristbands, flashing lights and klaxons when your time was up. We always tried to stay in as long as possible and were often whistled at by an attendant for overstaying our welcome. Dad would allow us to have hot chocolate from the vending machine after our swim. Halcyon days.

Gallowgate, *Green Eggs and Ham* and Sugar Puffs

Mum and Dad had friends called the O'Sullivans. I think Mr O'Sullivan was studying at the university as a mature student, possibly medicine. They lived in the university's married accommodation, which at the time was in the beautiful Georgian sandstone buildings on Leazes Terrace, right next to the football ground. At the time St James' Park was still all terraced, except for the wooden west stand, which had seating in the upper tier. The O'Sullivan sitting room window directly overlooked St James' Park, giving an almost perfect view of the playing surface – only the north-east corner was obscured by the roof over the Leazes End terrace.

Dad asked me if we wanted to go and see a game from the O'Sullivans' window. We'd visited their flat before and it was exciting enough seeing the pitch without a game on it, so the answer had to be yes. Seeing real footballers was a thrilling prospect and I arrived full of beans. Steve wasn't interested and preferred instead to play with Meccano. Chris sat quietly watch-ing the game, taking everything in, as we and the assembled O'Sullivan children crammed as best we could around the window frame, heads poking out into the street. I was only about four and Dad had to keep me informed. He pointed out all the stars: 'Look, that's Bobby Charlton, he won the World Cup …

and look, there's George Best, he's the best footballer in the world.'

It was nearly half-time when my misunderstanding of my Dad's excited commentary became clear. Newcastle was the *other* team.

Forty-five minutes proved too much for me at such a young age and I was introduced to Dr Seuss's book *Green Eggs and Ham*, which kept me so entertained that Mum and Dad later bought me a copy of my own.

My happiest times as a small boy were spent on the Northumberland coast. Mum and Dad had friends with a cottage at Low Buston, near Warkworth, where they would let us stay for our family holidays. I still remember the smell of the place and the joy of discovering both Action Transfers and Sugar Puffs while staying there. We would go on day trips to the spectacular beach at Bamburgh and have picnics on a red and white table and chairs that collapsed neatly to become its own carrying case. Steve and I found a dead starfish on the beach and took it back to the cottage where we buried it in the garden in a grave marked with a cross made of lolly sticks.

Mine was pretty much a normal 1960s suburban childhood. I was aware that my Mum was different, and that made us different as a family, but life was good in those early days.

West Jez

I became a pupil at West Jesmond Infant School in January 1969, schools at the time having intakes at the start of the calendar and school year. My first day came upon me as quite a surprise. Mum gave me an anorak to wear: it was nylon and blue with a diamond pattern made by lines of stitching. I absolutely hated it, refused to put it on and struggled as Dad tried to load me into his car. I took it off a number of times and wrestled with Dad every time he tried to put it back on me. By the time I returned home the blue anorak was my favourite thing in the world.

The day had been marred by only one further bout of tears. My teacher was absolutely lovely to me. Time has fogged her name, but it was something like Taysler. She told the class to get out their gym kits. I sat on the floor, not knowing what to do. Christopher Milne, a boy who had been in the class since September, told me I had to put my shorts on. I explained I had my shorts on (like all boys at the time I wore grey flannel shorts as a matter of course, winter or summer). He insisted I had to wear special shorts for gym. I didn't have any and started to cry. Mrs Taysler-Possibly noticed my upset state and fetched a purple bag, telling me this was my own plimsole bag, left for me by Dad. She unfastened the drawstring to reveal my name embroidered on it in white stitching. Inside was a pair of navy blue gym shorts and black elastic-topped plimsoles. I'd never seen them before and had no idea where they came from.

West Jesmond was a nice, friendly school and I soon settled into life there.

For Steve, however, problems developed both at home and school. He asked Mum if he could have hot chocolate one bedtime and she told him he was now old enough to make his own – just follow the instructions on the tin. Mum and Dad were in the sitting room when they smelled burning plastic. They found Steve in the kitchen, having put a plastic cup full of milk in the pan and turned on the heat. He explained that the instruction read 'Put a cup of milk in a pan and heat ...'

Mum's youngest sister Thea called in one afternoon. It started to rain and Steve had gone to school without his coat. Thea offered to take it to him and on her way found a mesmerised Steve watching some workmen fitting a new sign to the front of Boots. She told him she'd brought his coat and put it on for him. He never moved his gaze. When he got home, Mum said, 'Auntie Thea found you then?'

'No,' he replied, slightly put out.

'You didn't see Thea?'

'No.'

'Well, where did you get your coat from?'

Steve looked down at the coat, puzzled.

After a series of nights climbing into Mum and Dad's bed, he was told he was old enough to sleep alone and wasn't to come into their room again. The following morning Mum found Steve lying asleep across the threshold of their door, asleep, wrapped in his blanket. One again, he'd interpreted the instructions to the literal letter. He was an enigma.

Minty Bullets

Visits to Granny and Granddad's house in Lily Crescent were always a treat. The house was homely and, as with all the best things in childhood, had its own distinctive smell. Knowing it was the house where Mum had grown up added to its special quality. Granddad was Edwin Rickard, a retired clerk and former apprentice cartwright who was mild mannered, generous and kind hearted. He would always give children visitors Jesmona Black Bullets, a mint-flavoured boiled sweet that came from a tin. Granny was Dolly Rickard, née Robson, an active volunteer at St George's Church, where she and Granddad were married, as were Mum and Dad.

Dad's mum and dad were Nana and Pop. Nana was known to most people as 'Little Annie' Donald. She was a lovely woman and was always very welcoming. Pop, Fred Donald, had muscular dystrophy. I never saw him anywhere other than in his armchair in their flat in Pandon Court in Shieldfield.

Mum's condition meant moving to a house more suitable for her future needs. It was likely she'd eventually not be able to climb stairs, so a house with everything she needed on the ground floor would be a sensible choice. Granddad stepped in with an offer that my parents could buy 16 Lily Crescent, and he and Granny would buy a smaller house nearby. Number 16 was in the centre of a leafy Victorian crescent, facing the local suburban railway line, which was in a cutting bordered by wooded embankments.

I was unaware of all of the dealings that went on over the planned move. The first I heard, I was told we'd be moving into Granny and Granddad's house. I assumed they would still be living there and I was confused over sleeping arrangements. Dad tried to explain.

'No, your Granny and Granddad will be moving to number 20.'

I thought I had it all sussed now. We lived at number 20, so we were swapping houses. I was wrong. It turned out they had found the smaller house they were looking for just three doors away.

We would be moving to 16 Lily Crescent; Granny and Granddad to 20 Lily Crescent.

Welcome to the house of *Viz*

We moved in in time for Christmas 1970. Mum, with her history as a display artist, would always dress the house up in some style. A real tree filled the sitting room bay window and was decorated with beautiful glass ornaments and strings of coloured electric lights. Glass baubles hung from the ceiling, suspended invisibly on fishing line. On the shelves in the alcove stood a nativity scene inside a wooden stable that she had made herself: it had a rustic timber frame, a thatched roof of real straw and was lit from inside with a concealed electric light. It was all quite magical.

My 'big present' that year was my first ever record, an LP of The Seekers' *Live at the Talk of the Town*. Mum was a fan and played it for me on her blue and cream Dansette record player.

Apart from the Christmas decorations the house was completely stark and we clattered around on bare floorboards. I was most put out by Dad's 'modernising', having been quite settled with the idea of moving to a familiar house that I was very fond of. He ripped out many of its features, including the highly ornate seven-foot-tall marble fireplace in the sitting room, and the cupboard under the stairs where Granddad had kept his Black Bullets, a particularly difficult loss for me. The house changed completely and I didn't like Dad's reinvention of it much, but it soon felt like home.

Chris and I shared the front bedroom, which had two windows overlooking the front street and straight down the long, thin garden to the railway line opposite. Chris decided that he would have three quarters of the room to himself, so naturally I raised the issue with the conciliation service: Dad. He decided, as he often did, that there was no need to make a fuss. I was left with only the space to the side of my bed to call my own. I've never really understood this, and obviously I'm still bitter.

Steve got the small bedroom at the back, which soon became a workshop for building robots and complex Meccano structures. Mum and Dad had the middle bedroom, next door to mine.

Early days at Lily Crescent were one big adventure with all the building work going on. The smell of the foisty earth that came from under the lifted floorboards filled the house while the rewiring and central heating work was done. The central heating was an amazing new luxury and bath times spent standing shivering next to the paraffin heater were banished to history.

Lily Crescent was a very pretty street, inhabited by an interesting mix of people: older couples whose children had grown up; retired people who had chosen the street for its peacefulness; and a few new families with young children. Many of these were rather more liberal minded and somewhat left wing in comparison to the older, more starchy residents. Over the years the ratio of old guard to woolly liberal changed slowly but surely in favour of the Citroen 2CV-driving families.

Our immediate next-door neighbour was a rather dashing man called Jim Falconer, known to everyone as Jolly Jim. He was rather on the shady side, ran a plant hire firm and drove a bright red Jaguar. It was impressive enough that this sharp-dressing man lived right next door, and the fact he drove such a flashy car only added to his kudos. He was a cool neighbour. This was no ordinary Jaguar, either. Coinciding with our move to Lily Crescent was the making of the legendary British gangster film *Get Carter*, starring Michael Caine. The makers of the film had a red Jaguar that they intended to use, but it was not in good condition, as it had been bought as scrap and would be destroyed in the making of the film. They needed a car to double for it in the scenes leading up to its eventual demise. Jolly Jim was approached and his car was hired out. If you watch *Get Carter* you'll see his car – every time the villains' Jaguar is on the move it's his car; when the door is knocked off on the high-level bridge and when the car is finally destroyed that's the scrap car. In the scenes after the door is knocked off, when the car is driving again, what you see is Jolly Jim's car with its door carefully unbolted from its pillar. Not surprisingly, Jim Falconer was extremely proud of his car.

We awoke one morning after a very severe storm to see a most shocking vision. Lightning had struck a huge tree on the railway embankment, the trunk had been split in two and this tree of many tons had fallen straight down the middle of Jolly Jim's *Get Carter* Jaguar. It was completely flattened in the middle.

Dad's sister Muriel, a very cheerful woman with a blonde beehive of hair, was known to the children of West Jesmond School as Mrs Hudson. She was a dinner lady. In my early days at 'West Jez' I stayed for school dinners, but I rarely enjoyed them and later took to packed lunches of tomato sandwiches and Ski hazelnut yoghurts, prepared lovingly by Mum.

Dinnertimes were organised into two sittings, and I was on the second, so for the first half of the lunch break I got to run around and play and then eat lunch right up to the time of afternoon lessons beginning.

On one occasion I was sitting in the hall trying to force down the last mouthfuls when I looked around and noticed there were only two other children left. I looked out of the window. The playground was empty. I started to panic and munched away, keeping my eye on the other two children. To my horror, they both got up and left in a hurry. To make matters worse, a cleaner began mopping the floor. The empty hall, the deserted play-ground, the cleaner at work: these were all very unfamiliar to me and it was scary.

I got up and began my charge for the door. As I gained momentum my feet shot out in front of me. I had run straight through a patch of soapy wet lino. My head came down on the corner of one of the wooden bench seats. Confused, I tried to stand up, my head in great pain. I put my hand on the back of my hair and it felt wet; I looked at my hand and it was bright red. Things had gone from scary to horrific.

It was decided by the staff that the best course of action would be to take this panic-stricken child to a doctor for attention. Who better to take me there than Auntie Muriel? She put on her coat and took me by the hand, walking me the short distance to the remarkably named Yellow Fever Clinic, just off Osborne Road. She sat with me as a doctor put a few stitches in the split in my scalp. She then walked me the two streets home, whereupon she told Dad how brave I had been. I was very proud of myself. I didn't actually know what I'd done that was brave, but it was a compliment, so I was having it. The most special aspect of this whole incident was that I finally realised that Mrs Hudson, Auntie Muriel, was my Dad's sister.

My favourite lunchtimes by far began when I started to walk home for lunch with Mum. The school was under a hundred yards from our new front door – you simply walked to the end of our street, crossed the railway via the footbridge and you were there. Lunches with Mum were very special times as I didn't often get to be alone with her. She would make me Heinz Toast Toppers, a product from a small tin that you spread on toast and grill. We would sit together, listening to Radio 2.

My favourite time of the day was all spoiled by a rather unfortunate event on my way home one day. I saw a very fat woman in a beige three-quarter-length coat waddling down our street. She had some kind of terrible skin condition on her legs, and they looked exactly like the surface of grilled Toast Topper. I got home, Mum put down my plate in front of me, and I looked down at the toast with its bubbling cheese and ham. I felt sick. All I could see in my mind's eye was the woman with the Toast Topper legs. I couldn't bring myself to explain what had happened to Mum and I felt terrible saying I didn't want the food she'd prepared. I could never face Toast Toppers again.

Anything but *Top of the Pops*

Family holidays underwent a giant change around the time we moved to Lily Crescent. The Davidsons who owned the cottage at Low Buston had decided to sell it. However, their generosity to us continued, and they would often invite us to their lovely home in County Durham that boasted its own swimming pool. We had wonderful times there at summer parties, the pool filled with the many children of the family and all their friends.

Without the cottage at Low Buston we had no home from home any longer. We spent one sunny summer holiday at another cottage in Northumberland belonging to the parents of Jamie and Anna Ross, who lived at 6 Lily Crescent. The next summer we were invited to stay with Auntie Jean and Uncle Laurie in Oxfordshire. They were retired relations of Mum's – Jean was my Granny's sister – and lived in a lovely house with a huge garden in a picture-postcard village called Burford.

The journey was the longest drive any of us had ever known and Dad's peculiar driving habits didn't make it any more comfortable. By now Dad had a white Mark II Ford Cortina, in which he flatly refused to open the windows, saying traffic fumes gave him headaches. He even blocked off the air vents with pieces of foam and cardboard, just in case they weren't fully closed in the 'off' position. The glaring sun made my legs stick to the black vinyl seats and as it beat down into our travelling greenhouse the chemical odour of the baking seats filled the car, making me feel sick. All three of us would plead from the back seat for him to allow us to open a window. Rarely, he would concede, and open his own window by quarter of an inch. I would rise up in my seat as high as I could to try to get some of the trickle of fresh airflow in my face.

Then there was the overtaking. We didn't realise it as children, but our Dad's reputation as a phenomenally slow driver was legendary. Even on the motorway he rarely overtook a vehicle of any description, and when he did there was always quite a commotion. Firstly, he announced to us all that he was about to overtake, and we were instructed to be silent for the duration of the overtaking manoeuvre, which would take an eternity. These journeys really were epic, and the only entertainment was provided by a transistor radio that Mum kept propped on her knee. Dad didn't have a radio in his car, so her only option for listening to her beloved Radio 2 was to bring the radio from the house with her. The main problem with this was that the set was not designed to receive a signal whilst on the move, so it would go horribly out of tune every few miles and we would listen to nothing but static for as long as it took Mum to retune it manually. At the best of times the sound from this radio was awful, and the best of times were few and far between on the mammoth five-hour haul to Burford.

This was all forgotten when we got to the luxury of Barns Lane House.

Jean and Laurie were most definitely right at the posh end of our family and mealtimes were at a table with a linen cloth and napkin rings. Butter was served on a plate in curls and Uncle Laurie ate apples using a special knife to peel and core them. They had a colour telly, and seeing it for the first time was amazing. Auntie Jean was watching show jumping and the green of the grass and red of the rider's jacket were spellbinding. She would allow us to watch anything we liked, but not *Top of the Pops*, as it was, in her opinion, 'a load of *awful* noise'.

Jean and Laurie looked after a retired police dog, an Alsatian called Kim. She was the kindest-natured dog and came to wake me up on my camp bed daily at exactly 7am by licking my cheeks. She wouldn't lick my mouth or nose – she really was extremely well trained. I'd never had a pet and I fell for this adorable creature immediately.

Almost everything at Auntie Jean's was perfect: there was wall-to-wall carpet in the house and sunshine in the garden. We went on day trips on a hired riverboat, stopping off for outdoor refreshments at a waterside pub. There was another pub called The Grapes, where we were allowed to play records on the jukebox. 'Chirpy Chirpy Cheep Cheep' by Middle of the Road was a particular favourite.

To top it all there was a toyshop in the village with the complete range of Matchbox Superfast model cars, each costing sixteen new pence. We had an idyllic time staying in Burford and I was beside myself when I heard we'd been invited back the following summer.

Chris and I both had wooden money boxes and we began to save for the next Burford holiday. Chris was old enough to have a paper round and he began to save his wages. I was too young for delivering papers, but I earned what I could by running errands, cutting the hedges, mowing the lawn and washing Mum's and Dad's cars.

As the next holiday approached Chris and I compared the contents of our money boxes. I had saved what I considered to be a remarkable sum: a whole £3. I tried to do the maths to work out how many brand-new Matchbox Superfast cars I could buy for this, but the figures were beyond me. All I knew was that I would end up with more cars than I could dream of. Chris had saved a quite stunning £12. I couldn't begin to guess at what he would be able to buy. Although I was jealous that he had so much more than me, I couldn't wait to get to Burford and the little toyshop on the corner. I envisaged a holiday in which we played together endlessly with our new toys. Little did I know what was to follow.

At the end of the holiday I had spent all of my £3, having several Matchbox cars, a Dinky American police motorcycle and

15

a new safari hat to show for it. Chris returned home with his entire £12 intact. I can honestly say that I don't know what went wrong. Maybe he just got too old for toys, or maybe he became very attached to the money. Maybe he still has it now.

Chris was developing a very dismissive attitude at this time and began to respond to anything he didn't approve of, which seemed to be most things, by tutting loudly. He did this to such an extent that Dad nicknamed him 'Tutting Carmoon' after the Egyptian boy king, who was all the rage at the time.

My long-term memory is pretty good, although certain things do tend to merge and haze over slightly. I don't know if we stayed at Burford two or three times. I could probably work it out if I thought it was worth it, but the next incident certainly happened on what was to be our last visit there.

Uncle Laurie took Chris and me into his shed and showed us something that was like a dream come true for us. He had built what we on Tyneside know as a bogey: a home-made go-kart. It was beautifully built from plywood and pram wheels, with a rope attached to the front axle for steering. He said that we were free to play with it in the back garden. This was quite the best offer we could have imagined, as his back lawn sloped quite severely and was very long. I can't say exactly how long, as until very recently I believed that the counter at Jesmond Library was about eight feet high and only realised this wasn't the case on my first visit for over thirty years.

The inaccuracy of measuring things when you are yourself much smaller put to one side, the lawn was long, smooth and downhill. Chris, being my senior, would take first turn, Uncle Laurie having left us to our own devices. Chris sat in the bogey at the top of the lawn and set off, building up speed as he went trundling down and down the lawn. The wheels turned very freely and the speed at which he was travelling by three quarters of the way down the garden was getting too scary for me, and I was only watching. It dawned on both of us at the same time that there was no means by which to slow down or stop this now speeding vehicle. With hindsight, this is really something we should have given thought to earlier in the proceedings.

Chris began to shout for help, but from my vantage point there was absolutely nothing I could do. He continued in an arrow-like straight line, launching off the end of the lawn straight into the mature rose garden that formed the bottom of Uncle Laurie's prized plot. Still gathering speed, arms across his face for protection, he was lashed by endless thorny bushes before finally coming to a complete standstill in an instant when the front wheels hit the high stone wall at the very end of the garden. As this happened Chris flew upwards along with the back end of the bogey, pivoting on the now-static front wheels. Fortunately, the momentum wasn't enough to send him all the way headfirst into the wall, and gravity brought him and the back wheels thumping straight back down into the beautifully tended earth.

Dramatic as the incident was, when the dust settled the damage to Chris and the bogey was not too bad: the front wheels seemed to have kept their shape quite well and still turned freely, and Chris had been quite well protected by his adoption of the embryonic pose, although he was pretty scratched and his shirt was by no means in as fine as state as it had been earlier in the day. Uncle Laurie's roses appeared to have come off the worst. The petals that had moments earlier been part of a glorious display were now strewn untidily over the soil like confetti.

We stood and discussed how best to avoid a similar accident on the next run, which, of course, would be my turn. We concluded that the best way to slow down would be to turn sideways. Somewhat nervously, I climbed into the bogey and took hold of the steering rope. Before I knew it I was off and heading downhill at quite a lick. It felt even faster from inside the orange-crate-like seat than it did watching from the sidelines. Chris and I shouted to one another as I hurtled downwards, trying to judge what would be the best point to start steering. About two thirds of the way down the lawn I began the manoeuvre and I was very conscious that if I were to turn too sharply the bogey would tip me out. I pulled gently but firmly on the rope and began to turn to my right. All seemed to be going well. I looked up and instantly saw I had a problem: with the steering adjusted, I was now heading directly for one of the apple trees that lined either side of the lawn. I tried to steer further to my right to avoid it, but I now had the steering on full lock. The impact was similar to Chris hitting the wall. Uncle Laurie had planted these trees himself and watched them grow for years, and they were still young enough to be staked at either side. I felt sick as I heard the tree crack on impact. I looked down at my feet and saw the almost white colour of the young, soft wood inside the tree now exposed through the huge split in the bark. I dismounted immediately and chanced a glance at Mum, who was sitting on a park-style bench at the top of the garden. She stared, and rather ominously said nothing. I could now see the tree from a different angle, and a different angle was indeed what I'd created: it was leaning by a number of degrees and no longer stood in line with the others. Chris and I hastily attempted to straighten it with a less-than-pleasing level of success. I was panicking inside and it felt horrible.

Chris decided that the most sensible thing to do would be to pretend nothing had happened and say nothing, an approach that, given similar situations, he's stuck with through the rest of his life.

We were never hauled up over the tree incident but I was very sad to hear that we'd not been invited back for the following summer holiday. I guess the fact Auntie Jean had caught us watching *Top of the Pops* hadn't helped. Gary Glitter had been on when she walked into the room, only to storm straight out again. I'd always felt it was quite a harsh and judgemental approach towards us as children, but now I know Gary Glitter's a paedophile I feel significantly less hard done by. Well done, Auntie Jean. RIP.

So, after the bogey and Gary Glitter incidents there would be no more Burford holidays. To the rescue came another aunt and uncle. To be factually correct, they were my Mum's cousin and her husband. We knew them as Uncle Charles and Cousin Phyllis, the name Auntie Phyllis having already been taken by one of my Granddad's sisters, a wonderful, friendly old lady who lived over the railway from us in Lavender Gardens, and whose style of dress and manners made her appear to have stepped straight out of Victorian times.

Uncle Charles and Cousin Phyllis lived in a very tidy suburban cul-de-sac in Altrincham in Cheshire. Steve was by now a somewhat reclusive teenager and was no longer interested in family holidays, preferring to stay at home developing his film- and model-making skills. Chris and I spent one holiday in

Altrincham, but the following year would be my first spent holidaying on my own with Mum and Dad.

Phyllis and Charles were wonderful hosts, and Phyllis especially was always jolly and extremely kind to Mum, who she called Kate. No one called her Kate, but Phyllis was so nice Mum just smiled. Charles grew his own tomatoes, which would be served at the breakfast table every morning. He would invite everyone to pull out the stalk at the table in order to get the best possible chance of sampling the delights of his exceptionally sweet-smelling toms. Whenever I taste a good tomato I always think of Uncle Charles.

Chris and I went into Manchester with Mum and Dad, our mission to buy our first brand-new 45 rpm 7" single. We were to chip in and take shared ownership. Our first choice was 'Hypnosis' by Mud, but the first shop we visited had sold out of it. We opted for our second choice and bought 'Free Electric Band' by Albert Hammond. We later found another shop and got the Mud single too. Happy days.

The holidays in Cheshire would see us almost to the end of the 1970s. Elvis Presley died during one of our stays, and our final holiday there was in 1978. The following year I went to Filey with Mum and Dad. Mum's mobility was on the decline and we stayed in a specially adapted static caravan in a lovely garden. It would be our last family holiday.

Although I thoroughly enjoyed spending time with Cousin Phyllis and Uncle Charles, and the Filey holiday was also special, the magic of Burford was greatly missed, and I will always regard those wonderful summers spent playing in that idyllic Cotswold garden with Kim the dog as some of the happiest times of my life.

We were not amused

My time at West Jesmond School was in the main a pleasure. The building stood between the railway line and a graveyard, in which my great grandparents are buried. It was a typical Victorian school with tall windows and a concrete playground in which we played in all weathers. The teachers were all very nice with one exception, Mrs McKittrick, who was universally despised by all the pupils, and, I was to discover later, by the staff too.

I have so many memories of my time here that I could write forever and never get to the part of this book that you probably bought it for, so I'll push on, but I hope you'll allow me a handful more reminiscences about my childhood.

Dad decided to write to the school for permission to take me out of my class early one day in order that we could go and see the Queen. She was visiting the area, and although she wasn't stopping anywhere near us, Dad had seen that her route would involve driving up Claremont Road. His plan was for us to cycle to a vantage point in Spital Tongues and watch her cavalcade drive past.

The plan worked perfectly, permission was granted and we cycled across the Town Moor and took up our viewing position on a corner of the completely deserted Claremont Road. Bang on time, a small group of large, black and very shiny cars approached, and we were only feet away from them as the Queen's car passed. It was a Rolls Royce with an almost Lady Penelope-like expanse of glass; a car clearly designed so onlookers could get a good view.

The Queen was as plain as day to us as we stood waving. We were looking her straight in the eyes. For a child of eight or so, this was a breathtaking moment: just me and my Dad, just us, waving at the Queen. Unfortunately, her hands must have had other engagements at the time, and neither was available to be lifted out of her lap to return the favour. She looked at us for a moment and looked away.

Dad and I cycled home in silence. I imagine Dad must have felt humiliated. Short of winding the window down and spitting, or waving the 'wanker' gesture at us, she really couldn't have been ruder. There was I, a prospective royalist turned republican in an instant. Thank you, Ma'am.

My friend Sandy Chadwin had a colour television and invited me over one Saturday to watch the Munich Olympics. When his older brother arrived to collect me for some reason I panicked and decided I didn't want to go. Dad and Sandy's brother tried their best to persuade me that I would enjoy it once I arrived

20

there. I took the only course of action available to me: I shut myself in the airing cupboard and ignored their muffled pleas.

Some time later I saw the error of my ways and was taken to Sandy's house. The television, despite being colour, was something of a disappointment after the luxury of Barns Lane House. It was comparatively small and was in a cupboard halfway up a wall in the kitchen, and his mother was doing the ironing in front of it. Nevertheless, I watched Mark Spitz win some of his seven gold medals on it, and now I wanted to be a swimmer.

I was already keen on swimming, going every Saturday and whenever else I could get the chance. Dad found it hilarious when a letter came from the school saying we would be taken for swimming lessons at the start of our final year. The idea of teaching me to swim when I'd been at the pool every weekend since I was a toddler seemed ludicrous, but of course we were the exception – many of the kids in my class couldn't swim.

The upside to being ahead of the class was that only my future *Monty Python*-loving friend Julian Flear and I were capable of doing the top-distance swim for badges at the end of the term. We both swam 1,500 metres, 72 lengths of the pool, at the age of 10, which wasn't bad going. Julian's family were really serious about swimming: they got up at 5am to do time in the pool before school every day, and his sisters swam for the county. So I guess I was the only kid at school who didn't have to get up at daft o'clock who could swim a mile.

Our West Jesmond swimming lessons took place at Byker Swimming Baths, in the east end of the city, despite Jesmond having its own pool only a short walk from the school. As West Jez was late taking to swimming, the private schools in the area, and there are plenty of them, must have already been using the local pool.

The pool was one of Byker's only remaining buildings. The Byker Wall, a Scandinavian-style housing development, was under construction at the time, its purpose to replace the Victorian terraced housing stock that 1960s planning saw fit to demolish. The existing swimming baths were built into the new estate and one of our trips for a lesson there coincided with the official opening of the Wall. I was unaware of the event until, as we exited the baths, we walked straight into the throng of a

21

walkabout by comedy racist Prince Philip. Without so much as trying we found a place in his path and stood to watch him come past. To our surprise, he stopped and talked to all of us. Noticing our wet hair, he asked if we'd been swimming, then he pointed at my Newcastle United shirt asked me, 'Do you follow Newcarstle?'

'Yes,' I said, amazed that he knew one football shirt from another.

'And do you go to St James' Park to watch the games?'

'Yes. My Dad takes me and my brother.'

He moved on immediately to question one of my classmates. I was bowled over at the time – I hadn't realised he was the Queen's husband or I would have passed on the message that I thought his wife had been extremely rude to my Dad.

Paddington terminus

Sadly, not everything was rosy in my childhood. My mother's condition had its inevitable consequences not only for her but for all of us as a family. As the youngest by four years I felt particularly vulnerable to its effects.

Alongside lunchtimes with her, bedtime was a very special part of my day. Mum was at this time still sleeping in the bedroom next door to ours, and she would also make another trip up to my bedroom to read me a story at my bedtime. Our favourite books were Michael Bond's *Paddington Bear* series. She would read me the stories of the marmalade-loving bear from Peru, his friend Mr Gruber and his adopted family, the Browns. The stories were funny, well written and told of an idyllic, if somewhat eccentric, family life. I loved them, and most of all I loved having Mum sit on my bed reading them to me.

One night Dad appeared at the bedroom door instead of Mum. He sat down on my bed and told me that Mum wasn't feeling very well and wouldn't be able to come upstairs to read to me. I was very upset. He went on to explain that this wasn't just for today – she would not have the strength to climb the stairs twice a day any longer. She needed to save her strength for going to bed herself.

This was probably the most traumatic thing to happen to me in my childhood. It may sound trivial – the idea that the reading of a book was such a terrible thing to lose – but of course it went much deeper than that. I was losing part of my relationship with my mother, the best part. In my mind the fact that Mum was ill, and she too was losing out on our special time together, tortured me, but I had no one to turn to.

Dad had told me that if I was ever upset about anything I shouldn't trouble my mother about it. He told me that she had too many problems of her own and I should come to him if there was anything I needed to talk about. Unfortunately, I found Dad to be quite unapproachable about such things. I know he was only trying to protect Mum, but as a small child I was very close to Mum and suddenly being told I shouldn't speak to her if I was upset was an awful blow. I started to bottle things up and secretly I was a tortured little soul.

Dad offered to read *Paddington* to me, but it just wasn't the same. Mum offered to read to me downstairs, and this was better, but it wasn't the same in the living room, with my Dad sitting doing his paperwork and my brothers coming in and out. This wasn't my special time with my Mum. That was gone.

At about this time my previously unblemished school record began to get rather stained. It's difficult to know how much of it was down to problems at home, how much was down to learning difficulties and how much was a result of me naturally being an exhibitionist.

I was always right at the top with achievements in the class-room, and then, without warning, everyone had to sit a reading test in the school library. I was confident that I would sail through, as I seemed to do with all work up to this point, but there was a problem. I looked at one of the sentences I had to speak out loud and began to read. About halfway through the sentence I lost my place and flapped a bit. I put it down to nerves – after all, we were being tested, and this was a big and complex sentence. I tried to continue, and just about scraped through. I was disappointed.

Little did I know that this problem wasn't a glitch, and it wasn't about to go away. It would haunt me well beyond my school years.

Being silly

As for attention seeking, I'd always been something of an entertainer. I don't really remember how it started, but whenever Dad had friends round he would always encourage me to do my impressions for them. My best voice was Eddie Waring, but in front of my Dad's friends Tommy Cooper was the show-stealer because I could use props, which made for more of a show. Although I'd entertain people at home a lot, up to now, in the main, I'd been very sensible at school. This, though, began to change. I began not only to act the clown, but I also started getting into trouble. The first incident I remember was when I was playing in goal at the school playing fields. I say the school fields: they were actually public playing fields about a hundred yards from the school. The school had never had any need for its own.

Highbury playing fields bordered the Great North Road and we not only went there with school, but Dad would take us there as many times in a week as he could manage, and when I was older I would go with Chris and the boys from the street. We would play football until we couldn't see the ball anymore. When we weren't playing at the fields we'd be playing in the front street until we were called in for tea. I got to be quite good in goal – because I played with older boys, they would relegate me to goal because they didn't rate me as a player, but spending so much time there, I got pretty adept at it. I was also tall for my age, so it was certainly my most useful position.

Anyway, playing in goal in the school game, I was having a very quiet time. My team was demolishing the opposition and I was getting bored. The goalmouth was, as all goalmouths were in the 1970s, a mudbath. Often they would have set like rock, which made for very uncomfortable landings, but on this occasion it was all soft underfoot. In my uninterested state I began to practise diving. The full backs laughed as I stood up, covered in mud. I'd got a laugh, and my instinct was to carry on. It was good practice whatever, and besides, my kit was already filthy. I threw myself into the mud time and time again. I got lots of laughs and it was great fun.

The teacher in charge, Mr Curzon saved his 'hairdryer treatment' for the wooden changing rooms in which we used to get

24

dressed. He accused me of 'deliberately' throwing myself in the mud, and then the bombshell ... my behaviour had been 'silly'. This was the first time the word had been used against me in a negative sense. I didn't like being told off, not at all. School was the thing I was good at, the thing I got praise for. It looked like that was starting to change, but here was something else I knew I could excel at – being silly.

Mud wasn't the only thing I threw myself into to impress people. Our front street was a popular route for a lot of children walking home from school. As our house was right in the middle and we had a long path, I saw an opportunity to entertain. We had a ball-catch on our front door and if anyone was at home, which Mum always was, the door wouldn't be locked. It could be pushed open quite effortlessly. I learned that a dramatic way to open the door was to charge it with my shoulder. I began to do this from further and further away, the door flying open and me landing inside. I was eventually taking great run-ups and successfully convincing a number of people that I was forcing entry. I was a hero.

There was a girl in my class called Jessica Machin. She sat next to me and she was the first girl I ever fancied, provided you don't count the dark-haired one out of The New Seekers. She lived around the corner. In order to impress her I told her she could watch me force a door open with a manly and dramatic shoulder charge. My moment came and she stood on the pavement watching as I took my biggest run-up yet. This was going to be *amazing*. I hit the door with some considerable force. It was locked. My shoulder, followed instantly by my head, clattered off it and I landed on my feet, dazed and in some not-inconsiderable pain. She laughed. I was heartbroken.

I'd forgotten that Mum and Dad had gone out and I was supposed to go to a friend's house. I sat on the front step for hours. To make matters worse, Jessica emigrated to Australia and added insult to injury by 'going out' with Gavin Partington before she left. He became a TV reporter. The bastard.

Before I left West Jez I was to get into rather more serious trouble for the first time. I was a perpetrator of vandalism. There was a wooden park bench in the corner of the school yard and someone pointed out to me that it had a crack in it. The damage was right in the centre of the front. I don't really remember how it came about, but I was at one point surrounded by a baying crowd as I jumped aggressively and repeatedly up and down above the crack, trying to break the bench in two.

The tribunal, led by Mr Curzon, concluded that I was 'the straw that broke the camel's back'. I suppose my previously squeaky-clean record had gone some way to saving me from any serious punishment.

At home, my silliness began to cause trouble too. For some reason there was a supermarket trolley in the street, so logically enough it became a plaything. I persuaded Timothy 'Tinhead' Wickens to climb into it and I began to push him down the middle of the road as fast as I could. Unfortunately, like most supermarket trolleys, it didn't steer very well. It swerved out of control wildly to the left and crashed straight into the front of Mum's car, smashing the headlamp.

Once again, I didn't get the kind of telling off I was expecting. I guess at the time I just wasn't 'that kind of boy'. This was to change at secondary school.

2

Oh Dear. Big School

All three Donald boys attended the same secondary school that Mum had been to as a girl. When she was a pupil the school was two separate establishments, a boys' grammar school and a girls' high school, sharing a red-brick building opened in 1928 by King George V on the same day he opened the Tyne Bridge.

Shortly before we began our time at Heaton it had been converted to the comprehensive system, a changeover resulting in pupils from both a larger catchment area and a wider range of social backgrounds. Sadly, in Steve's early years there his eccentric nature and awkward social skills led to him being the focus of attention of a number of bullies, becoming known as 'Professor Posh'. The seventies was a time when aggro-boy culture was rife and violent gangs were commonplace. Hooliganism was almost a career path for many boys, and indeed some girls – something in which you could make a name for yourself. For a kid like me, with a gentle suburban upbringing, being thrust into the cauldron of Heaton School was traumatic.

There were a number of pupils in each year that were branded 'remedial' or 'non-examinable' and it was from this 'stream' that most of the problem kids came. We knew troublemakers as menties (from mental-cases), later abbreviated to ments. Breaks and dinnertimes were often a cat-and-mouse game of avoiding menties.

Chris, as I'll go on to explain in greater detail later, would begin his cartoon career depicting menties in cobbled-together comic books he would pass around his class.

Both of my brothers were seen as rather eccentric by the staff, most notably Steve. Chris, though, was not short of his own flamboyant moments and during games lessons wore a football shirt with the number 3 on the back, under which were the words 'Cowgate Circle'. This is a bus route joke.

For many years I looked back on my time at Heaton with little more than contempt. However, now that I'm older I have developed a more balanced view, and see this time as an important part of my development. I took almost nothing from the education system itself, but the characters that inhabited the school, pupils and teachers alike, were so much larger than life that to this day I still have to pinch myself to verify I wasn't dreaming.

On my first day I encountered class hatred for the first time. As a kid from one of the posher neighbourhoods, this was only to be expected from those from poorer neighbourhoods. Kids on both sides of the class divide would naturally defend their own kind. However, this particular character assault was from a teacher.

The first half of the first day was spent touring the school and meeting our form teacher, Mrs Hogg, who was a very warm and welcoming younger teacher with a friendly face and long wavy blond hair. After the dinner break we had normal scheduled lessons, the last of the day being metalwork. At this time girls weren't allowed to study woodwork, metalwork or technical drawing, despite the Sex Discrimination Act already having been passed earlier in that same year, 1975. Likewise, boys couldn't study cookery or needlework. The failure to implement the new law properly would lead to serious trouble at the school within weeks of my arrival.

When we boys got to the metalwork lab we were asked to sit along a bench, facing the teacher, whose name I've changed to Mr Todd. He began by explaining that our uniform list had omitted the metalwork apron we would all need. He said this was nothing for us to worry about: we could buy one before the next lesson. He asked for a show of hands from anyone who could name a shop where we could get one. I eagerly raised my hand – I knew that Isaac Walton & Co was where Mum had bought my shirt and jumper, my trousers and blazer being rather comedic hand-me-downs. I was ready, hand eagerly raised. He chose Phil Robson first.

'Farnons?' said Phil.

'Good one, yes – Farnons.' Mr Todd approved.

Most of the class had hands raised by now,

'Fenwicks?' suggested Richard 'Lam-bee' Lambert.

'Yes, Fenwicks is another,' Mr Todd replied,

This continued until almost all the department stores in town had been named. By now I was doing that thing that kids do when they're so eager to get their raised hand noticed that they try to lift themselves off the ground by their own arm. Another kid was selected.

'Isaac Walton's?'

Disaster.

Arms were dropping like flies as the list of shops dried up. I didn't want to miss my chance to be seen as a willing and knowledgeable contributor. I remembered there was a shop that sold only school uniforms, but I didn't know its name. I looked at the label on the back of my tie. Raymond Barnes School Supplies. Joy. My hand shot back up. Instantly I was selected.

'Raymond Barnes?' I announced proudly.

'Raymond Barnes? Posh shop, that. You don't want to go there, lads. Posh shop. I think we've got a posh lad here.'

He continued as if nothing had happened as I tried, and just about managed, to suppress my tears. I couldn't work out what I'd done wrong. Never in the supportive environment of my primary school had I received anything but praise for trying. I tried to hide my tears from Mum and Dad too, but eventually burst into tears that night as I showed Dad my new schoolbooks. When I explained what had happened, Dad thought it better not to say anything to anyone at the school about it, thinking it may only cause more trouble.

How is an eleven-year-old kid supposed to deal with cursory humiliation from an adult put in a professional role to help him develop? But this incident did make me realise what it was like to be alienated. It made me determined that in my life I wouldn't make snap judgements about people or follow the divisive class boundaries that this teacher was trying to use to alienate me from my own friends.

29

Kojak or Sweeney?

In my early days at Heaton bullying took the almost innocent form of the '*Kojak* or *Sweeney*?' assault. A kid, or a gang of kids, would approach you and ask '*Kojak* or *Sweeney*?' and your answer would determine your fate.

This system was based on the two most popular telly police shows of the time. If your allegiance was to the wrong programme, without so much as a nod to the Magna Carta you would be pushed down a steep, but thankfully not too high, bank.

I discovered quite early on that some of the kids using this excuse for introductory-level violence were really quite stupid, and I took to asking them which was *their* favourite before sentence was passed, taking advantage of the forthcoming information when deciding on my answer. Some kids grew wise to this and refused to tell me, so the lottery was reinstated. I was sick of being pushed down the bank, so one day I decided to say *Police Woman* instead of the choices offered. Confusion abounded when I explained that I had started a new gang, and I followed Angie Dickinson as the sexy-yet-liberated detective. *Kojak* and *The Sweeney* were both old hat. It actually worked, but just the once.

Later a ruddy-faced blond-haired kid called Michael Rowntree, who unbeknownst to me had a reputation as a hard lad, came up with a remarkable novel twist. He decided to simply push anyone and everyone down the bank, no questions asked. He caught me completely unawares and, as I picked myself up from the tarmac road at the bottom of the bank, I just snapped, probably for the first time in my life. I chased after him and swung a punch at him, making a decent contact with his right ear. I then caught him with a left before he could retaliate. He caught me with a couple of punches, which for some reason I hadn't expected. In what seemed like an instant I was in the grips of a wrestling scrap at the centre of a sizable crowd chanting 'Scrap! Scrap! Scrap!'

It was all a bit surreal. I'd seen this happen a few times before, but I wasn't the kind of kid that did this sort of thing. I was a nice boy, surely. It was over as quickly as it started. We were separated by a passing lab technician, whose presence dispersed the crowd. There were two great things about his intervention: he stopped the fight before Rowntree could take advantage of his experience, and as he wasn't a teacher he didn't dish out any discipline. I'd started a fight and not got into trouble for it. This was quite a result. Such an offence would normally have meant the belt at least, or more likely the cane.

The best thing to come out of the whole incident was the development of my reputation. I was no longer seen as a total softy. I wasn't a troublemaker, but I wasn't easy prey for bullies either. I'd stood up to a tough kid and not lost. If you bullied me I might snap and punch you in face. The bullies moved to easier targets and never troubled me again.

I made friends with most of the kids at school easily, and my humour certainly helped. I would try to make all the kids laugh. I was the 'class clown', that's for sure. I always wanted to do something creative with the jokes. I felt it was a natural thing; comedy came easily to me. My friend Gordon Poad and I would recite *Monty Python* at one another endlessly and eventually kids would ask us to act out whole sketches for them during break times. We eventually got a new English teacher, Miss Gajdus, who brought drama lessons to the school for the first time, and unlike the other teachers fanned the flames of our thespian behaviour, which had previously been seen as a nuisance at best and disturbing at worst. We wrote sketches and performed them in front of the class. Using the skills we were learning at the local People's Theatre (more on that later), we involved anyone in the class who was willing to take part in the productions. Miss Gajdus was delighted, and Gordon and I were selected for a special drama course that took us out of lessons for a while and culminated in a performance at the Gulbenkian Theatre in the city centre. This was a very proud moment for us both and the others involved, and of course for my parents, who saw me perform on stage.

Miss Gajdus was an exception at Heaton – she was friendly, supportive and quite normal. Most of our teachers seemed to be a random collection of social misfits.

Tekkas!

Raggytash

There was a teacher known as Raggytash, due to his unkempt moustache. One day he was struggling to control his pupils. The problem seemed to emanate from one particular corner of the class. He singled out a girl who was continually starting conversations and giggling with her friends and shouted, 'Tracy! Will you stop being so immature!'

Tracy responded instantly. 'How man. Fuckin' Raggytash. Divven't fuckin' caall me immature. I've had more cocks than ye've had hot dinners!'

She was suspended. Not expelled, just suspended.

Stretch Armstrong

There was Mr Armstrong, known as 'S-t-r-e-t-c-h Armstrong!' after the elasticated action toy, or more commonly 'Fitter' Armstrong due to his unbelievable ability to go from mild-mannered bespectacled boffin to Nazi commandant on speed in a split second. It was often a hot topic before his classes if he would 'tek a fit' that day. His glasses would steam up as he screamed at us in rage as he 'threw a dickie mint', his pitch getting higher and higher as he warned us all of the terrible consequences of our misbehaviour and disrespect. He would bang his fist or any available object against the desk as he went into his crescendo. On one occasion he picked up Ian Brumpton's brand-new wooden ruler and smacked it repeatedly on our bench as he 'hoyed a wobbler'. As he finished his 'blue fit' he turned to walk back to his own table, returning to Ian a piece of wood that was still a ruler at one end but a frayed fan of split timber at the other.

Dozy Dawson

Then there was 'Dozy' Dawson, a technical drawing teacher, who really was quite an eccentric, even amongst the bizarre haul of other-worldly weirdos who staffed the school. He was remarkably forgetful and pretty thick skinned. I always thought he'd make a great Dr Who. He picked up a new nickname, 'Two-Ties' Dawson, when he arrived one day, you guessed it, wearing two ties. My friends Peter and Andy were both in his form as he tried to take the register.

'Sir! Sir!' Andy shouted.

'Shut up, boy! Can't you see I'm taking the register?'

'But Sir! Sir! You're ...' Andy pleaded.

'Be quiet at once!' Dawson cried.

'You've got two ties on, Sir!' Peter piped up as the class all tittered.

'Don't be ridiculous, boy!'

He continued to call out names. More and more kids began to shout out.

'Sir! Sir! It's true!'

'Have a look, Sir! You've got two ties on!'

Eventually he reached down with one hand and felt clumsily around the front of his neck. He confirmed to himself by means of incoherent mumbles that he was indeed wearing one tie too many. He simply tugged at the top one until it untied and came free and stuffed it into his pocket, never once ceasing his work filling in the attendance register.

Mr Mackay

Music was subject in which you fell into one of only two extreme categories: very lucky, or very unlucky. The school had two music teachers: Mr Young, whose age befitted his name, and Mr Lewis, who was old. Mr Young had long hair, played the guitar, encouraged his pupils to embrace music by creating their own, and gave special free guitar lessons during his lunch breaks. Mr Lewis was a humourless Scottish disciplinarian dressed in a tweed suit and orange brogues that creaked when he walked. His nickname was 'Mr Mackay', which makes little sense unless you're familiar with the TV series *Porridge*. Mr Lewis's entire demeanour was exactly that of the zero-tolerance prison guard. Lewis's lessons comprised of his pupils standing to attention and singing hymns, tedious lectures on the life of Beethoven, and being forced to listen for hours to his hideously scratched vinyl opera records on a Dansette record player.

Mr Young's room was big and airy and full of instruments, with walls covered with interesting colourful pictures. Mr Lewis's room was as stark a contrast as is possible: bare, with nothing but a piano and the Dansette in one corner and a blackboard on the wall with rows of seats facing it. These were divided down the centre – boys on one side, girls on the other. No child in Mr Lewis's classes ever got to touch a musical instrument. Pop music was a forbidden subject.

At the beginning of each year the kids would all scrum around the timetables to see who they had to teach their subjects. There was always a feeling of sinking like a stone if Mr Lewis featured on your rota. Sadly, I got him every time. With my love of music being as strong as it is, and with my ability to play instruments, something I've picked up in recent years, I can't help feeling that I could have really done something in my life with music if I'd had the encouragement. Sadly, this wasn't a word in Mr Lewis's vocabulary.

Brasso

Mr Hully had a very shiny face. We called him 'Brasso' and put the word about that his wife buffed up his face with metal polish every morning before school.

Miss Shite

There was Miss Wright. She was a very attractive young woman with tumbling light brown curls and a penchant for slightly hippyesque clothes. She taught me history in my fourth year. She was one of the softest teachers we ever had, but we really liked her, so we took full advantage of her, but not in nasty ways. One day she popped out in the middle of a lesson to get a textbook. Paul Simms suggested we light up a tab in the classroom. It was an unusual classroom known as the 'audio-visual room' and unlike all the others it didn't have any windows along the corridor, just a door with a glass panel, so was more secluded. A lad was sent to the door to 'keep toot for tekkas' and Simmsy lit up the cigarette. He passed it around to me and Paul Smith and we all had a few 'drags'. The alarm went up from the lookout. 'Tekka!' He returned swiftly to his seat.

With a rather blasé attitude, we decided on a very quick last round of drags, wafting wildly at the smoky air with exercise books, but as Simmsy was passed the tab for the last time Miss Wright walked back in. In a panic, he put the lit cigarette into his mouth. This was a trick some of us could do – if the lit end faces backwards, you can hold the other end between your lips or teeth, keeping your tongue well out of the way. However, it could only be kept there for a few seconds. All of the class's eyes were secretly on Simmsy. None of us were able to believe what we were seeing. It seemed to go on forever. His face went red and then gradually turned grey, then waxy white. Smithy and me were pissing ourselves, trying to keep silent and not draw any attention to him. A little puff of smoke came out of Simmsy's right ear before he coughed out the saliva-soaked remains of the tab under his desk, along with a dense cloud of fumes. Fortunately, Miss Wright's attention was distracted by activity on the other side of the room. We were all bemused that she never mentioned the smell. Simmsy wasn't at all well for the rest of the day.

Gravyface

There was one youngish teacher; I don't remember his real name. He had a browny-red, short-yet-scruffy beard and we called him 'Gravyface'. Poor Mr Gravyface was assaulted by two of the school's less notorious but most sinister ments. They ambushed him by leaping off the roofs of the bike sheds as he patrolled around 'on duty' one dinnertime. The reason they gave for their actions was simple: in an attempt to leave school as soon as possible they had ensured, by absenteeism and a total lack of interest in all education, that they weren't entered for any exams. However, this sterling effort had been for nothing, as by law they wouldn't be allowed to leave until their sixteenth birthdays. So, as logic would have it, their only course of action was expulsion. What finer way to achieve such an ultimate goal than GBH on a 'tekka'?

The Riot

When the Sex Discrimination Act of 1975 was passed the school's decision wasn't to banish the belt and the cane to history, along with sex discrimination, but to mete it out to girls as well as boys. This led to our school's infamous riot, which made the front pages of the national press during my first months there as an innocent Jesmond softy.

After a swimming lesson at a nearby pool, our bus pulled up back at the school. A large crowd had gathered on the front field.

It consisted mainly of older girls, probably fifth formers, some lads of the same age and parents, mainly women, who were at the front. They chanted 'Haway the lads!' and I, in my innocence, assumed it was some sort of football-related gathering.

The teacher we were with, Mr Quickfall, was clearly flustered and gathered us close to the school gates before deciding what to do. As we stood there, a boy appeared from the school building, making a beeline for the chanting crowd. In hot pursuit was Mr Wisbach, who would later become my form teacher and was most famous for having a non-speaking role in *Get Carter*.

The boy made it into the crowd, which opened up and closed immediately around him as the pursuant teacher arrived. Mr Wisbach pushed his way in and the crowd swallowed him instantaneously. I watched in horror as the fists of unseen assailants rained down into the area where the teacher had disappeared from sight. Shortly afterwards, a bedraggled Mr Wisbach beat a hasty retreat to the building.

The repercussions – calls to the radio, letters in the press, pupils still angry at the corporal punishment decision – would carry on for a long time. The phone lines to the local radio station were on fire for the next few days, with claim and counter-claim being made by each side on the James Whale programme.

Opinion seems to be divided over the riot's seriousness. Some say there was overblown reporting and exaggeration; others reported some very ugly scenes. Those pupils I've got accounts from saying it was much ado about nothing importantly didn't witness the beating of Mr Wisbach, and neither did the press. I saw a scene far more violent than that reported in the local paper, which seems to have thought little happened and claimed it was all over in an hour. The school suck to its guns about the decisions for years, at least until a change of headmaster in about 1979 or 1980.

The comedy racist art teacher

Mr Massey-Taylor wasn't a regular attendee of his own art classes and would often turn up halfway through a lesson, if at all. My Dad once saw him shopping over two miles away from the school during lesson time. Obviously he had more important things to attend to than our education. In 1978 a new girl arrived in our class. She was Asian, which was a rarity in our experience. Of the two thousand pupils in the school there was no more than a handful of Asians and even fewer pupils of African descent. In the art lesson the new girl took a seat and some of the other girls showed her where to get some paper and paints, as Massey-Taylor was nowhere to be seen, as usual.

Eventually, he marched into the room. He was an imposing figure to say the least, very tall, about six foot four I'd say, and sixty-ish years old with a shock of silvery-white hair and a huge white regimental moustache, curled up at the ends. He wore tortoiseshell glasses and invariably dressed in a tweed suit and leather brogues. He walked purposefully around the room, looking over people's shoulders at their work. When Massey-Taylor was present the class was always silent: his presence alone drilled fear into us all. He arrived at the new girl's table and performed a comedy double-take. Standing directly behind her, he asked abruptly, 'You're new aren't you?'

'Yes, Sir,' she replied politely.

'What's your name, girl?' he snapped.

'Kameljit, Sir.'

'Kameljit what?' he retorted impatiently.

'Kameljit Boghul, Sir.'

'And where do you come from?' he boomed.

'Jesmond Park West, Sir.' She had given the name of her street.

'No. Before that,' he jabbed angrily.

'Leicester, Sir.'

'No – before that.' He was losing the very little patience he had.

'I was born in Leicester, Sir.' She was becoming more uncomfortable and the whole room was by now crawling with unease.

'No, no, NO, no, *no* ... No! What bloody tribe do you come from!?'

We never found out if her family made a formal complaint, but certainly many did over the years. It was always a mystery how he stayed in the job.

I recently bumped into an old teacher who finally cast light on the matter. Apparently, Massey-Taylor would regularly be called into the headmaster's office to account for his behaviour. The head was a mousey little man called Mr Askew who would explain that a complaint had been lodged and that disciplinary action would be inevitable. However, both men had served in the armed forces and Massey-Taylor had outranked Askew. Massey-Taylor would boom at Askew, saying he would not be spoken to like this by an inferior officer. He would then turn on his heel and march out of the room.

I was once walking along one of the school corridors with Paul Smith and two other lads, one of whom was Andrew Li, popularly known as 'Soofy'. I think this was because his full name was Andrew Su Fi Li, or something along those lines. Soofy was a quiet lad who always minded his own business. He was so quiet that we really never heard him speak until one day I asked him what page of the textbook we needed to turn to. To us, whose only experience of Chinese culture was watching David Caradine in *Kung Fu* on a Saturday teatime, his reply revealed the most amazing accent. He sounded like Confucius speaking in Geordie dialect. 'Di-vin-knaaa … hev-in-go-aa-book.' For most people two stages of interpretation are called for: firstly, into the Geordie he was attempting to pronounce. 'I divven't knaa, I haven't got a book.' And again into English: 'I don't know, I haven't got a book.'

As we walked along the corridor Soofy suddenly flew forwards and where he'd been walking appeared a large leather brogue on the end of a long, tweed-clad leg. Massey-Taylor had walked up behind us and kicked Soofy so hard in the arse that he jumped about a metre forwards. Massey-Taylor then bounded forwards and repeated the action on a bemused and sore Soofy. This time, as his leather-soled shoe met the poor lad's arse, he turned and bellowed back at the rest of us: 'How about this for Chinese torture, eh boys!?'

This wasn't poor old Soofy's only taste of the bizarre and nasty racism of Mr Massey-Taylor. One day Paul Smith and I were packing our bags at the back of our classroom. We'd been serving a detention in another room, returning just to get our books. The room was empty but for us and Soofy, who was standing over his own desk about three metres away, packing his things. The sound of marching feet approached. There was never any mistaking the sound of Massey-Taylor: he had an enormous stride and the metronomic pace of a centurion. The side of the classroom that faced the corridor was made up entirely of windows, so we were able to watch him as he passed by in solo military formation. As he strode the length of the room he cast a glance our way. He continued for a few paces until he was just out of sight. Then we heard him abruptly stop and turn on his heel. Suddenly, he appeared at the door, which he violently kicked open. As the door clashed against the wall Massey-Taylor stood to attention, filling the opening with his giant frame.

'Donald! ... Smith! ... You're not getting muddled up with this bloody coon are you!?'

I've never known a moment like it. I can still hear the silence. Unlike the Chinese torture incident, it appeared that this wasn't one of Massey-Taylor's 'jokes'. He was staring at us, waiting for an answer. I looked at Smithy, who looked back at me. We both looked at Soofy, who looked at us, and then we all looked at Massey-Taylor. Certainly we all shared the shock at this un-precedented and outrageous outburst, and I guessed we might be sharing the confusion over how a full-time racist could make the fundamental race-hate error of calling a Chinese boy a 'coon'. I eventually spoke, not really knowing what I was supposed to say.

'Erm, no, we're just packing our bags, Sir.'

Strangely enough this seemed to satisfy the old twat and he turned and walked away. I look back on this incident and I still find it hard to believe that it could ever have happened. But, as I have done so many times over the years, I give you my every assurance that it did.

Later Massey-Taylor had a heart attack whilst walking past a classroom and ended up with his face and hands pressed against the glass as he slid to the floor, choking for air. The entire class stood and cheered.

On me head, son! Nice shot!

One day a lad in my class brought a muzzle-loading Gat air-pistol to school. Not surprisingly, this was in clear breech of school rules.

A number of us used to congregate in a ditch at the bottom of the front playing field. It was just deep enough to stand full-height in without being seen by patrolling teachers. It was our smoking den.

The lad with the gun wasn't a smoker, but he brought the weapon down to the ditch at dinnertime to show it off. He had pellets too, and we took it in turns to try shooting pop cans and tab boxes in a makeshift gallery along the ditch. Then we turned our attention to the game of football being played a few yards up the field. We decided to try and shoot the ball while it was in play. It was a hilarious idea. Everyone was keen to have a go, visualising our historic comic moment as the ball instantly deflated at the feet of a player in flight.

Three or four lads tried a shot, but all missed. I volunteered next. I was a pretty good marksman, and still I have a medal to this day to prove it. However, the trouble with the Gat was that its muzzle-loading design resulted in it being hideously inaccurate. This was something I was, as yet, unaware of.

A lad called Nigel 'Nig' Richardson was on the ball, tearing up the wing. I took careful aim at the ball, steadied my hands, checked my aim, squeezed … Bang! Nig twisted in mid-air as he fell to the ground, clutching his head.

Two questions struck me at this moment. 'How the fuck is it possible for a pistol to be that inaccurate over less than twenty yards?' and 'Have I just shot someone in the head?' The answer to both was, unfortunately, yes.

My luck was in on this day as never before or since. The wound was a graze across the temple, the pellet only glancing his head. My heart was in my mouth; my mates all rolled around in the ditch, pissing themselves laughing. My good fortune was extended when Nig decided not grass on me. To this day I don't know why. He went to the first aid room, telling the nurse he'd grazed it on a wall as he tripped.

Homo-erratic behaviour

Of all the most fearsome ments in the school, one of the scariest was ironically one of the most effeminate. Billy Bloater (name changed to protect my personal safety) was an overweight and particularly camp individual who had a gang of hangers-on who were, strangely enough, exclusively masculine girls. Young and naive as we all were, we never raised questions about the sexuality of Billy or his fearsome sidekicks.

Billy was a strawberry blonde, quite short and very fat lad. He wore a tan-coloured, full-length leather riding coat, half-mast Oxford bags and brogue-patterned oxblood 'dealers'. He was quite an imposing figure. His sidekicks dressed in men's northern soul/bovver boy fashions, high-waisted bags with dealers, riders or monkey boots and lumberjack jackets (otherwise known as 'pitch invasion' jackets, so called as whenever there was pitch invasion at a football match the first kid on to the playing surface was always wearing one). Billy Bloater and his bizarre gang always congregated around the radiator outside the girls' toilets, in a back corner of the building with no classrooms nearby and not on any pedestrian thoroughfares, so it was always quiet. As you walked past you would always feel the very public stares of Billy and his cohorts. Occasionally they would shout abuse if they considered you didn't conform to their fashions, so punks, mods and generally anyone they didn't consider 'normal' were always likely to come under fire. One day as I approached the corner where Billy's gang gathered there was a kafuffle and Billy Bloater himself beat a very hasty path directly toward me. I hardly had time to be frightened: he pinned me against a wall with his big fat belly and prodded me repeatedly with his stubbly little chipolata fingers.

'Are ye the fuckin' one who called wor kid a fuckin' puff?'

His voice was so camp it was comical. He continued.

'Are ye the fuckin' one who called wor kid a fuckin' puff?'

It was all happening so fast that I was hardly able to take in what was being said.

'Sorry? What?' was all I could blurt out.

'Ye fuckin' did, didn't ye? It was ye that called me lirril cousin a fuckin' quee-a!'

I had no idea what he was talking about. To this day I'm not sure if it was mistaken identity or whether I had actually committed the crime. One of his sidekicks, with dark curly hair, a pitch invasion jacket in brown and black Oxfords, decided to up the stakes.

'Fuckin' hoof him man, Billy! *Fuckin' hoof him!*' she exclaimed as she rounded Billy's girth from behind to land a vicious kick in the side of my calf with the toe end of her monkey boot.

41

'Fuckin' hoof him man, Billy! *Fuckin' hoof him!*' She landed another kick, this one into my thigh.

In his high-pitched voice Bloater was going ballistic. 'Nee-one caalls wor kid a fuckin' puff! D'yu hear us?!'

His sidekick continued to swing kicks at me.

'Fuckin' hoof him man, Billy! *Fuckin' hoof him!*'

The rest of his gang of female hoodlums were screaming abuse at me and goading Bloater to further violence. He then pushed me away up the corridor, warning me not to insult members of his family again. His assistant swung one last kick at my arse and it was all over. Bruised and confused, I went about the rest of my day.

I had a run-in at the school gates with a fearful ment known as PD. I was on my way to the shops one dinnertime and as I passed through the school entrance PD appeared from behind one of the huge brick pillars supporting the gates. A tall fifties throwback with a black, greased quiff, he stood right in front of me, his chest touching mine.

'Haway then!' he barked.

'Haway then what?' I asked, stalling for time.

'Fight,' he replied factually.

'Fight? Why?' I tried to sound like I couldn't possibly know what he meant.

'Well. You're a fuckin' mod, aren't ye?'

'Why do you say that?' I played the innocent.

'You're wearing a fuckin' tie!' He pointed out my skinny purple crepe tie, with a roundel, or 'target' badge, on it.

'I just like wearing ties,' I declared.

I was determined not to deny being a mod, but at the same time I didn't want to get my head kicked in, so I tried to be vague.

'What about the badge?'

'Oh, that? It's a book club. The Target book club.' This was true. Target, the publishers of the *Dr Who* books, had run a club I'd been in as a younger kid. But the reason I wore the badge as a teenager was that it was the unmistakeable mod symbol.

'Well, what are you then?' He was getting confused.

'Well, I suppose I'm an individual.'

Good answer, I thought. True, but vague and not provocative.

'Do they fight?'

'No. Not really.'

Remarkably enough, he was satisfied with my answer and allowed me safe passage to Denton's bakery for my lunch: a nutritious meal of half a loaf of bread hollowed out and stuffed with a packet of crisps.

I guess, unlike the bullies, PD may have been a fighter, but he wasn't interested in fighting anyone unwilling. There was an ethical code of sorts in play here.

Knob joke with extra cheese

After the third year we were all 'streamed' into either O level classes or CSE ones. I found it very difficult to understand why I was put in the CSE stream. I'd started Heaton with seven As in my first report and I'd always been very keen to learn and to take part in lessons. I wasn't long into secondary school that I began to become frustrated. My teachers continually told me they expected better of me, putting on record that I was lazy with my written work.

Looking back now, it's so easy to see that all of the issues revolved around reading and writing. My writing was good but painfully slow; my reading almost non-existent. There's no point in dredging through the past, though. I could have benefited from an understanding of my reading problems, but the milk is long spilled.

I developed many really good friendships after my demotion to the 'fuckin' CeeeZeees', as Dad kindly called the CSE stream the night I dropped the bomb. I found being surrounded by less-privileged kids suited my personality better. The working-class kids were not judgemental about me being thrown into their world – they accepted me straight away. The reverse happened with the middle-class kids, some of whom began to pass me by, or joke about me now being a ment.

I began to enjoy the fact there was less intellectual expectation on me and started to thrive in the subjects I'd already done well in. I was awarded two school prizes in one year: the woodwork prize for best project and the fourth-form prize for the most improved all-round school performance.

The prizes took the form of books, which you went and chose from the school supplier's bookshop. My prize-winning wood-work project was a children's bedside cabinet, painted on one side with a picture of Superman. I chose for this prize a coffee-table book of graphic images called *Masters of Comic Book Art*, and for the form prize *The Bumper Book of The Two Ronnies*.

While I was working on the bedside cabinet project there was an incident that I'll never forget. I shared several lessons with a real character called David, known to everyone as 'Ducka'. It was rumoured that he got the name because he had an arse like a duck, but this wasn't something you asked the man himself about. Ducka joined Heaton mid-term with a fearsome reputation as a hard case. He was heavily tattooed with DIY designs, including on his face, neck and ears. He had been through a rough upbringing, living in care and reputedly spending time in borstal. A lot of people feared Ducka, but I found him to be a very friendly lad with a great sense of humour. He had a very positive attitude despite the challenges he'd faced.

We were in a classroom early in the school day and Ducka said to me, 'How Don. Ye knaa when yu shag a lass and yer knob gans aal cheesy?'

Not knowing quite what had just happened to me, this question coming out of the blue as it did, I tried to maintain a straight face in order to see where this was going.

'Yes?'

Shagging lasses wasn't anything I'd yet done, but I got the picture.

'Smegma,' Ducka proudly announced.

I could tell that he wasn't making a joke but was showing off the fact he'd learned the proper word for something. I managed to keep my cool and replied, 'Yes. Yes, I know.'

I had a few laughs to myself throughout the day about the bizarre way he'd launched into the smegma conversation. We all found the word hilariously funny at the time, but Ducka's opening gambit kept cracking me up.

'How Don. Ye knaa when yu shag a lass and yer knob gans aal cheesy?' kept echoing around my head.

Later on I was in the woodwork room, working on the cabinet. Ducka was opposite me, on the other side of the bench, working on his own job. Once again, totally out of the blue, he asked quite seriously, 'How Don. D'yu like cheese?'

'Yes,' I replied.

He cupped one hand around of all three items of his marriage furniture through his trousers, thrusting his hips forward as he did so, and exclaimed, 'Well, here's half a poond!'

I was instantly beside myself with laughter. I laughed so hard that I wanted it to stop because I was in fear of being sick. The teacher, the jovial but very strict Mr Venables (not his real name), had left the room, slipping into his office next door. I was in fear that he would hear me laughing and come back and dish out a punishment, so I put my head inside my cabinet to muffle the sound. All around me I could hear Ducka and the other lads working at our bench howling with laughter.

Inside the cabinet, I had one hand firmly over my mouth. I was still getting huge spasms of laughter, which made me bang my head upward against the wood. This went on for some time until I noticed the sound of the other lads' laughing had stopped. I began to withdraw my head slowly, assuming Mr Venables had come back in. I thought if I took my head out carefully and looked sensible he'd probably just think I'd been working on the inside of my job. The room wasn't just quiet now, though: it was silent. The first thing I saw was a pair of big brown shoes immediately behind me. With the rather-too-short brown trousers hanging above them, I knew this could only be one person. I stood up and faced Mr Venables, quickly wiping a tear from my eye. All around the class stood to attention, stony faced. Venables rocked back and forth on his heels a few times, as he always did when giving matters consideration. He finally spoke.

'Is this a joke you'd like to share with the class?'

I spluttered out a laugh, which I quickly stifled, realising only too well the severity of my situation. Spontaneous titters burst out around the room. I then tried to speak.

'No … Not really, Sir.'

My voice quivered.

Venables replied very sternly, 'Not really? Well, perhaps you'd like to go and stand outside the staff room until you're prepared to share whatever has tickled you.'

I stood for the remainder of the double period in the area of shame outside the main staff room, where each teacher who passed in or out would ask the purpose of you being there. I have to say I did rather enjoy my shame that day.

Detention deficit and disorder

By the time I was fifteen, in most classes I sat next to a girl called Angie Jenkison, a very pretty and effervescent girl with bags of character and, although she'll kill me for saying so, more than a little rough charm. On Saturdays Angie worked as a hairdresser at Fenwick of Newcastle, where Mum worked.

We were in the same art group together, organised by a rarity at Heaton School in 1979: a good teacher, Mr Dixon. He was friendly, bright and always instilled confidence in his pupils. My project in the art group was a screen print based on a photograph of The Jam, who I was pretty much preoccupied with at the time. Angie and I would stay friends for life, and the Jam would play a big part in our future story.

Next to me and Angie in that class sat Paul 'Smithy' Smith. Paul was a great friend of mine and we spent hours laughing together. He loved to walk into Gannon's sweet shop on Newton Road and ask how much a particular item cost. When, for instance, told a Mars Bar cost 12p he would ask quite frankly, 'So is that 12p each or three for 36p?'

He would do this with any number of items until the shop-keeper lost patience. This made me laugh so much that we used it on the front of *Viz* years later, the cover price marked as '35p or 3 for £1.05'.

On our final day at Heaton School, after walking out of the gates for the last time, Smithy and I continued straight into Jesmond Dene, where we ceremoniously burned the bibles given to us by the school on our first day. We both felt the school had done little for us, and at that time our feelings towards the place were purely of anger and resentment. We were lucky though, as despite our schooling we would both go on to do very well.

Paul was a gifted sportsman. He left Newcastle immediately to join Warwickshire County Cricket Club, where went on to win every trophy in first-class cricket, including the treble in Brian Lara's legendary team of 1994.

3

The Exuberance Of Youth

Dave, the ace of clubs

I consider myself very lucky to have been a member of St George's Youth Club. The club was run by a man called David Hall, or Dave, as club members knew him. Dave had been a member himself in the early 1950s. In those days the club had been closely associated with the church and was called the AY, which stood for Anglican Youth. My Mum and Dad met at the AY and Dave was one of their best friends. He was Dad's best man in 1956.

Dave came from a wealthy family and lived most of his life on inheritance. He decided, having completed his National Service, to reinvent the club, free of the church, in the early 1960s. He took over a wooden ex-Scouts building behind the church and set up a club with very few rules. You could be forgiven for thinking that there was a lack of discipline. Dave allowed members to swear and to smoke in the building. However, there was more discipline in this place than anywhere else I've lived or worked. There was a weekly fee that had to be paid, whether you attended or not. Alcohol was strictly forbidden, and anybody who drank on a club night, either before or after attending, would be barred for good.

The club itself was not funded in any way by the wealth of Dave's family. The National Association of Youth Clubs had one annual charity week, 'Club Week', in which they could collect money from the public to fund their entire year's schedule. St George's Youth Club won the prize for the club that collected the most during Club Week in each and every year that Dave was in charge. Other club leaders could never fathom the reason for this, and it was often suggested that it was because the club was in a wealthy area, but this had nothing to do with it. In fact, the wealthy areas don't produce the best results on door-to-door collections, not because the rich are tight, but because in streets with big posh houses there are far fewer doors to knock on. The real reason was really quite simple. Dave put in far more effort than anyone else.

As a member of St George's you were obliged to collect door-to-door during Club Week. If for any reason other than genuine illness you didn't collect, your membership would be terminated, and you'd not be allowed back in as a guest of another member.

In the weeks leading up to Club Week a show was put on in the main room and all members were obliged to attend. The purpose was to inform members of the club's proud history of self-funding, to explain how the system operated, the need for members to take it seriously, and the dangers collectors could face when out on the streets. Club Week took place in autumn and the streets were dark and cold.

Through Dave's hard but fair teachings, members realised their club's existence was in their own hands.

St George's was without doubt the best learning experience of my teenage years. I learned that hard work pays dividends, and I learned if you treat people well they'll return the favour. Every ex-member who had a car would volunteer to drive collectors.

From the parents' and neighbourhood's perspective the club's work was hugely beneficial. It didn't just keep kids off the streets – it taught them responsibility.

Kids need clubs

Sadly for Dave, as the 1980s moved on, kids in the membership bracket of fourteen to seventeen began to want to go drinking on weekends and the club became unfashionable. Membership dropped to record lows, and regrettably in the early 1990s the club closed. Dave had nothing to work for any longer. He'd sold the family house and moved to a smaller one and eventually was living in a rented flat. He was still seen on a regular basis on Acorn Road, just a couple of hundred yards from the site of the club, always cheerful and always well turned out. One weekend he went camping alone and never returned.

Dad and Dave's brother were involved in trying to establish what had happened leading up to the disappearance. My Dad suspected Dave's inheritance had dried up and this may have led to personal problems. But this was speculation. No one really had any answers.

Dave's body has never been found. It's a very sad story. None of us who loved and respected him have had the chance to say goodbye: we don't even know if he's alive or dead. I often wonder if he knew how much he'd done for so many young people. The world needs more people like Dave who can give kids boundaries. Every time I see problems caused by anti-social behaviour, I think, 'Give them a club, for fuck's sake.'

In the health and safety culture we have today, funds couldn't be raised by sending kids out in the dark knocking on doors. I accept that. But the alienation of kids from their own communities is such a fundamental part of society's ills that youth work should be receiving massive planning and funding from national government. We need to give kids their own spaces where they can do what they want without disturbing anyone else, and crucially, they need to run these spaces themselves.

How did keeping young people off the streets and helping them to develop social skills become so unimportant?

Thespian tendencies

In the summer of 1976 my classmate Gordon Poad suggested that I join him at the weekend at the People's Theatre, an amateur theatre near the school. They had classes in theatre skills on Saturday mornings that he'd been attending and said I'd really enjoy it. He wasn't wrong – it was very engaging and unlike school there was no written work. Before long they couldn't keep me away. For three years I was there every minute I could be, helping out in any way possible: dismantling sets, helping build new ones, running errands ... One of my favourite jobs was painting the sets, mixing the paints by hand. It was hard, messy work, but fun. I acted as Assistant Stage Manager for the RSC's first visit to Newcastle in 1977. They sent four actors to the People's to perform a piece of work. I did their dressing room calls and got all their autographs. I recently looked through them to see if any had become famous and sure enough John Nettles out of *Bergerac* was in there.

One of the real highlights of 1977 for me was seeing Morecambe and Wise live at Newcastle City Hall. A friend called David took Gordon and me to celebrate his birthday. During the performance they opened the floor to questions. I managed to get my voice heard and I asked Eric, 'How long have you been together?'

He turned to Ernie, looking a little confused, looked at his watch and said, 'It's about forty minutes, isn't it, Ern?'

It got a huge laugh and between them they then told me how they'd first met and just how long they had worked with one another. That was a special moment. I couldn't wait to get home and tell Mum.

In my time at the People's I acted too, appearing as Tommy Hepburn in Alan Plater's *Close the Coalhouse Door* and as both Friar Laurence and Peter in *Romeo and Juliet*. Mum and Dad came and saw me in both plays and despite not being theatre fans they were impressed by the cast's professionalism and very proud of me.

My devotion to the theatre didn't go down well at school. I was told by Mrs Currel, a fearsome geography teacher, that I must make a decision. If the theatre was taking too much of my time and affecting my schoolwork then I must choose which was more important. I think I was supposed to decide on school, but in my mind there was no contest. I loved the theatre, I learned things there, I was useful and appreciated there – the opposite of school.

Having chosen the stage I was later put off it by the levels of luvviness that abounded. I guess it was that, the appeal of the youth club and later my band that killed my interest, but it was an experience for which I'm most grateful.

Two pints of lager and a welly of sick

I have no idea quite what was going on in my parents' minds at the time, but they allowed me to go camping, unaccompanied, with five school friends at the age of fourteen. It was Easter on the Northumberland coast, and consequently it was bitterly cold and our camping equipment was hopelessly inadequate.

We all took the bus from Newcastle and set up camp at Waren Mill, a beautiful but exposed site. Of the three tents we had, mine was the worst: it was Dad's, from the 1950s, and made of canvas with no zips, just lace ties, some of which were missing. It had a separate ground sheet, so there was an exposed area all the way around the bottom, and no flysheet. It wasn't in any sense waterproof. On setting it up we abandoned it immediately and used it only for storing our bags. Of the two remaining tents, one was half-decent and the other was, in theory, the king of tents. Its owner, Poady, constantly sang the praises of its ex-army pedigree. Phil Dangermouse and Stephen 'Richie' Richardson slept in the half-decent tent, and the rest of us were left with Poady's ex-army palace, which was built to sleep two.

We all indulged in smoking cigarettes and drinking beer, and it wasn't long before Richie, who'd quaffed his way through two whole cans of lager, was retiring early, having waved a packet of blobs (condoms) in the air, saying, 'You never knaa when yu ganna need 'em, eh, lads?'

Well, one time and place I could say we all knew we wouldn't need them was on a freezing campsite in the middle of the night with the potential of female company set firmly at zero.

I spent the worst night of my life in that tent, freezing cold, jammed in like sardines, lying on stony, hard ground, exposed to the howling wind at the sides where the ground sheet was meant to be fixed to the tent but wasn't. Nobody got a wink of sleep.

In the other tent Richie woke in the night and stuck his head out of the tent to vomit. He was sick directly into Phil's wellies. The whole thing was a disastrous nightmare.

We somehow managed to learn by our mistakes and camping became a regular adventure. We found a pub called The Lobster Pot that was happy to serve us beer. We were all pretty big and mature-looking lads for our age, but we didn't really look eighteen. The pub was in the middle of nowhere, though, and we were often the only customers. We would walk back to our tents through the fields, daring each other to touch the electrified cattle fence.

We later moved up in the world and started to camp at Beadnell, a site right on the coast, but surrounded by a stone wall that provided good shelter. Our equipment improved, as did our chances with the opposite sex. We met a group of girls from the Central High School, a rather high-class private school for girls in Jesmond. One of the girls' parents had a holiday home in the village and the girls would be allowed to stay there. There was a comical scramble to impress them and in truth no one really scored, but we spent time together in an attempt to do so. We were all rather jealous of Poady's ability to charm girls, for which we gave him terrible stick. He was a heavy-set chunk of a lad and quite sensitive with it. The girls liked this, so naturally we didn't.

In the girls' house one night we were all sitting around talking. Poady was in an armchair and, as a result of sleep deprivation, the signature of these adventures, he fell fast asleep.

For a group of fourteen-year-old boys made jealous by his vaguely less-unsuccessful advances on the girls, the opportunity couldn't be missed. I got the ball rolling by tying his shoelaces together, to thunderous laughter. Poady remained fast asleep. My next mission was to tie one of the belt loops of his jeans to the drawer handle of the sideboard, using a piece of string. The laughter continued. We found a felt-tipped pen. Could we draw on his face without waking him? Remarkably, this proved quite easy, and before long I'd drawn a swastika on one cheek and Steven 'Benny' Bennet had drawn a rudimentary penis on the other. We were convinced by now that the laughter would wake him any second, but, bar the occasional stirring, he remained fast asleep. Now it was time for the big one. On his forehead I painstakingly wrote, in reverse to read in a mirror, I AM FAT. It was difficult to do, not only because of how gentle I had to be, but because I was laughing so much.

Job done, he still stayed asleep, like a giant in a fairytale. He began to snore loudly, increasing the humour levels considerably. Benny and I put cigarette ends from the ashtray into his open mouth. Astonishingly, we managed to get four in before he finally woke up. Spitting the butts out, he looked around the room, his eyes trying to tell us he was above this kind of thing,

'Yeah, very funny,' he declared dismissively, wiping ash from his tongue with his sleeve. He glared angrily at each of the lads in turn as we all roared with laughter. He then attempted to get up, wobbled slightly and fell back into the chair. More laughter, more dismissive comments, more laughter. He untied his laces, got to his feet and went to take a step. The sideboard drawer flew out and he jolted back into the seat. Whilst untying the string, he took time out to stare very seriously at each of us again, his face, twisting with despair at our childishness, unknowingly baring the penis, the swastika and the legend I AM FAT. I can't begin to describe how funny it was. It was painful.

He eventually made his way to the bathroom. We all sat in silence, punctuated by titters, listening. We heard him use the toilet, but still nothing telling, and then suddenly the single word '*Bennnnnetttttt!*' boomed through the house. Poady and Benny were neighbours and were always at each other's throats. He blamed Benny for the incident and I got off scot free. Great times.

Say Waah!

Another little hobby was a game called 'Say Waah!' This was a simple game of dare in which, at any place and at any time, if one of your friends was to say your name and then declare 'Say waah!' your mission, should you choose to accept it, was to scream 'Waaaaaaaaaaaaaah!' absolutely as loudly as your body could muster.

One Saturday afternoon in town I was sitting in Mark Toney's ice cream parlour and café on Percy Street with Andy Storey and some other friends. It was a big café, unchanged since the early 1960s, with Formica tables and lino floors, and it was very busy. Andy had ordered fish and chips. Everyone else was just drinking tea. He had just begun to eat his meal when I said, 'Andy, say waah!'

In our teenage world, in order to save face, it was out of the question not to respond to the call. Andy, without hesitation, delivered the loudest, longest 'Waaaaaaaaaaaaaah!' I'd ever heard.

The café fell completely silent. Absolutely every pair of eyes in the place was on us. Andy attempted to pretend nothing had happened and continued to eat. As if we'd somehow slipped into a Tex Avery cartoon, a chef, dressed in the full regalia, including the big hat, appeared, complete with a meat cleaver. (By the way, I haven't made this up.) Not only was he straight from a comedy sketch in appearance, but he had a heavy Italian accent and spoke in broken English.

'What-a zee fack eez go-eeng on 'ere? Who screamin'? Who screamin'? For fack-a-sake? I theenk someone eez being fackeeng murdered!'

'It was him, mister,' I offered pathetically.

The index fingers of everyone at our table pointed at Andy. The chef turned his attention to him.

'You-a fackeeng idiot! Why you fackeeng do thees? Get-a out of my fackeeng place, you-a scare all my customer!'

'Can I finish my fish and chips?' Andy asked politely.

Seconds later we were on the street, having walked through a sea of dirty looks and threatening mutterings. Andy, now hungry and penniless, had gone down in teenage legend.

Rock 'n' dole star

There was a period that seems extremely dark, looking back at it now. I remember my overwhelming feeling at the time was one of helplessness. My entire family was unemployed. Only my Mum didn't sign on, although, like the rest of us, she lived on benefits because of her disability. But she didn't have to go with the rest of to the downright depressing Swan House in Newcastle city centre. The year was 1980. I'd just left school, Dad had been made redundant, Steve had finished college and had come home and Chris had left his job at the Department of Health and Social Security. Because we all had the same surname and lived in the same area, we were all allotted the same time to sign on: 10.10am, Box 5, Department of Employment Office, Swan House. It was a family outing like no other. We all caught the number 33 bus together. Well, we did for a while, maybe once or twice. Chris and I decided to hang about and be fashionably late. Being seen out with all the men in your family was bound to draw the question from anyone we bumped into: 'Where are you all off to, then?' It wasn't a question any of us would have felt proud to answer.

Johnny artpants

In the first year of signing on, I was 'actively looking for work'. In the second I started at Newcastle College of Arts and Technology as a 'part-time' student. At the time this meant you could study up to twenty-one hours per week without getting a proper grant. You just kept signing on for the same benefits.

I studied art A level for a year, completing the course and passing the exam by the same time I could have taken it had I stayed at school, but without the additional year of study. My dream was to go on to take the Art Foundation Course, which my eldest brother had done six years earlier. Students got to work in each department of the college, effectively doing a crash course in each subject. The idea was that once the course was completed you'd know which subject was the one for you. Steve had gone on to study film and television in Bournemouth, enjoying photography and sculpture the most, and eventually utilising both in his career as an animatronics wizard. (Unfortunately, I didn't get accepted.)

Chris, post-DHSS, was also studying art A level at the college's Bath Lane site, as the art side of the college was always known. The building was Victorian and decrepit, standing between the almost-forgotten remains of the city wall and one of the seediest streets in town. It was draughty and cold in winter and unloved, but it had lots of character – just right, I always thought, for an art school.

Its corridors were full of interesting people: punks, goths, old hippies, eccentric lecturers with big woolly jumpers and beards who looked like they belonged in a beat poetry club in Greenwich Village in the 1950s. I loved the mix.

In my time at college the technology buildings stood a good mile or so from the art building through a run-down area of town, which sadly has almost all gone now. Parsons was the main academic building of the college. Its canteen was great, the social centre for all the students, where everyone checked everyone else out: the clothes, the music talk, the party invites, the fanny.

Shy bairns get nowt

I met Andrea, my first long-term girlfriend, in the Parsons canteen. Well, I say I met her there: the truth is I first met her on the street in Marlborough Crescent, having spent weeks secretly fancying her across the room. I told my good friends Wendy and Libby and they took it upon themselves to force me into asking out this object of my desire.

One day they made me promise that I would ask Andrea out before the end of college that afternoon, in the end forcing me out of my seat and marching me across the room, pushing me out of an exit door through which Andrea had just left. I now had to approach a total stranger from behind and ask her out. I was terrified. I walked down the stairs from the canteen to the exit, left the building and hid behind a pillar. After a few moments I headed back to the canteen to say I'd lost her. As I stepped out, Wendy and Libby were standing right front of me, arms folded in the style of angry, dominant housewives on a seaside postcard. They womanhandled me in the direction she'd gone, telling me that I was not to return until I'd asked her out.

Somehow, I did manage to muster the strength to approach her, on a street corner, and in a very nervous state ask her if she would go out with me. She told me she was seeing somebody else. I was devastated. Worst of all, I had no idea what to say next, and must have just muttered 'Thanks' or something and wandered off.

Over the next couple of weeks I would stop and chat with Andrea and her friends. I was delighted that she was happy to give me so much attention.

As I left a class one day, the girl who sat behind me said, 'Why don't you ask Andrea out again?'

I was very surprised that anybody knew I'd asked Andrea out.

'She's seeing somebody clsc,' I replied.

'No, she's not,' she insisted. 'She thinks you're lovely, and if you don't ask her out again, she's going to ask you out.'

It was less of a challenge second time around, and Andrea and I were to stay together for four years, the first three of which were very happy.

Johnny Shiloe's Movement Machine

Aged seventeen, I dived headlong into the crazy world of rock 'n' roll. I don't actually remember exactly how Johnny Shiloe's Movement Machine came into being. It was around the time I started college, but I knew the lads in the band from school. Drummer Dave 'Rosie' Rose had been a classmate, his younger brother Paul, also known as Rosie, was with our guitarist, and the bass player was Gary Shaw. Dave and Paul lived close to 'Shawsy' in High Heaton. I would walk through the Dene to the Roses' house and sit with Dave to put the songs together. Dave would play guitar and work out the music and I would fit in lyrics from Chris and his friend Jim's poetry (Jim Brownlow became a fellow *Viz* founder; more about him and the poems later), moving on later to writing words of my own. Shawsy also contributed his own songs occasionally.

From the word go our ambition was not to be serious, although all three musicians were very talented. We were annoyed at how seriously most teenagers took music. We all loved it, but we really wanted to poke fun at those who took their rather narrow and clichéd musical cliques far too seriously. We had many songs that were fundamentally piss-takes of other musical styles.

There was our rockabilly song 'Shakin' Blue Suede Hound Dog Mamma', our blues song 'The Ready Brek Blues', our disco number 'Disco Disco Disco Baby' and Shawsy's amazing heavy metal composition 'Rocking With the Devil in the Bowels of Hell'. As well as these, we had songs that were simply based around funny lyrics rather than taking piss out of musical style. There was 'My Room', based around one of Chris's great poems, and 'Dum de Dum Parts One and Two', using Jim's wonderful Spike Milligan-like nonsense words.

We rehearsed in many different places, amongst them friends' houses, a farmer's disused glasshouse and a derelict room on Newcastle Quayside, open to the elements from holes in the roof. In this hovel, used by Arthur 2 Stroke and many of the top local bands at the time, rats could be seen running in the mountains of rubbish piled against one wall. There's now a café there, and a very posh estate agent, and an art gallery. How things have changed. I liked the Quayside when only a handful of us ever

58

went there. It was vast, industrial, historic, jaded and empty. That made for a hell of a lot of character.

We began to drink in the Baltic Wine Cellar, just off the water-front, which was a ropey old boozer, but friendly. The Quayside in those days was pretty rough: there were no trendy drinking establishments, just run-down industrial buildings, long-forgotten shipping offices and a handful of pubs frequented by Russian sailors, tramps and the odd one-time gangster. The artistic set began to take it over: the actors from the Live Theatre and Bruvvers; the bands who rehearsed in the rats' nest; and the general shitterati of post-punk Newcastle. Arthur 2 Stroke took up residency on Mondays at The Cooperage.

Johnny Shiloe's Movement Machine played their first gig at Newcastle's Guildhall on 23 December 1981. It was an enormous benefit in aid of Amnesty International. We would appear in between the two main acts, The Hostages and Arthur 2 Stroke.

Arthur 2 Stroke had by this time metamorphosed from the edgy bass-less trio of 1979 into a pulsating seven-piece soul band with bass, brass, keyboards and percussion. They developed an enormous following in Newcastle and were close to their peak at this time. It was an honour to play on the same bill as them – such a major event was a real scoop for us. Phil Branston, aka Arthur, had suggested we appear after hearing a tape of our Christmas song 'Santa is Coming'. He thought with the gig being so close to Christmas it would be absolutely perfect to set the mood before they came on stage. We planned to perform three songs, opening with 'My Room', straight into 'Disco Disco Disco Baby' and finishing with the Christmas number. Phil had been a great supporter of my performances on stage and had invited me to appear as master of ceremonies at some of his biggest gigs, which meant an awful lot to me. He was a bit of a legend and was one of the great inspirations behind *Viz*'s launch, the comic having been partly a fanzine running stories on Arthur 2 Stroke on a very regular basis.

Between us we came up with the idea that I should open my band's set with a piece of character stand-up. I had been enter-taining mates in pubs for some time with a character I had created, who would complain relentlessly in a thick Northum-brian accent about the frequency of buses.

Once The Hostages had finished their set and my band were ready, I wandered on to the stage dressed in a flat cap and muffler and began a lengthy complaint about once having waited 33 minutes for a number 33 bus. It went down really well and I got loads of laughs, but the plan was to continue until the crowd was worn down by the one-dimensional joke. Once people began to heckle, the band would walk on. As soon as they were ready I threw off the cap and scarf and Dave counted us in.

Nine minutes later we walked off to rapturous applause, the crowd chanting 'Shiloe! Shiloe! Shiloe!'

I shall never forget that moment. In fact, I think it's one of my happiest and proudest memories.

Scouting for boys

Sadly, we would never play another gig in quite such a splendid setting, and I guess we never played to as many people again, but I have some wonderful memories of some very special times. We played at a venue long gone called Spectro Arts Centre and at a one-day music festival in Heaton. The High Heaton Rock Festival took place in St Francis Church's hall. (Somebody somewhere has a recording of that show that belongs to me, by the way.)

We played a couple of memorable gigs at a pub called the Newton Park Hotel. First was a triple bill with a couple of young blues bands. It was one of our best performances, and one of my most enjoyable gigs. The place was packed and with the room nicely geed up by the first band we went on and played a storm-ing set. The crowd, many of whom were blues fans, loved Paul's playing and as they were young they really got our humour. Even the lasses dragged along by their boyfriends danced to 'Disco Disco Disco Baby'.

But the mood was to change. A local 'radgee' called Sean came into the room and as the headline act struck up he took an instant dislike to their singer, Johnny Wright. Sean was a neighbour of the Roses and came to our table to speak to them. He was clearly drunk as he said his hellos, turning his attention straight to Johnny. Gesturing at the stage he snarled, 'What does this fucking comedian call himself?'

'Johnny Wright,' Dave replied.

'Johnny Wright? Johnny fuckin' Wrong.'

Johnny was a very lively singer and would constantly dance, regularly straying out into the crowd. He was a great performer with a fine gravelly blues voice.

Sean went to the bar and as he turned away carrying his pint Johnny, in mid-performance, danced past, unknowingly nudging Sean and making him spill some of his beer. Johnny turned round and looked like he'd seen a ghost as he clapped eyes on the notorious Sean, who very hastily put the remains of his drink down on a nearby table in order to get hold of Johnny with both hands.

I don't remember what the level of violence was. Maybe Sean threw a punch or two, maybe he just a shook Johnny by the throat, but whatever, it was over quickly.

It changed the atmosphere in the room instantly. Sean, however, seemed satisfied and Johnny went back to his singing. But when he stepped back to the microphone his voice was no longer that of the Alexis Korner-style blues man but more like Minnie Mouse on helium. You had to feel for the lad, but it really was an absolute treat to watch.

The final movement

Our second gig at the same venue was also memorable, but for very different reasons. During our sound check I stepped back into the room to get an idea of what the levels were like. Paul began to sing and then began a jerky dance movement reminiscent of David Byrne. Everybody laughed. As he danced away he knocked the microphone out of the stand, but instead of it falling to the floor it stuck to his guitar. I immediately knew something was wrong, grabbed the cable into the mains and pulled it as hard as I could. The plug flew out of the socket and Paul fell in a crumpled heap. He'd had a massive electric shock.

He was still conscious but extremely dazed. My immediate response was to call an ambulance and cancel the gig. Paul refused both, despite the guitar strings having heated up to such an extent that they had burned into his fingers. After walking several circuits of the car park, supported between me and Shawsy, and then necking two pints of beer, he decided to go ahead and play.

This would have been the most legendary rock 'n' roll come-back if the gig itself hadn't been a shambles. That night only nine punters came to see us and three of them left during our set. Dave refused to play one of the songs and we ended up squaring up to each other over the drum kit.

A bloke called Graham Lines, regular gig attendee and one of the six remaining audience members, spent a great deal of time rolling an entire packet of Old Holborn into one giant cigarette before joining me on stage, putting it in my mouth and lighting it for me: a fairly unusual highlight of an otherwise altogether forgettable event.

After the show we retired to Shawsy's mam's kitchen where we divided up the gig funds over some of her homemade scones. We pocketed £1.12½ each before the inevitable 'musical differences' conversation. Paul and Dave didn't really want to be in a comedy band any more. Shawsy was happy to carry on, but there was no point if half the band were against it. We agreed to call it a day. It was the end of an era in my young life that had been a lot of fun.

On reflection, I think perhaps I should have considered the idea of continuing as a rhythm and blues outfit as we'd begun to play some really good hard-edged up-tempo guitar blues. Paul went on to great things as a guitarist. The Paul Rose Band continues to tour to this day, Paul often playing a Fender Strato-caster that was gifted to him by Rory Gallagher.

Moving away from home

On a bitterly cold February night I went out for a drink with Dave Rose and another old school friend, Phil Dangermouse (name changed due to Civil Service employment). They invited me back to the flat that they'd recently moved into, just off Chillingham Road in Heaton. Their flatmate had recently done a runner.

I'd been arguing with Dad even more than usual, and this very day Dad had shouted, 'If you don't like it here, why don't you move out? Go and get this bloody flat you're always talking about!'

As I stood surveying the very basic flat, imagining what it must be like to live independently, I realised there was a room spare. Immediately, I asked if they would take me as a lodger. So, in this very haphazard fashion, I began my life as an independent adult.

I've never felt wholly comfortable about the way I left home. Not having university as an option, I had no obvious point at which to break my ties. I don't regret moving out, but to this day I wrestle with the fact that I was leaving my mother behind. Maybe that's hard for everyone, but Mum was becoming more reliant on help, and I'd been providing more of that. I was helping her with cooking: the first dish I learned to prepare was spaghetti bolognese, which I took to making for her every Wednesday. I took her to town every Thursday morning for some grocery shopping, but more importantly to visit Fenwicks, where she still had good friends. She always liked to have lunch in the café there. As simple a thing as this might seem, it was definitely one of her great pleasures in life.

I did keep up helping her, riding my bike the two miles home each Wednesday and Thursday for the cooking and trips to town. However, I continued to feel guilty about having left. I knew that she was proud of me for gaining my independence, but I also knew it meant a great deal to her to have me around. Steve was living away by this time and Chris spent almost his entire time in his bedroom, being tempestuous if ever asked to help, so it was down to Dad and me.

I try not to let my feelings about leaving Mum haunt me. I know people will tell me that I did nothing wrong, and sure enough I don't believe I did do anything wrong, but that doesn't stop me being troubled. Around the time Mum's condition confined her to a wheelchair she told me that her life had been very difficult, but she considered me her consolation prize. Knowing how much she doted on me for this reason alone is enough to make me feel bad about leaving her even now.

Although I've so far painted a fairly bleak picture of this time and my mixed feelings about leaving home, things in the flat were fantastic. The freedom to do absolutely as I pleased was wonderful and I took full advantage of it, as did my housemates. Some of the laughs that we had form some of my most enjoyable

63

memories, and there are many moments from that time that make me laugh out loud every time I remember them.

Breaking the news to my parents wasn't easy. I remember just sort of blurting it out. I don't remember what happened next, maybe a stunned silence, maybe I walked out of the room. I don't really know. I don't remember any particular reaction from them, but there is an uncomfortable feeling associated with the moment in my memory.

As far as I remember I moved out pretty much straight away. Dad drove me to the flat with my things, stopping at Joseph Hughes' Coal Merchants at the top of Chillingham Road to buy me a sack of smokeless fuel for my bedroom, which rather romantically had an open fire. Less romantic was that the flat had no form of heating except a gas fire in the sitting room and my original little Victorian bedroom fireplace. It was quite a shock to the system to wake up on a regular basis to ice inside the windows. I was the lucky one, though: I could light a fire at night before going to bed and in the morning the room would still retain some of its heat. The rest of the flat was indescribably cold.

The day Dad took me to the flat, bought my coal for me and gave me £5 to help me settle in was a rare day of peace between us at the time. It reminded me of how fond I was of him and I sometimes wonder how much more of the good side of Dad I would have seen if it hadn't been for Mum's illness. Dad didn't come into the flat and indeed, despite my many invitations, he never visited anywhere that I lived for the next eight years.

116 Simonside Terrace was far from glamorous. It was a typical upstairs purpose-built Victorian Tyneside flat. The rent was cheap, £33 a week between the three of us, but we were in the unenviable position of living in an upstairs flat with our landlord below. This would be bad enough had the landlord not been a chronic alcoholic and had his tenants not been three nineteen-year-old tearaways with a penchant for late nights, loud music and alcohol.

Our landlord was called Charlie Foreskin (not his real name). He was not a handsome man and had the ugliest wife I have ever cast eyes on. He was always very eager to get the rent from us in cash by 11am on Saturday, the relevance of which never dawned on us until Dave called Phil and me into his room at about half past nine one Saturday night. We all lay on Dave's bedroom floor with our ears pressed to the boards listening to Mr Foreskin vomit violently and repeatedly. This was an event as predictable and dependable as the sounding of the one o'clock gun at Edinburgh Castle. We would often hear him coming in his front door, jump up from our seats and run through to Dave's room, where we would roll around the floor laughing at the almost pantomime-like sounds of Mr Foreskin hurling up £33 worth of beer.

Shortly after I moved into the flat Phil Dangermouse celebrated his nineteenth birthday with a night out with his brother-in-law. Eventually we heard him scrabbling to get his key in the front door. This particular challenge passed, we heard the front door slam behind him.

We heard Phil making very slow progress up the stairs, planting his feet in the stamping fashion popular with very drunken people. He refused all offers of help that we shouted to him from the sitting room.

Although we didn't actually see what happened, it's safe to assume that the drunken Phil encountered trouble when he reached the sharp bend at the top of the stairs. It wasn't long before he was making his way back down the stairs again, this time by means of gravity. The noise was absolutely thunderous as he fell brutally right the way to the bottom. Dave and I rushed out of the sitting room to find Phil lying upside down at the bottom of the stairs, head against the back of the front door, at the centre of a bomb-site-like proliferation of Coke tins and Chinese food.

'Nah, nah! ... I'm absolutely fine. I've got egg fried rice, man!'

We collected together, as best we could, the food parcels and dented tins of pop and assisted Phil to the top of the stairs. He assured us he was absolutely fine again and that, being in a celebratory mood, he had bought each of us a can of Coke. We thanked him, suggesting that we might hold off opening them until such time as the potential for explosion had lessened.

We all settled down in the sitting room, Phil now laying out his food on the coffee table. In a very boisterous mood, he decided to exchange his seat on the sofa for a position standing on the opposite side of the coffee table, dipping into the various containers of food whilst talking frenetically, occasionally doing little comedic dances. All of a sudden, without any warning or explanation, he unfastened his jeans and began to pick handfuls of fried rice and onion rings from the table and deposit them down the front of his underpants. Massaging the food suggestively into his crotch, he announced, 'What about that, eh? What about that, eh? Fried rice and fucking onions! What about that, eh?'

This behaviour was very much out of character. As we sat, crying with laughter, Phil began to swagger around in front of us, doing his best comedy Geordie headcase impression. 'What's the matter there, lads? Is there summik wrang wi' yu balls?'

I was rudely awakened the following morning by a noise that wouldn't go away: the sound of somebody repeatedly banging on the front door. It took all of my effort to drag myself out of bed, suffering as I was from the most appalling hangover.

Trying not to open my eyes fully, I gingerly made my way to the foot of the stairs, expecting to see the landlord at the door, wanting his rent. However, instead I was confronted by a uniformed stranger.

'I've come to empty your meter.'

Our gas was on a slot meter that stood at the top of the stairs on the landing, where all the doors to the bedrooms and the sitting room met. Every so often the gas board would come and empty it and a rebate would be returned to us in cash from the coin box.

Reluctantly, I showed him in. He made his way straight to the meter and I left him there to go into the sitting room to fight back waves of nausea. The gas man spoke to me from the landing.

'Is there somewhere I can count out the coins? A flat surface, like a table?'

I got to my feet and stood in the doorway, looking down on him as he knelt by the meter. Before I had a chance to answer, the door immediately behind him opened, and there stood Phil, dressed in nothing but his underpants, which were very brief and navy blue in colour. Phil's skin was the colour of a peeled potato, he was as skinny as a rake and had an absolutely crazy mop of the thickest and darkest curly hair, which hung down past his shoulders like something from the *Fabulous Furry Freak*

Brothers. His hair completely covered his face, like Cousin It's from *The Addams Family*. There were absolutely no features visible. He paused for a moment, then walked very hurriedly through the sitting room and kitchen, into the back corridor, straight past the toilet and into the bathroom.

This all happened in an instant. I answered the gas man as if nothing had occurred. 'You can use the kitchen table, it's just through the sitting room.'

The gas man carried the coins to the kitchen table and began to count them. I sat in the living room with my eyes closed, the silence interrupted only by the gentle chink chink chink of the 50p pieces.

Suddenly, there was an almighty sound from the open door of the bathroom – Phil vomiting violently into the cast-iron bathtub. It was absolutely chilling, and the gas man was only about a metre from the open door. There followed a further two equally outrageous bouts of vomiting. The gas man quietly went about the business of counting coins.

Phil then fell silent.

The gas man walked out of the kitchen and approached me across the sitting room floor, telling me of the sum of money taken from the meter, the total cost of gas used and the figure that would come back to us as our rebate. He presented me with a form and asked for my signature.

His behaviour it was entirely formal, flat and without any emotion in the delivery of his words. I took the paper and pen and I began to look for the place I had to sign.

At this moment, I saw over his shoulder the figure of Phil emerging from the back corridor. He staggered, arms and legs stiff, his dark curls hanging in front of his face as he loomed towards us through the kitchen, dressed only in his skimpy underpants. He climbed the single step up from the kitchen and stood framed in the doorway.

I handed the signed form back to the gas man, who ripped off the top sheet to hand it back to me.

Phil, swaying slightly from side to side, reached into his underpants and produced, as if from a magician's hat, a few very limp-looking onion rings, half coated in rice.

The gas man was still facing me, sorting out his paperwork, as yet unaware of Phil's presence.

'Right! Who's been putting onions and rice in my fuckin' underkex?' Phil boomed very suddenly.

After a brief, nonchalant glance at Phil, the gasman politely announced, 'Thank you Mr Donald, that's all. I'll be leaving now.'

4

Mags To Riches

It was a very exciting day when Chris told me that he and his friend Jim were going to produce a 'proper' comic, and they wanted me to do some work for it. Between the ages of about nine and thirteen I'd been obsessed with the idea of being a comic artist. My interests had moved on slightly by the time I reached fourteen or so, and although still an avid comic collector, I was now more interested in listening to loud music and trying to get my tops and fingers.

Chris had been very keen on making magazines since an early age. His first effort had been the *Lily Crescent Locomotive Times*, a magazine with a rather limited target readership, specifically the children living in Lily Crescent, more specifically the children living in Lily Crescent who were interested in trainspotting. Readership totalled about six, including Chris himself. The limited print run was in truth a good thing, as the reproduction method used to create the entire run was carbon paper. (For those of you too young to know what carbon paper was, it was a very primitive method of reproducing documents written using a typewriter. Carbon paper, of a very flimsy dark blue material, was slipped in between the document you were typing and another piece of plain paper. As you typed, the ink was transferred from the carbon paper to the paper underneath.)

This rather brutal method meant that the magazine's entire contents had to be typed and there could be no photographs or illustrations. By using additional sheets of carbon paper in the typewriter you could only get a maximum of three copies of a reasonable standard, so Chris had to type the whole magazine out twice without error in order to produce six copies.

The *Lily Crescent Locomotive Times* did have one contributor other than Chris, and remarkably this reporter wasn't even a resident of Lily Crescent. Jim Brownlow was the paper's Heaton Sidings Correspondent. He had grown up in Lancashire, moving to Newcastle at the age of eleven, becoming Chris's classmate at Heaton School. Their friendship and love of bizarre and extreme humour would bring about the birth of *Viz*.

In about 1975 Dad took me to the Central Library in Newcastle to show me one of the wonders of the space age: the photocopier. He told me to go off and find a book with a nice picture in that I would like to keep. I didn't understand – I couldn't tear a page out of the book, and even if I borrowed it I wouldn't be able to keep the picture. I selected a line drawing of a flying dragon, Dad put it on the copier and he told me to wait by the tray to the side. I couldn't believe my eyes when an exact copy of the picture appeared. It was more amazing than the pocket calculator he had brought home weeks before. The photocopy cost 10p, about 50p today. The photocopier would also play a pivotal role in the origins of *Viz*.

Chris had produced a number of comic strips at school called the Fat Crusader books. These were passed around his friends and featured many of them in cameo roles, the hero himself being the alter ego of one of his classmates, the extremely mild-mannered Chris Scott-Dixon. The strips usually involved some trouble beginning with one teenage social group or other turning up (skinheads, bikers, teds etc.). In graphic, gory detail the Fat Crusader would despatch them by varied and most imaginative means, a bit like one of those predictable horror films popular at the time. These comic books weren't publications as such; they were one-off pieces of artwork that weren't reproduced. Chris's next publishing venture would up the stakes in distribution by utilising the magic of 'the Xerox machine'.

In 1978 Chris and Jim compiled a single page of cartoons with the intention of photocopying it and selling it at cost around friends. This first comedy collaboration between them was called *The Daily Pie*.

70

The Daily Pie was a pretty good production, considering it was a first attempt by teenage boys. Many of the cartoons and features on its one A4 page were later reproduced in the first *Viz* comic, including 'Tommy's Birthday', 'Colin the Amiable Crocodile', 'Your Stars with Gypsy Bag', and, most significantly, 'Rude Kid'.

The single page of artwork was reproduced on the photocopier at Jesmond's Prontaprint, a high-street print franchise, at a cost of 10p a sheet, and priced to sell for the same. Chris and Jim then took it around the pubs of Jesmond and sold it to their friends who drank there.

My first contribution to *Viz*'s beginnings happened at this time, although not in the pubs, but at St George's Youth Club. I got permission from Dave Hall for *The Daily Pie* to be sold there, so one weekend Chris and Jim came down and we went around the club together, pushing our filthy wares on unsuspecting youths. We tried to persuade them that their pocket money and paper-round wages would be better spent on a sheet of puerile humour than on Hubba Bubba or Curly Wurlys from the tuck shop. The problem we faced trying to sell *The Daily Pie* was its price. For a single sheet, 10p was a lot of money at the time, and certainly put people off.

This problem was solved soon afterward as the photocopier became less of an exciting gimmick, which led to the price of copying going down dramatically. Its unstoppable march led to Chris and Jim's next venture being far more saleable. *Arnold the Magazine*, another single-page photocopied publication, was priced once again at cost, but at a much more affordable 2p. Combined sales can't have been more than a few dozen, but the seed had been sown. The desire and means were in place to put together, and reproduce for sale, a publication based around a shared love of extreme and surreal humour.

My parents had introduced my brothers and me to the comedy of Spike Milligan when we were just children. Dad also drove us all to see *The Morecambe and Wise Show* every week at the Carmichaels', television-owning family friends in High West Jesmond. Goons and Stan Freberg records were never off Mum's Dansette. Comedy was something to which we seemed to be naturally drawn. As a family we loved to watch the films of Peter Sellers, Woody Allen, Mel Brooks and Laurel and Hardy, TV shows such as Peter Cook and Dudley Moore's, *The Morecambe and Wise Show* and *The Two Ronnies* and the great sitcoms like *Dad's Army*, *The Good Life*, *Porridge*, *Fawlty Towers* and the wonderful *Whatever Happened to the Likely Lads?*, surely one of the most poignant chronicles of twentieth-century life committed to any medium. But for young lads in the 1970s it was really *Monty Python* that was our comedy god. It was a love of *Monty Python* that drew together Chris and Jim, and I too have loved it from the moment I first cast my very young eyes on it.

At primary school the only other person who had ever seen *Monty Python* was Julian Flear. Julian's parents (the ones who went swimming at five in the morning) were very liberal. His father was a doctor and had long hair, and their house was full of amazing furniture, Corbusier chairs, beanbags and a colour TV set. I would often go there for tea after school where I would be fed strange and wonderful foods like knotted bread with poppy seeds on top, which wasn't cut into slices but was torn at the table. This was an outlandish and eccentric household in which Julian was allowed to stay up to watch *Monty Python*.

My parents, like those of every other child at school, thought the show was on far too late and always sent me off to bed long before it started. Of course, I would never go to bed. I was terrified of going to bed alone. I would sit on top of the stairs, listening, and would sneak down a stair at a time, retreating in haste into the darkness if necessary. If my parents stayed in the room we called to the living room, I would be able to sneak into the sitting room, where the telly was. This took some bravery, and I would occasionally get caught. However, one time, on hearing one of my parents approaching, I hid at the end of the sofa in the gap between it and the wall. I had a perfect view of the telly, whilst remaining hidden. The downside was I had to wait until Mum and Dad either left the room or had fallen asleep before I could make good my escape.

This became my regular hiding place until, for reasons lost to history, Chris decided to grass me up. Not long after this I was allowed special permission to stay up late to watch the show, provided I had my pyjamas on and was ready for bed. *Monty Python* was then moved to an earlier slot and would no longer be the exclusive preserve of the children of West Jesmond's most eccentric families.

My love of *Monty Python* was such that I named my first pet Monty. He was a brown mouse and was very small and cute. One day he was dead. I cried. I got another one, a white one. He was called Monty the Second. He stank and so I had to keep him in the spare bedroom, which meant I would forget to feed him. Dad found a new home for him through his work, with a teenager in Sunderland, the son of one of his clients. Dad was most entertained as the woman reported her son was a 'punk rocket'.

The best way to get your *Monty Python* fix when it wasn't on telly was to listen to the LPs (that's 'long playing' vinyl records to you youngsters). Chris and I were both members of Conway's record library on Holly Avenue. Dad had bought Chris, Steve and me cassette recorders for Christmas and we used them to listen to copies of LPs borrowed from this very strange emporium. It was an almost Dickensian library, its window filled with ancient cobwebbed displays, long since sun-bleached of all but the tiniest hint of their original colours. It had dark, dusty shelves and a polite-to-the-point-of-never-speaking owner, Mr Conway. His very frail and elderly wife sat silently in a corner behind the counter, like some dusty spinster straight from the pages of *Great Expectations*.

I used the library to record all of The Beatles' albums, for which I made my own cassette inserts and labels. Chris was into heavy rock for a short time and borrowed Deep Purple and Led Zeppelin LPs from Conway's, but it was the *Monty Python* albums that saw us through all short-lived trends and teenage musical whims. Whatever else was going on, there was always *Monty Python*. At weekends Jim would often come round and we would listen endlessly to the albums. The team put so much effort into their records. They weren't just the soundtracks of something previously released on film. The *Holy Grail* album, for instance, is an almost entirely new piece of writing. These records were very special to us.

Chris came back one day with something that would push completely new boundaries: Peter Cook and Dudley Moore's *Derek and Clive*. It was by no means as cleverly put together as *Monty Python*, but the outrage caused by the use of constant expletives and dark, explicit sexual subject matter is difficult to explain in this day and age. It's almost impossible to bring home to people how much of a shock it was to our world when nowadays anal sex is fair game for jovial conversation, providing it's after the watershed.

Chris and I had already been involved in creating some comedy together. Using our cassette recorders, we had made several audio versions of TV shows, most commonly *Dr Who*, as I had a 45 rpm single of the theme tune. Rather like Chris's Fat Crusader books, these would inevitably end in extreme violence, a trait of our writing that would continue through the early years of *Viz*. I also recorded a stand-up comedy show based on *The Comedians*, a popular TV show at the time. My 'Funny Joke Show' featured comedians whose jokes were all terrible. There was a Cockney who made useless jokes about his wife being so fat that she couldn't even get through doors and a racist South African whose preoccupation was how black people were. Even though I wrote these jokes when I was twelve or so I still use some of the ideas in my stand-up today.

The Gosforth Hotel

The Daily Pie and *Arnold the Magazine* had given Chris the taste for production of something bigger, with a number of pages and the exciting addition of staples. The means to produce a comedy magazine were almost in place.

Chris and Jim had taken me to see bands play at The Gosforth Hotel on Monday nights since the summer of that year, 1979. I was only fifteen, but the function room where the bands played was upstairs, accessed from the street. It was easy for me to sneak in. Looking underage was never a problem for me really, as I've been almost five foot ten since I was thirteen and I was never refused service in a pub. Many people thought I was older than Chris, which always annoyed him.

Viz, at its birth, was to be something in between an underground comic and local music fanzine. Anti-Pop was a post-punk music cooperative responsible for putting on gigs at The Gosforth Hotel. This was a vibrant scene and all of Newcastle's movers and shakers were to be seen in there on sweaty and noisy Monday nights. The Gosforth had previously been home to resident band Last Exit, featuring the one and only Mr Sting out

74

of The Police. Mr Sting had upped sticks and moved to London before Anti-Pop moved in.

In the months leading up to *Viz*'s launch I began to perform comedy poetry on stage with Pig Sani, a band made up of lads from school. Poady, who I'd written comedy sketches with at school, and who was also my good friend at the People's Theatre, was the singer. My job was to go on stage while the musicians set up and to read some comedy poems. I would then introduce the band and they'd start their set.

The poems I used on stage were written by Chris and Jim. They had originally been part of a fictitious poetry competition they'd posted on the school's sixth-form centre notice board, another stage in their burgeoning comedy writing partnership. (I also used a number of these poems as lyrics to songs when I formed my own comedy band a couple of years later.)

Chris was forever looking for new mediums for his comedy writings and his obsession with stationery and form filling led to the creation of The Bumph Club, a letter-writing club inspired by my copy of *The Book of the Goons*, featuring hilarious letters that Spike Milligan and Peter Sellers sent to each other from fictitious people and companies. Chris had a vision that we could do something similar, but his trainspotter's brain would insist on it being formalised and categorised with membership cards and numbers and a rule insisting that a letter didn't count as a piece of 'bumph' if it hadn't been sent through the Royal Mail. Bumph Club membership was to peak at three: Chris, Jim and me. I had to apply in writing, via the Royal Mail, to The Bumph Club's office, which was Chris's bedroom, across the landing. I received my membership card by return of post. Chris had made a lino-print to create the membership cards, and his use of this basic print medium, one up from potato printing, would soon play its part in the creation of the *Viz* brand.

Anyway, the day I received my Bumph Club letter of acceptance and membership card, in September 1979, I was appearing at The Gosforth with Pig Sani, reading some of Chris and Jim's poems. Before I went on stage I wrote a joke about Poady having done a course in apathy but he didn't turn up for the exam. I wrote it on the back of The Bumph Club acceptance letter, which I had in my pocket at the time.

Once again, this thirty-year-old joke, written by me as a teen-ager, appears in my stand-up act today: it's part of the set of my humourless comedian character Jeremy Jitler.

Chris had insisted, typically enough, on further rules and regulations in The Bumph Club. One of these was that no member was permitted to use a real name in any correspondence connected to the club. In the early years of *Viz* this was a tradition that was upheld, with Chris, Jim and I never using our real names in the credits. One reason for this was the fun we had making up names for ourselves, but it also had the additional benefit of disguising our real identities from the DHSS.

The false identity I chose for myself when joining The Bumph Club was to stick with me for some time. I took the name from an episode of *The Wonderful World of Disney* that I watched in horror one Saturday teatime. It was the most syrupy piece of American sentimentality and stomach-churning child acting I'd ever seen. It was set in the American Civil War, and was the story of Johnny Shiloh the Lovable Little Yankee Drummer Boy. Johnny was remarkably brave and cute in equal measures, and the entire debacle was finished off with a cheerful musical number singing his praises as Johnny marched bravely onward with his comrades being blown limb from limb all around him (in a sanitised Disney fashion, obviously). As I'd watched this on the day that Chris asked me to join The Bumph Club under a false name, Johnny Shiloh came straight to mind. As these were the days before Sky Plus, domestic video recorders or even Ceefax, I was unable to go back to the beginning of the programme in order to see how this adorable all-American hero's name was spelled. I guessed at Shiloe, and Johnny Shiloe became my pseudonym for the next twenty-four years, my cartoons for *Viz* all being signed 'Shiloe'.

Chris had left school after staying on into the sixth form for two years. Jim had stayed on for a year, but left at seventeen. Chris had applied to universities, but was, and still is, narked at not getting accepted where he really wanted to go. An offer from Loughborough seemed to particularly annoy him for some reason. None of us had done well at school, my brothers had failed to achieve their desired targets, and Jim was much brighter than his education would suggest. I was now heading for the lowest finish of all, leaving school at sixteen with only two O levels in English and Art. As a CSE student I was entered specially for these, my best subjects, along with woodwork. However, the school did me the honour of forgetting to inform me about the date of the woodwork exam. They later did me what they seemed to consider a great favour: instead of arranging for me to sit the exam at another time, they had the examining board delete the 'fail' entry from my results and certificate. They knew how to treat kids back then.

Chris had not taken the Loughborough student opportunity and had instead, after a while looking around at train- and bus-related careers, taken a job at Newcastle's single biggest employer of persons lacking the desire to live – the notorious 'Ministry'.

The headquarters of the Department of Health and Social Security in many ways suited Chris. For a start, there were lots of forms to fill in. As far as I can tell, work at the Ministry went something like this. You spent all day working at a job that was neither interesting nor rewarding, but there was the benefit of a varied social life. During the 1970s the site employed 10,000 staff and contained banks, a post office, a hairdressers, a garden shop and a staff canteen with licensed bar. It was basically a well-equipped prisoner of war camp for people with families to go home to. It was even built like a POW camp, the premises having been established on the site in a hurry during the Second World War.

Chris's job at the DHSS was another keystone in *Viz*'s birth. He'd been stumped momentarily at the job interview when asked why he wanted to work there, but came out with the perfect answer – he simply needed a steady and solid job he could rely on, allowing him to spend time on his hobbies during weekends and evenings. Apparently, when you're applying to work in a place that no one has ever desired to work in, this is the best answer you can give.

Chris became involved in many activities at the Ministry, including working on an internal magazine as a football reporter, but the DHSS's real contribution to *Viz*'s birth was to pay Chris wages.

Just like *The Beano*?

My invitation into the world of *Viz* was quite understated. Chris had told me of his plans to make a 'proper' comic and invited me to become a contributor in pretty much the same breath. I remember being stunned. It sounded almost unreal. I would have my work as a comic artist *published*. Amazing. I immediately asked what sort of paper it would be on.

'Proper comic paper.' A welcome answer.

'Just like *The Beano*?' I asked.

'Yes. Just like *The Beano*,' Chris replied, beginning to lose patience, as he does.

Chris and Jim, whose work I admired hugely, wanted me to work with them on a real comic? I couldn't believe it. I asked Chris what he wanted me to draw and was amazed when he told me that would be up to me.

I walked out of Chris's room and across the landing to my own. I had to both write and draw my own cartoon. What would I produce?

I wasn't without experience, having produced a few copycat comic books called *Baddie Killer Man* in the style of Chris's Fat Crusader books, although by my own admission they were greatly inferior. I'd also practised drawing comic characters since I was about nine, so I believed I could make a go of it.

My first piece of work took a couple of days. I have no idea why I chose the subject matter. I guess I wanted to do something like what Chris and Jim had created for *The Daily Pie* and *Arnold the Magazine*, yet was different and in some way my own. What I produced was a bit *Monty Python*-like in so far as it was a genteel British suburban scenario violently interrupted by both the surreal and the violent. 'Afternoon Tea with Mr Kipplin' was a four-frame strip in which the narrative went as follows:

Mr Kipplin was a jolly nice chap. He asked me over one Sundry Sunday afternoon to sample his new Bonfreit Slices.

He sported some wizard sex aids and was decent enough to let me have a quickie with his wife.

Then I tucked into his gorgeous goodies.

> But unfortunately I ate so much grub that I bowked
> rich brown vomit well into the night.

It wasn't brilliantly drawn, or indeed written, but the final frame, in which the narrator is leaning over the toilet bowl, spewing a quite ludicrous amount of 'rich brown vomit' into it, does make me feel happy that at fifteen years of age I was doing something with my life I could always be proud of.

I delivered the artwork to Chris's bedroom and was delighted when it received a nonplussed silence, meaning it had been approved.

The rest of the comic was put together in Chris's bedroom, using work taken from *The Daily Pie* and *Arnold the Magazine*, with lots of new work produced by him and Jim.

Martin, the singer of The Noise Toys, one of the bands we regularly watched at The Gosforth Hotel, was an art student and asked if he could contribute a page. He was one of a very small number of contributors to the first issue and was to become a regular cartoonist in all the early editions of *Viz*. His artwork was quite stylish, more like that in what we'd call a graphic novel today. It was very different from mine and that of Chris and Jim.

His first contribution, 'Revenge of the Steel Skull', differed from the rest of the content of that first issue, being very dark both in its appearance and its subject matter. Martin adapted his style as *Viz* continued, remaining dark, but introducing a much more *Beano*-like element with the introduction of Tubby Round.

The contents of what was to be the first issue of *Viz* were quite mixed, and not all of a very high quality, but one thing that shone was the humour, and, maybe more importantly, the attitude. We were right in the middle of the post-punk music explosion, which brought with it an ethic that touched everything creative. We were doing something for ourselves. No businesses were involved, no one told us what to produce, or why. Our heads were filled with nothing but the thought of making people laugh. We wanted to be in The Clash and we wanted to be in *Monty Python*. We'd taken a bit of each and made something of our own. *Viz* would develop very rapidly in style, but for now it was just a very rough-and-ready vehicle for the humour of three comedy-obsessed teenagers.

It's important to realise at this point that this comic was not intended as a long-running publication. It was nothing more than a natural progression in our efforts to better each of our previous attempts to make each other laugh.

The idea of being involved with the local music scene attracted us into producing something that would give us some status in that world. Chris also saw the music scene connection as being a useful way of attracting fans of the bands to buy copies of the comic. He needed to make his money back, having decided to price *The Bumper Monster Christmas Special* at 20p – 10½p less than its cost per copy. Sensibly enough, he saw this as a reasonable price for buyers. Better to lose 10½p a copy than sell no comics and claw nothing back. As for it not making business sense, it wasn't a business, it was a hobby. Or perhaps another way to look at it is as a very shrewd investment.

Chris had searched around the local printers to see who could do the best deal. Prontaprint proved prohibitively expensive, as did all the other high street shops. However, an alternative was found in a little hidden-away square just off Westgate Road. The Tyneside Free Press Workshop was a non-profit-making co-op run by socialists, hippies and professional printers.

The cost of printing nowadays is remarkable compared to 1979. Chris paid almost £50 to have 150 copies of the comic printed, at just 12 pages and only using black ink on the cheapest paper. It was a lot of money. Nowadays it's possible to have 10,000 flyers printed in full-colour on both sides, on high-quality glossy paper, for around the same price.

Seeing the printed copies for the first time, knowing that inside them was a piece of my own work entirely of my own making, is a memory I shall always treasure. Chris handed me a copy and, as I sit here writing, I remember the smell. It didn't smell like the comics in my collection: they had a unique smell I now realise comes from the ageing paper. *The Bumper Monster Christmas Special* smelled of ink and brand-new paper. But it was unmistakably a comic. The dream of my childhood was a reality. I flicked through the flimsy pages and sure enough, there it was: 'Afternoon Tea with Mr Kipplin', in print. I was a comic artist.

There had been a certain amount of guesswork involved in putting the comic together. Chris had laid out the artwork initially not realising that the printer requires a layout of the pages as printed, as opposed to the way they will be read. For example, in a twelve-page comic, page 1 will be side by side with page 12. The other side of this sheet will be pages 2 and 11. Page 3 is laid out next to page 10, and so on. Chris was sent home from the Free Press to rearrange the artwork to fit this pattern, from which the printers would make the plates.

Having insisted that Chris do his part of the job properly, the Free Press then proceeded to get their part wrong. The plates were all made properly, with all of the pages corresponding as they should. However, they were collated wrongly, with pages 3 and 10, backed with pages 4 and 9, being laid the wrong way round before the paper was folded and stitched. The result of this was page 9 where page 3 should be and page 4 where page 10 should be. Unfortunately, Martin's very dark and not particularly representative 'Revenge of the Steel Skull', which had been scheduled for page 9, now appeared in the extremely prominent position of page 3. Comic collectors now look for this mistaken layout when trying to identify if a *Viz* issue 1 is from the first print run.

This wasn't the Free Press's only incident of the same mistake. Their solution next time, but for another customer, was to lock the door, turn off the lights and hide under their desks.

Chris's plan was to start by selling some of the comics at The Gosforth Hotel. The two bands that always topped the bill on a Monday night were The Noise Toys, featuring *Viz* contributor Martin, and Arthur 2 Stroke.

All three of us headed along to Gosforth High Street carrying about half of the print run with us. On arriving at the hotel we went in the side entrance and straight up the stairs to the door of the function room. There was a small landing outside, with a little table, at which Andy Pop sat to take payment from customers before they entered the room. He had a rubber stamp bearing the legend 'ANTI-POP ENTERTAINMENTARAMA', which was used to stamp the backs of the hands of the gig-goers. Andy had granted Chris permission to sell our comics at the door, so we all adopted positions around the landing to ensure anybody coming up the stairs to the gig would pass all three of us, each holding the comic, and each of us doing our best at a hard sell. Nowadays this would probably be equated most closely to the tactics used by *Big Issue* sellers, although to be fair it's not in their interests to work in teams.

Being the most outgoing of the three of us, I found it very easy to be pushy, but in a friendly way. If people said no I would always quickly turn to one of the funniest things in the comic and say, 'But look! It's funny!'

This method had a remarkably high hit rate, although it tended to infuriate Chris, but then so did most things that I did. He and Jim were both naturally very quiet people, and not disposed the hard sell. I saw my icebreaker as creating a great opportunity to talk to people.

Many of the people going into the gig had bought the comic. The most amazing trend was now starting to develop. People who had declined were now coming back out to buy a copy, having seen other people laughing and passing it around. Before long we realised we only had a handful left. The obvious thing to do would be to get the rest from home. However, Lily Crescent was a half-hour walk from the pub, and there were no direct buses. Fortunately, the only person that we knew with motorised transport happened to be at the gig. Paul Webster, one of Chris's old school friends, had a blue Ford Escort van, and very kindly drove me back to the house to collect the rest of the print run.

Before the end of the night the whole lot had been sold. It remains only for me to say 'the rest is history'.

So, *Viz* had arrived. It wasn't called *Viz* yet, but that was soon to change. What we'd produced had been intended as a Christmas novelty. Selling out as quickly as it did, the option to leave it as a one-off would clearly have been a mistake. Andy Pop, who unlike us cartoonists was a businessman, suggested that we move immediately to produce a second issue.

When Chris announced his intention to go ahead and produce another, I was absolutely bowled over. I was part of something successful. We'd made something that people wanted. They thought our work was funny. This was another hugely significant moment in my life: not only had I produced something that I was proud of, but other people, and not just people that I knew, wanted to buy it because it made them laugh.

The Bumper Monster Christmas Special had featured a logo in the top right-hand corner of the cover denoting the fictional publisher of the product. Chris had produced this logo using a linocut. It read 'Viz Comics'. Logically, this was a great title to use for all future products, but naming our new product was by no means a straightforward decision. Chris, Jim and I all put forward suggestions for a title. My favourite was *The Daily Pie*. I'd always loved that name and I still do. That said, the simplicity of *Viz* surely worked in our favour.

There has been much speculation about where the name *Viz* came from. Contrary to popular belief, we had no idea that 'viz' had any meaning. (It's from the Latin that means 'namely', 'that is to say' or 'as follows'.) Chris has said that he chose it because all the letters had no curves, therefore the linocut was much easier to make. However, this was clearly nonsense, as the lino image not only uses a lower-case 'i', which has a circular dot, but the word 'Comic' appears in all of its curvaceous and circular glory beneath.

The sadly uninteresting truth is that we thought *Viz* sounded like a comic's name.

As *Viz* grew in circulation Chris, Jim and I would become very familiar with the Free Press workshop. A do-it-yourself service that they offered proved particularly useful to us, as with only a few minutes' training we would be able to fold, collate and stitch all of the printed pages ourselves, not only reducing the cost of printing, but greatly increasing my feeling that we were doing something that felt like a proper job. It was a lovely place to work, and on our three or four annual visits we were treated as if we were always there.

It's funny to look back and realise how unplanned the whole venture was. It wasn't entirely without organisation, but there was no real long-term goal, no business plan, no sales targets, no desire to take over the world – just a lifelong love of laughing and something of a gift for drawing.

The fact that Chris and I are quite anal was also very important. A lot of people see our creation as the result of having a 'right laugh' and lots of trips to the pub for 'production meetings'. Although we all socialised in those early days, it's not possible to be productive or to be a good judge of your work if you're spending too much time in the pub. There is a need for relentless discipline in sitting down to draw out your ideas as cartoons. It must be one of the most tedious processes you could imagine, to sit and draw out in fine detail the same faces, the same bodies, the same pubs, the same everything time and time and time again. Not that I'm complaining.

Welcome to the Bigg time

One of the great joys of the early days of *Viz* was throwing our launch parties. Our social circle, much of which remains in place today, was in the main bonded by creativity. All the people we knew were involved in the world of music or art. Apart from the usual gigs at The Gosforth Hotel, there were many house parties in the creative hotspots of Jesmond, Sandyford, Heaton and Fenham, but my favourite events by far were the *Viz* parties that we would put on at the launch of each new edition. These were known as *Viz* receptions. *Viz* was not a regular publication. We were driven only by our passion to create a new edition and there were no regular deadlines in those days. One of the results of the irregular appearance of the comics was the fact that a new issue felt like an event, so it was always a good excuse for a celebration and letting people 'on the scene' know that a new copy was out.

The receptions began in a very modest way with a drinks party in the office of Anti-Pop one Friday afternoon, probably for issue 3. Chris, Jim and I carried the cardboard boxes containing the entire print run the short distance from the Tyneside Free Press down to the Bigg Market and up the dark, winding stairs to the pokey little office, in which about half a dozen of the usual suspects were congregated. A box was opened and comics were passed around, followed by cans of beer and smokes. The good times were here: I was involved in the production of something of which I was truly proud, something that gave me some real status in my peer group, despite the tenderness of my years. Here

I was, enjoying the company and congratulations of those older than me, and becoming one of them as I drank and smoked my way into adulthood.

The Anti-Pop office was very long, thin and dark with the door at one end and the window at the other, a row of built-in cupboards up to about waist height, Andy's desk and two or three office chairs. It was a remarkably scruffy place. Chris, Jim and I had once spent a week looking after it and tidied the place up. It was littered with papers, the window into the Bigg Market was opaque with filth, and on the windowledge outside, amidst a three-inch-deep layer of pigeon shit, was a filthy old trainer, presumably thrown there in the distant past. We picked up all the papers and filed them in an orderly fashion, swept the floor, decorated the walls with posters advertising the gigs the business had promoted, cleaned the window and replaced the trainer with a nice new clean one. We waited in anticipation for the return of Andy and The Chart Commandos, who had been away on tour in Scotland. Our week's work was greeted with a few words of mild disgruntlement by the ever-effervescent Andy Pop.

As the *Viz* launch party began I'd been lucky enough to get one of the few chairs in the Anti-Pop office. The other partygoers sat along the top of the three-foot-high cupboards. On the chair next to me was Davey Bruce, drummer with The Chart Commandos, and an almost unbelievable stereotype: wild, scruffy, loud, brash, loads of fun, completely mad and with an ability to continue drinking alcohol after what he had already consumed would have felled the strongest carthorse. He was also a quite stunning drummer. As the party progressed and the drink flowed, I was filled with a wonderful feeling of happiness and warmth. This was soon replaced with a mild feeling of panic. I was suddenly very aware that I was going to be sick. Unfortunately, the only toilet in the building was shared by all the other offices, and was a single cubicle down a winding and narrow flight of stairs. Therein I endured my first experience of drink-induced vomiting. Oh, the joys of youth.

When it all comes true man – wow! That's something else

The feeling that *Viz* would be more than just a hobby for us was driven home to me when we were invited to take part in a national BBC television programme. *Something Else* was part of the late 1970s and early 1980s 'yoof' genre. Chris, Jim and I were to visit London for the first time as part of the filming. *Something Else* was famously 'the programme made by young people for young people', although in truth this was something of a gloss. Each programme featured a different UK city. Researchers had found that *Viz* was something of a buzz amongst Newcastle's teenagers, so had opted to include us.

The trip to London was the greatest adventure I'd ever been on. None of us had ever visited the capital before, and we all found the journey very exciting. As a boy I'd had a children's map of London on my bedroom wall, illustrated with fantastic colourful cartoon drawings of landmarks. I used to lie on my bed and look at it, dreaming that one day I would visit this magical place.

In 1951 Mum was taken to London by Auntie Ella to see the Festival of Britain. She often talked to me about it. She was seventeen, the same age I was during my similarly wondrous adventure thirty years later. It's said that first impressions last. I fell in love with London the moment I arrived.

We arrived at King's Cross on the train that as boys we had watched set off for London so many times. It was only the third time I'd ever travelled on an Intercity. On arrival the first thing that struck me was that almost all of the staff on the platform were black. In the north east of England in the 1970s, black faces were very few and far between. I had known a girl called Anna, who lived along the street, and a handful of other black children, mostly adopted by the wonderfully loving hippy–socialist mums of Jesmond. Strange and unexpected as it was to suddenly be confronted with all these West Indian faces, I saw it as exciting and different. We were no longer in a familiar place: we really had travelled, even though the journey was only 300 miles. We were about to experience something akin to landing on an entirely different world.

Looking back, seeing how the presence of the black population of London surprised me, I realise that this was a time when the media really didn't fairly represent the existence or importance of black people in British society. Television hadn't prepared me for a London as cosmopolitan as this. The only images of the streets of London we had were in *The Sweeney*, and everyone on that was white, except for the occasional criminal. No surprise, really, that the Brixton riots happened in the spring of this year, 1981, and race riots would trouble much of the country in the following years.

It was summer and the weather was amazing. I had no idea there was such a temperature difference between the north and the south of England. The place felt tropical to us.

Our first port of call was the BBC's Community Programme Unit's production office to collect the keys to the flat where we would stay for three days – the home of the show's producer, Jane Oliver. The flat was in a converted Victorian terrace in Hampstead. Its previous owner had been Errol Brown out of Hot Chocolate. Hampstead reminded us of Jesmond: it was cosmopolitan, wealthy and inhabited largely by middle-class socialists. We dropped our bags and set off back to the tube, went to Notting Hill Gate and strolled down Portobello Road. I was familiar with the Portobello Road from my fondness for Paddington Bear. Mr Gruber, Paddington's antique-dealing friend, had a shop there, where they would drink hot chocolate together on his old settee.

We wandered along through the market, taking in the vibrant colour, noise and bustle. Our mission was to find Rough Trade Records, an independent record retailer, and one of the only shops to sell *Viz* outside Newcastle. We couldn't believe our eyes when we spotted, amongst the littered array of punky promotional material, a *Viz* poster advertising the comic for sale. Jim and I posed for photo next to it. This was a fine day.

The following day we boarded the underground and set off for Leicester Square. It sounded pretty central. We found Trafalgar Square and were suitably impressed. I took photos with my old Bakelite Box Brownie camera, acquired from a jumble sale, and Chris took some with Dad's old 35 mm. I spotted Big Ben just down the street and we made a beeline for it. Halfway there, we

87

found Downing Street. Glancing at the map Chris had cleverly brought, we discovered Buckingham Palace too was only a short, and extremely glamorous, walk away. We had a quick shufty at Buck House and then walked into Green Park, where we sat down, enjoyed the sunshine and reflected on our amazing discovery that all of these things that I knew from my childhood bedroom map were only yards apart.

The best, though, was yet to come. Sunday was to be spent at BBC Television Centre, the entertainment Mecca of all school children of the 1970s. We were in absolute disbelief when we were shown into the studio and told it was where *Top of the Pops* was filmed. Not only that, but I immediately recognised the studio walls as being those in the background on *The Old Grey Whistle Test* when the likes of David Bowie, Alice Cooper, Lindisfarne and Bob Marley and the Wailers had played live in the early 1970s.

The bands that appeared on our show were the fantastically named, not-insignificant, but rather dated by this time, Angelic Upstarts and the truly dreadfully named, no-holds-barred astonishingly awful Tygers of Pan Tang. These choices were a rather sad state of affairs when you consider how good the music scene was in Newcastle at the time. The Upstarts came from Sunderland. This seemed to be an irrelevance to the producers, who treated Sunderland as part of Newcastle, which as anybody from either city will tell you is far from the truth.

Whilst the studio was set up for the bands we were invited to the BBC bar for a drink. The Angelic Upstarts had brought some of their entourage along, one of whom had a live snake wrapped around his shoulders. I can't say I know why, and I'm also assuming BBC security was somewhat laxer in those days. Looking down from the bar's terrace, I couldn't believe what I saw: the *Blue Peter* garden, instantly recognisable with Percy Thrower's comparatively new Italian sunken garden, which had been added only a couple of years before. It was another massive moment on this amazing trip. Unsure of what I was supposed to do with my life, it was an enormous adrenaline boost in my teenage world.

The initial filming for the programme had taken place in Newcastle, with Mark, a Sunderland lad, interviewing all three of the *Viz* team in Chris's bedroom. Before the arrival of the camera crew we went to The Collingwood Arms for some lunchtime Dutch courage. On our return to the house, with a couple of pints inside us, we decided it would be funny if we all wore wigs, glasses and false moustaches for the interview. Chris took a pair of sunglasses and broke out one lens, cracking the other for full comedy effect. He then put on a false moustache, which he lined up at a jaunty angle, half being pasted over one cheek. Jim wore a Beatles wig, off to one side, and I wore a long dark one, with plenty of my own blonde spiky hair protruding, and a pair of circular sunglasses at a fashionable Eric Morecambe angle. Looking back, it was all quite Goons. Our first national television interview was to be a glorious shambles.

Over the years I've learned to deal with television interviews and media coverage quite well. I wouldn't recommend, given a few moments to speak to the nation and put across your message, that you should prepare by going to the pub and give no thought whatsoever to what you want to say.

That said, being rather anarchic teenagers, and representing an irreverent and heavily sweary publication, we did ourselves no harm.

Chris, despite dressing up, decided to be quite sullen once the camera was rolling, and was offended by everything I said. He and Jim both fielded questions about the comic's foul-mouthed content with quite serious answers, while I deliberately played up to the camera, inspired by the hippyish wig. I did a right-on piece about our mission being to make the world a better place to live in. It still makes me laugh now. Chris, though, took it upon himself to tell the crew that I was drunk, despite the fact we had each had an equal and insignificant two pints of beer. Chris's moods – from wacky and laugh-a-minute to dark, judgemental and morose in the blinking of an eye – were something I would have to deal with for many years to come. He very rarely offered words of support or encouragement.

Viz was not the only success story of *Something Else: Newcastle*. Mark Rough, the Sunderland lad who interviewed us, went on to be a successful stand-up comedian. Andy Inman, aka Andy Pop, interviewed on the show about his promotion of music in the city, went on to distribute *Viz* nationally and developed a very successful business supplying record shops with merchandise. Tracey Wilkinson, from South Shields Youth Theatre, went on to star in *Our Friends in the North*, *Bad Girls* and many other dramas. The show was a great experience.

We'd been welcomed into Jane's home by her six-year-old daughter, Jemma. Jane asked her what she thought of her Geordie houseguests. She replied, 'I love them all really, but I love Simon the most because he's the jolliest.'

I didn't see Jane or Jemma again for twenty-eight years. Recently, I tried looking up Jane on Facebook. I didn't find her, but I did find Jemma. After becoming friends I randomly bumped into her at the Edinburgh Festival in 2009. Then I bumped into her again outside my local shops in London. It turned out that we were neighbours. This is one of those stories that should naturally end with the legend 'It's a small world.' However, she was moving to Australia the next day, which somewhat negates the possibility of using the cliché successfully. Jane has since come to see me at one of my stand-up shows, and I finally got the chance to thank her for giving us the opportunity to put our work on TV for the first time.

In the next two hours ... the next thirty years

The term 'alternative comedy' hadn't reached Newcastle in 1981 when Andy Pop told us he had a new exciting venture. He'd seen an opportunity for getting crowds into the rather forlorn Jesmond Cinema, standing at the end of Sunbury Avenue, and in which I'd spent so much of my childhood and adolescence. Putting live entertainment on there would pose a problem, as the cinema wasn't licensed for music, but comedy bypassed this issue. Andy had become aware of a touring comedy troupe called The Comic Strip and showed me an unbelievable photocopied press pack with scores of five-star reviews. They'd also sent wonderful posters depicting a falling bomb, with space at the bottom for Andy to write the gig details in with a marker pen.

Chris, Jim and I were sceptical about the possibility of stand-up comedy being funny. Stand-up was old hat: it was for outdated working men's club comedians who appeared on TV shows like *The Comedians*, telling predictable and often racist jokes. Or so we thought.

90

The event was very well attended – everyone who was anyone on the Newcastle scene was there. As the show opened we were hit with the astonishing, lightening-paced, aggressive, political and foulmouthed Alexei Sayle, compère. His material and attitude hit me like a cricket bat. It was apparent from the word go that there was actually someone else out there who saw the world they way we did. The acts and comedians that followed beggar belief from the viewpoint of hindsight, and I guess it's no surprise that I've never since seen a comedy show with such impact. It comprised Nigel Planer, Peter Richardson, Ade Edmundson and Rik Mayall, then there were French and Saunders, the first women to make me hurt with laughter, and finally Arnold Brown ... and why not?

'The Dangerous Brothers' was possibly the funniest thing I've ever seen. When they lined up Ade's final act of dangerousness, headbutting the mic out of the stand, I thought I might die laughing. It was truly wonderful.

In those two or so hours we had, in one fell swoop, witnessed the backbone of British television comedy for the next two decades and more. It was the most remarkable live event I've ever experienced, and it all happened on the street where I was born.

Unfortunately, I didn't get to meet any of the performers, and I never have since, with the exception of Arnold Brown at a book launch – a very nice man indeed. I would have loved the chance to thank the others too for one of the best nights of my life.

For your information ... For your entertainment

The *Viz* receptions became more organised over the next few issues. They would always take place in the afternoon in rooms that we were able to hire free of charge. These included the back room of the Baltic Wine Cellar, the function room of the Grosvenor Hotel in Jesmond and Dingwalls on Waterloo Street. Unfortunately, when *Viz* became a regular publication these parties came to an end, but they really were a big part in the comic's early history and I will always have very fond memories of them.

We were still very young and driven at the time and *Viz* was, of course, a home-grown product. We did our best to make these

91

parties as professional as we could, but with a cottage-industry, *Viz*-signature, openly cheesy feel.

We recorded cassettes to play during the receptions, mix tapes of our favourite tunes – lots of Motown, northern soul, Dexy's, The Jam and so on, sprinkled with obscure favourites and some good comedy tunes. I used to record pieces as a comedy DJ in between the tracks. He was based on the graveyard-shift DJs on Metro Radio at the time, with a bit of Alan Robson thrown in. He was your classic shit local radio presenter, the type inescapably associated nowadays with Alan Partridge. I don't remember the character's name, and I don't believe any of the tapes still exist, although I may be wrong. His catchphrase I remember very well: it was based on that random horseshit DJs talk when they need to fill in 'dead air' while they're thinking. 'Never the mind … the none the nevertheless!'

I also recorded a very serious-sounding voice artiste character who only ever had one line, delivered in the style of the bloke who always used to voiceover the really cheap local TV adverts. He was basically a shit actor trying to sound like Richard Burton or something. The wording of his line was, '*Viz* comic reception, for your information … For your entertainment.'

We had fun inserting this announcement rather too often into the tapes, which was a great test of people's humour. With very repetitive jokes some people begin to find it even more funny at the exact same moment that other people begin to find it absolutely intolerable.

For one recording Steve Nash, guitarist and later trumpet player in Arthur 2 Stroke, better known at the time as WM7, introduced us to the outrageous 1940s recordings of Spike Jones and the City Slickers. He invited Chris and me to his flat in the west end of Newcastle specially to borrow a Spike Jones LP and a Kenny Everett compilation of the worst records ever made. Two significant things happened on our journey, one being that in the particularly rough end of Benwell where Steve was living I spotted a shop called The Community Shop, which didn't seem to sell anything, but appeared to be more of a liberal-thinking community drop-in centre. Chris and I filled our journey walking through the streets of Benwell with images of an unshaven man in a vest and slippers trying to buy cigarettes there. At the time we were particularly amused by what we called 'woolly liberals'

92

trying to enforce their middle-class hippy thinking on the less-than-receptive working-class people of the area. Chris later turned the imagined unfortunate man trying to buy his tabs from a woolly-jumpered ethnically aware non-profit-making shopkeeper into an absolutely brilliant cartoon called simply 'Community Shop'.

The other significant moment, possibly more significant to those of us who were fans of Arthur 2 Stroke at the time, was Steve Nash showing us the packet of washing powder from which he had taken the stage name WM7. It was a 1960s pack of Omo, which proclaimed to contain the ingredient WM7, which was revealed in the small print to be the wonder formula Washday Miracle 7.

It would be years later that Phil Branston revealed to me where he took the name Arthur 2 Stroke from. He was sitting in a pub in Clapham and an old fella walked in. The locals all said hello to him, and he was introduced to Phil as Arthur 2 Strokes. Phil discreetly asked why the man had such a name. He was told that it was quite simple: his name was Arthur and he'd had two strokes.

There was little in the way of organised entertainment at the *Viz* launch functions: they were little more than an excuse to get drunk in the afternoon whilst celebrating the creation of another comic. One thing we did was to run little competitions and we made special prizes to give away to the winners. At the reception for *Viz* issue 7 or so we gave away as prizes two bottles of beer for which Chris and I had made our own one-off labels. His was called Britain's Brew and featured early *Viz* favourite Billy Britain. Mine was called Parkie's Piss, and not surprisingly featured The Parkie. More than ten years later I was in a friend's house in Gateshead. Davey Whitaker had played in the aforementioned not-insignificant band The Hostages, who in 1985 they were signed to EMI for the very short time it took them to spend their entire advance on drugs. On Davey's mantelpiece I spotted the Parkie's Piss bottle. I was very touched that he had considered it worth keeping after winning whatever competition it was we ran that day, but he was outdone by Davey Bruce, who had won the Britain's Brew by doing the best impression of Billy Britain. Davey Bruce to this day has the Britain's Brew bottle, but unlike Davey Whitaker's bottle, it still miraculously contains the original beer. Which, it has to be said, was not looking particularly appetising the last time I saw it, about ten years ago.

Your products are shit. Advertise with us

The progress of *Viz* was steady both in terms of our production and sales. Sales were particularly of interest due to the fact that they almost always seemed to go somewhere beyond our expectations. The initial print run of issue 1 famously sold out in a couple of hours. Chris informs me that this was never really true, and there were actually quite a few left in the house, but these kinds of claims do tend to work in your favour. It wasn't a million miles from the truth, anyway.

Issue 2 was a limited edition of 500, although we weren't aware at the time that when you print a limited edition nobody's really counting. Unless everyone's in one room at the same time, nobody will ever know how many came off the press. As a result issue 2 has become the rarest of all collectable *Viz* comics. Issue 1 was reprinted twice, selling around 750 or 1,000 in total, and issue 3 had a print run of about 1,000, so 2 will always be the most desirable.

In these early days the comic continued to be a loss-making venture. Issue 1 lost 10½p per copy, 2 worked out a little better due to the increased print run, but we were far from earning a living from our work.

Listen Ear was an independent record shop on Ridley Place in Newcastle, and it became the first shop ever to sell *Viz*. However, when *Viz* went on sale at legendary teenage hangout the Handyside Arcade things changed dramatically.

Brian Sandals was an eccentric, bespectacled, suit-wearing man looking rather more like a civil servant than someone who sold second-hand records, patches, badges, posters and general hippie and drug-related paraphernalia to teenagers. His shop, Kard Bar, had been at the centre of Newcastle's swinging scene in the 1960s, when the Club A'Gogo was in the same building: this saw the likes of The Rolling Stones, John Mayall and most famously Jimi Hendrix play on a tiny stage to a crowded room full of Geordie teens. The arcade itself, a beautiful horseshoe-shaped two-tiered Victorian building, always filled with natural light by

94

its cast iron and glass roof, remained the place to be seen on a Saturday afternoon until its shameful destruction in the mid-1980s to make way for a soulless extension to Eldon Square shopping centre. Perhaps there is some poetic justice in the fact that the shops there appear to find it very difficult to attract customers into this remote outpost of the shopping centre that destroyed so much of Newcastle's centre in the 1970s.

Brian was always good at keeping the teenagers supplied with whatever bits and bobs each generation had a particular interest in. During the early rise of *Viz* we used some of his old stock of posters to give away as an insert in issue 10½. It was amazing to discover that Brian never threw stock out. The arcade was a low-rent facility due to the development of Eldon Square, so he had whole shop spaces dedicated simply to storing things he'd never sold. We took advantage of this by giving away Bay City Rollers posters in the mid-1980s. Not only were these posters ten or more years out of date, but they were twice or four times the size of the centrespread of the comic, so we guillotined them to fit. Lucky readers buying the comic that carried the legend 'FREE FULL-COLOUR POP POSTER INSIDE' got half of the Rollers' legs or a quarter of David Cassidys' face.

Brian's policy was to pay great dividends in the late 1980s and early 1990s when his early-1970s stock of smiley face badges, patches, posters and so on sold by the barrowload. He once asked me in a very calm and matter-of-fact way why was it that this stock he had carried for twenty years was suddenly so much in demand. I told him it was all down to acid house. He looked at me and smiled, and said, 'Oh. That.'

He clearly had no idea what I was talking about. But that's Brian – never knowing what he's selling, or why, but always doing a very good job of it.

Brian was to suggest something that would really change *Viz*'s fortunes. He asked why we didn't carry any advertising in the comic. We said we didn't want to be involved with anything that didn't fit with what we were doing. It was alright to promote the bands we went to see, but beyond that it didn't seem feasible to whore the comic. It might pay the bills, but what would the comic become?

The answer to this quandary was simple. We would take ad-verts, but there would be a set of rules. If you didn't follow our rules your product would not be advertised in *Viz*. The rules, although never written down, went something like this:

1) We design your advert. You have no say over its contents.
2) Your product or service will be openly scorned in the advert.
3) If you don't approve of your advert and refuse to pay we'll print it anyway.

It was a policy that proved remarkably successful. Businesses wanted to be seen in the comic. They wanted to be seen to be with the in-crowd. *Viz* was seen in the hands of teenagers, a group of people who are notoriously difficult to advertise to. The minute you try and be cool or try to impress teenagers, they will shoot you down in flames or run a mile. The person who tries to be cool when advertising to a teenager is the least cool person. This is one of life's constants. So, for instance, if you try and put across in your advert that your shop is cool or trendy, teenagers will automatically never come.

In our policy shops appeared to say something along the lines of 'If you come to our shop to spend your money we'll think you're a cunt.' Or 'Everything we sell is crap.' The making of claims that were not impressive and the honesty and humour in the messages really got across. Teenagers don't like to be told anything, so they liked *Viz*'s 'non-adverts'. They admired the honesty of unimpressive claims. The advertisers became cool for being brave enough to be seen being mocked.

Rule three only came into force once that I remember. Chris and I used to work doing illustration for various people as a sideline, and one ran a clothing distribution warehouse and shop called Phaze. Martin Keegan was a quiet and slightly eccentric reclusive businessman and was most taken aback when Chris presented him with the artwork for his advertisement in *Viz*. Martin's shop was a post-punk fashion boutique that took itself rather seriously. The advert was a photograph of me dressed in the worst 1970s fashion disasters I could find and Chris laid it out as badly as possible. Martin was not happy. Chris said he would go away and come back with something different, but instead simply published the ad. After a stream of customers came into Phaze to say how much they had enjoyed his advert, Martin decided the piss-taking ad was a good idea after all.

The adverts sat amongst the rest of the comic's contents perfectly and made a statement about what *Viz* was. Its anarchic and irreverent attitude wasn't contrasted by having serious adverts. The fact that local businesses were so happy to come on board and be part of the madness, the silliness, did both our and their reputations no harm at all. It created a little niche market for businesses to be seen as part of a local phenomenon. Students and local kids could all see which businesses and services were cool.

As the early 1980s moved on all the local record shops began not only to stock the comic but also advertise in it. Listen Ear, the first shop to sell *Viz*, became Volume Records and a regular advertiser. Virgin in Eldon Square at the time was run almost like an independent shop and the manager was allowed to advertise wherever he chose. HMV's manager was not unaware of what he was missing out on, but the store's stock and advertising was controlled by a remote head office. Keith Armstrong, however, was a bright, entrepreneurial young man and did not miss the opportunity to sell and appear in *Viz*, against the wishes of his bosses. He placed the comics directly next to each till, giving his staff the opportunity to hide them under the counter should any HMV management personnel appear. Keith also took adverts out that very definitely went against HMV's corporate advertising style and standards, and to make matters worse and even more entertaining he even used their branding and logos and took the piss out of the company's campaigns.

My favourite ad was a half page that Chris designed for him in the style of HMV's ads at the time. The ads had black backgrounds with a white square graph pattern and very simple words appearing in random, diagonal strips. The corporate HMV ads would all have smarmy, pretentious, clever words. Keith's ad read simply 'THE HMV SHOP. ONLY PUFFS SHOP ELSEWHERE.' Chris also added a little extra to HMV's famous logo, in which the mystified pup stares into the speaker of the gramophone. Just behind the dog's tail sat a *Viz* trademark steaming turd. Quite how Keith managed to get away with this and the rest of his behaviour is a bit of a mystery. Perhaps a blind eye was turned because of his entrepreneurial skills. He went on to found

Kitchenware Records, the most successful independent label to ever come out of the north east, famous for acts like of Martin Stephenson and the Daintees, Prefab Sprout and more recently Editors.

I loved the way these ads sat amongst non-genuine ads – ones that were just jokes, part of the editorial. *Viz* in those early days was entertaining and mysterious in almost equal measures. A genuine advert could appear right next to one reading 'Balding on top? It's a scientific problem. If it affects you ... fuck off, you baldly bastard.'

The adverts were an integral part of *Viz* in those early years. Nobody else did anything like we did; nobody seemed brave enough or imaginative enough to fly in the face of accepted methods of doing things. Going against the grain seemed to be completely natural to us as a family.

Tyneside's silver-tongued cavalier

One of the regulars at The Gosforth Hotel was the aforementioned giant-cigarette-rolling Graham Lines. He was a bit older than us, in his late twenties, and lived just around the corner from Lily Crescent, on St George's Terrace. He was quite an eccentric and first person we knew to own a video recorder. We would often go round to his flat and watch Laurel and Hardy films on this space-age machine. He was studying maths at Newcastle University as a mature student and to fund his studies had taken a job working at the Byker Reclamation Plant, otherwise known as the Bin Depot. His job was to answer enquiries on the phones and in person over the counter. He was always full of colourful stories from his work there, like the one about the man who walked in saying, 'I've got a deed durg. In a box.'

There wasn't really anything to this story other than a man walking in and saying he had a dead dog in a box, but it was the stuff of legend at the time.

Despite Graham's intellectual leanings, his sense of humour was clearly being moulded by his time spent at the rough end of working-class life in the Bin Depot. There was another side to his humour that was, to say the least, pretty bizarre. When he was drunk, he would often be difficult to comprehend. On one occasion Chris and I left The Trent House, the legendary soul pub in town where we spent a lot of time in the 1980s, and walked down St Thomas' Street with Graham. We were about to part and Graham began to cross the street. He stopped in the middle of the road and announced in quite a serious tone, 'Think red, think red.'

This was expanded on.

'Eat them fuckin' sausages.'

On seeing we were confused, he began to sing.

'New York, New York, it's a wonderful town!'

He went on to confirm, 'Think red, think red ... Eat them fuckin' sausages.'

We later deciphered that he was referring to the Barbeque Express, a late-night takeaway. It sold sausages that had an unprecedented reputation. Legend had it that Jimi Hendrix bought one when he played at the Club A'Gogo.

The shop had a neon sign with red lettering. So we had the red, and the sausages. The 'New York' connection remained a mystery, and to the greater extent still does. My personal thoughts on the matter are that it might have been a celebration of sausage availability, New York being the city that never sleeps. Who knows if I'm right? It doesn't really matter. But at the heart of the Think Red Eat Sausages New York Mystery was a man who would become a legend throughout Tyneside.

There was a peculiar juxtaposition between Graham's rough-diamond Geordie humour and his shyness around women. He once wanted to ask out a girl called Sandy, one of Arthur 2 Stroke's biggest fans. Along with the two other girls that she shared her student digs with, she was one of the three-strong Arthur 2 Stroke Fan Club.

Having brought the subject of Sandy up, Graham talked about her quite a bit without mentioning again the idea of asking her out. I eventually asked him if he was going to do this. He was very nervous about the whole idea and didn't seem keen on my suggestion that he should just tough it out and go and call at her door. He didn't like the idea of ringing her either. I'd used all of my very limited experience of asking women out to give advice, so I said, 'Don't think the worst. Just be confident, remember the worst that can happen is that she'll say no, but be flattered that you wanted to ask in the first place.' I quoted this pretty much verbatim from what Wendy and Libby had said to me when I was terrified of asking Andrea out. Graham wouldn't have it, instead changing the subject time and time again.

Then, out of the blue, he produced a piece of paper from his pocket, declaring, 'I can do mirror writing, you know.'

It was a curious statement, and I waited patiently as he unfolded the scrap of limp paper. He continued, 'Do you think this'll do the business?'

He handed it to me. It was a note to Sandy, reading something like this:

DEAR SANDY. I'D LIKE TO GO TO THE PICTURES WITH YOU. I THINK IT WOULD BE VERY NICE. IF YOU'D LIKE TO GO PLEASE CALL ME. FROM GRAHAM.

I really didn't know where to look. It was something of a mystery why he'd looked to either of us for advice, Chris not having a girlfriend, and no history in that department, and me only just having started seeing Andrea. I said the only thing I felt I could, given the circumstances.

'Well, Graham. If that's the only way you can face approaching her, then just do it. You've really got to stop worrying about this. You'll make it harder for yourself. Just get around there and put the note through the door.'

After more coffee and smokes, the shy, retiring Graham set off down our long garden path to deliver his note. About halfway down, he turned back towards Chris and me, pulling the note from his pocket. He shook it triumphantly in the air. 'This note's ganna fuckin' pull me some totty t'neet!'

It was a giant moment in my career. Born in my mind's eye in this instant was the rough-arsed Geordie who feels he has to impress his mates with his patter but is inflicted with a chronic shyness around women. Sid the Sexist was born.

Abandon hope all ye who enter

Chris and I were soon to meet a man who could never have been turned into a cartoon character. It would be futile to exaggerate his lifestyle for comedy as it was already beyond belief. He was a proper headcase.

Around the time of *Viz*'s birth Anti-Pop had launched an album by an artist calling himself Wavis O'Shave that had become something of a cult. This renowned album, *Anna Ford's Bum*, was a collection of surreal compositions, some very cleverly put together, others ludicrously crass, none musically competent. Its title track was a recording of a radio phone-in call by Wavis, or possibly one of his cohorts, to radio's favourite fat fuck James Whale, who was at the time the Metro Radio Night Owls DJ in the slot later made famous by ginger hero Alan Robson. In the call the listener says he wishes to discuss the diction of TV newsreaders and brings up a female newsreader whose name he forgets. Whale names her as Anna Ford. As soon as her name is mentioned, the caller begins to moan repeatedly, 'Anna! ... Anna! ... Anna! ... ooaaaagh! Anna!'

Whale bizarrely allows him to continue, presumably assuming the joke will soon dry up. The caller continues relentlessly, eventually reaching a muffled climactic groan, finishing with a final 'Annnnnaaaa!'

Whale then breezes into some light-hearted local radio banter with himself and the track ends as he says, 'Who do we have on line three?'

Wavis was a reclusive eccentric, hailing from South Shields. Strangely for a performer he never played any gigs but wasn't afraid of a publicity stunt now and again: being photographed with celebrities whilst wearing an eighteen-inch-long false nose, supported with a bent wire coat hanger, was his particular favourite. Wavis had recently gained national notoriety on Tyne Tees' groundbreaking live music show *The Tube*. He appeared regularly in inserts filmed in his back yard, in which he declared himself to be 'The Hard', a man so hard he wore two pairs of Dr Martens at the same time and was able to hit himself on the hand with a hammer and announce proudly, 'I felt nowt!' During this period Wavis had changed his name to Foffo Spearjig and also appeared on *The Tube* as Mr Ordinary Powder, amongst others.

With his national minor celebrity madman status, we thought it would be a good idea to feature Wavis in *Viz*. Chris decided we should visit him at home to photograph him in his televisually famous back yard. Little did we know what we were letting ourselves in for.

It wasn't hard to spot the house where TV's popular cracker-jack lived. Written on the faded yellow door in small letters with a marker pen were the words 'Abandon Hope All Ye Who Enter Here' and cut into the cement of the doorstep was the number 666. Wavis answered the door himself. He was taller than I'd imagined and very tanned. It soon became apparent that his madness wasn't an act he could simply put on and then drop at will. He had short dark cropped hair and a goatee and was dressed entirely in black.

As we were shown into the small, dark and damp flat, I caught a glimpse of a small elderly woman in the back kitchen. She looked like Terry Jones in drag, short, with greying curly hair and horn-rimmed glasses, and wearing a nylon house coat. I later based Sid the Sexist's mother on her.

Wavis took us into his room, immediately to the left of the front door. Although it was daytime the curtains were closed and the walls were painted black. It was gloomy and rather smelly and it was difficult to comprehend exactly what met our eyes. The entire chimney breast was buried to some considerable depth with what looked like a rather sinister and unconnected collection of photographs, magazine cuttings, dolls, masks, old radios, Rod Stewart records, plastic toys and God knows what else. It was like a pyramid of rather unsettling pieces of junk, assembled in the style of Peter Blake.

'Do yuz like me satanic altar?' Wavis asked in a matter-of-fact kind of way.

'Oh, erm … is that what it is?' I replied.

A *Monty Python*-esque woman's voice interrupted from down the hall.

'Will your friends be wanting tea?'

Wavis turned the conversation back to the satanic altar.

'Aye, Pan came to see us the other day.'

'Sorry, what?' I asked.

Wavis's mam's voice came again.

'Do they want tea?'

Wavis replied with a loudly spoken question.

'Isn't that right, Mam? The Greek god Pan came, I saw him the other night, didn't I?'

'Yes, love. I've put the kettle on. I'll bring the tea through on a tray.'

Her tone of voice suggested to me that these kinds of questions were quite the norm in this most peculiar household.

Wavis then invited us to sit on the edge of his most uninviting bed. I felt more than a little uncomfortable, with the altar bearing down oppressively only feet away. He then spent what seemed like hours showing us endless photos he'd taken in the park, in which he believed he could see fairies. He made us study each one until, in an attempt to get this over with as quickly as possible, we agreed that we could see the fairies. This backfired, as with us having an eye for such things, he relished the opportunity to show us even more of them.

Eventually, swedes well mashed and tea drunk, we proceeded to the photoshoot in the back yard. Remarkably, as soon as the idea of becoming The Hard came into his head, Wavis became a fully functioning comedy performer. You could easily be forgiven for totally forgetting all the horrendous discomfort of the previous forty-five minutes or so.

Years later Wavis went on to appear on *Stars In Their Eyes* as Steve Harley. He didn't win, but he put in a pretty convincing performance.

Wavis O'Shave was a truly bizarre man, intelligent, with a sharp level of social observation and self-awareness, both put to great use in his comedy work, but sometimes the madness he would play up for his routines was all too apparent in him, and without a hint of irony. He now lives a comparatively normal life in Lincoln. However, there's more of his insane prime to come later in this book.

Young sparks

In 1983 we were invited to take part in another BBC yoof-genre programme called *Sparks*, which celebrated the entrepreneurial efforts of three different groups of youngsters in each half-hour show. The researchers had picked *Viz* as one of the subjects to be featured due to our increasing circulation through independent record shops and student unions.

The crew would film most of the show on location in Newcastle, and this time we had much more control over the its content, providing we covered how we put *Viz* together and how it was distributed. It was a fantastic opportunity. Rather than filming us sitting drawing at our desks and interviewing us in a predictable fashion, we decided to dress up in white coats, like the people who did scientific tests on toothpaste in television adverts. We were filmed walking into the Tyneside Free Press workshop, and chose to do so walking in single file in marching pace with one another. As we entered the building I turned to the camera and pointed at the business's sign with the most serious face I could muster. Once inside the building we stood by the printing presses watching the latest issue of the comic flying out of the end, just like every newspaper headline montage in every film you've ever seen. We pulled one off the conveyor belt and, once again utilising serious faces, we examined it carefully and pointed at it with pens. This was the accepted testing method used in the toothpaste adverts. The crew also filmed in Brian's Kard Bar and in our office. We didn't have an office at such, we still used Chris's bedroom, so we borrowed a proper office from a drunken photographer who we used for a short period before he drove himself into the gutter. It was in the Quayside Exchange Buildings, then verging on dereliction, but now part of a luxury hotel. In the 'office' Chris, Jim and I each made mission statements to camera, once again utilising our most serious faces.

I said, 'Extensive tests have proved that, to the ordinary man in the street, *Viz* comics are better fun than a jammy bun.'

Jim said, 'Unlike the gutter press, we don't print the truth, we print only what people want to read.'

Chris said, 'It has taken us years of scientific research and development to produce our unique comic formula, and we think the results speak for themselves.'

I then pointed with a stick at a huge sales chart on the wall, saying, 'As you can see, the green line, which is far more curvy than the red line, crosses the red line at this point, before leaving the chart completely in the month of August.'

There was a little bit of straightforward interview time, but only brief quotes were used to pretty good effect, describing what *Viz* was like to those who hadn't seen it.

Chris and I got our second trip to London out of this show, when the crew asked us to come and see the filming of an actor who would play Roger Mellie (one of Chris's famous creations). He would appear on a spoof live-action version of *What the*

Papers Say, a serious news programme that reviewed print media. In the spoof, Roger Mellie would introduce our film.

Chris and I were to visit London without Jim, BBC budgetary restraints coming into play. We would also not get to stop overnight.

The actor who was to play Roger Mellie was called Charles Pemberton, and Chris, being Roger's creator, got to choose him personally. Charles was a professional and he was luvvied right up to the bollocks. The recording was to take place at BBC studios at Ealing Broadway and we met Charles just before lunch. We were taken to a nearby pub to eat and Charles ordered a gin and tonic. He then began a very theatrical rant about how he had recently been in the north and it had been frowned upon most darkly when he had ordered a G&T. He continued, 'They thought I was some kind of creature from another planet when I spoke the words. But of course, in this heat I find it's absolutely the most refreshing alcoholic beverage.'

I thought to myself, 'Are you some kind of creature from another planet?'

Sparks was a great triumph for us, showing our work in a very good light. Without appearing pretentious or too showy, we managed to put across the spirit of the comic's content and give a good account of the way in which it was distributed through independent outlets. The attitude of the ten-minute film was just right and Charles Pemberton's performance as Roger Mellie, dressed in a black-and-white horizontally striped jacket, made especially for him by the BBC costume department, was wonderful. He pronounced the word twat 'twot', which was a first for us. We were about to correct him, but then we decided it quite suited Mellie to pronounce it that way.

Although I didn't know it at the time, *Sparks* would be one of the most significant things to happen in my career. Not only did it draw attention to the comic generally, but it was also seen by the man who would go on to carry *Viz* to its meteoric high point.

5

Mind The Gap ... In The Market

IPC Magazines was responsible for fifty per cent of all the publications sold to young people in the United Kingdom at the time. After *Sparks* was broadcast I took a phone call from a man from IPC called Bob Paynter, who informed me, 'You have something that we don't have: you can sell magazines to young men. We have something that you don't have, money.'

What struck me the most was how awful his timing had been in the delivery of the word 'money'. It seemed obvious to me that one beat of silence was the minimum necessary for dramatic effect, but he had left virtually none. It was like the 'What's the most important thing in comedy, timing' joke. (I'm sure this is mostly lost when committed to paper.)

More importantly, Bob was referring to the trend at the time for men aged between sixteen and twenty-four not to buy magazines. The magazine market for men today is absolutely huge, but in 1984 young men simply didn't buy them. If they were younger than sixteen they would buy comics; if they were older than twenty-four they would begin to move into special-interest magazines – fishing, motoring and so on. There was no such thing as a general interest magazine for young men. Some would buy the *NME* and *Sounds*, but unless you were a bit of a music fanatic these would be of no real interest.

Bob Paynter said he would be posting us – me, Chris and Jim – enough money to buy first-class return tickets to visit him and the board of IPC in London. He made it very clear there would be no *need* for us to buy first-class tickets: 'If you see what I mean, you can buy cheaper tickets and keep the remaining money. We don't have a problem with that. Do you see what I mean?'

I saw what he meant all right. For us, this was no insignificant amount of money. We would be setting off for London for a third time.

Chris and I waited at Newcastle Central Station for Jim to arrive. We waited and waited and began to worry as the time of the train's departure approached. Jim lived with his mother on Chillingham Road and they didn't have a phone, so we had no way of contacting him. It was literally only seconds before the train departed when Jim came hurtling through the station looking extremely bedraggled. It turned out his alarm had failed to wake him and he had woken with under fifteen minutes until the train left. It was a good five to ten minutes' journey to the station in a taxi, but without a phone he had no means of ordering one. He rushed straight out of his door, across Chillingham Road and burst into the shop opposite, demanding he use the phone, as it was an emergency.

He arrived at the station unshaven, having thrown on what clothes he could grab. He'd unfortunately put on a *Sounds* T-shirt, the arch rival to *NME*, which was published by IPC Magazines. This faux pas amused us momentarily.

Once again London was very warm. We made our way from King's Cross straight to the gleaming headquarters of IPC. On arriving at Kings Reach Tower on the South Bank we were greeted by Bob Paynter himself, a middle-aged, straight-laced gent who was very warm and welcoming. He showed us around some of the offices and most notably the desk of one of IPC's top comic artists, who was away for lunch at the time. The artist was in his eighties. Bob told us to not forget that this man had been working in comics for sixty years or more: 'Don't think there isn't a career to be had in what you are doing.'

This was a magical moment. It was the first time anybody had told me that what I was doing could earn me a living.

Paynter showed us into the River Room, a vast glass-walled boardroom on the top floor with a stunning view across the Thames. The room had a giant wooden table running along its centre, and to one side was a row of about seven or eight chairs, at the other stood three. We were greeted by a butler. Yes, a butler. One more time: a *butler*. The butler, for indeed that was what he was, offered us drinks, opening a wooden cabinet at one end of the room. There was no beer. We didn't know what to do.

I opted for a vodka and orange, a drink I was familiar with via buying for girls. Having ordered my alcoholic drink, Jim ordered something similar. Chris then opted for a fruit juice. I realised at this point that it may have been good etiquette to do likewise, but you learn by your mistakes. We were joined in the room by the board members of IPC Magazines Youth Group – a load of middle-aged men in suits. We were invited to take our seats for lunch. Not surprisingly, the three seats that sat alone at one side of the table were for us, and in a rather oppressive fashion we sat to eat with the suited board members all facing us across the vastness of the table. At the centre of the IPC team sat John Sanders, and no prizes for guessing that he was a middle-aged man in a suit. He had a bunch-of-grapes hairdo in the style of David Pleat.

We felt seriously uncomfortable in these surroundings, and the attentions of the waiter moving our seats for us and unfolding our napkins only made matters worse. The conversation that followed was no more comfortable. Sanders began by breaking the ice.

'So, you fellows come from Newcastle upon Tyne?' he asked.

'Yes, that's right,' I replied.

'I know the work of a comedian from Newcastle,' he continued.

'Really? Who would that be?' I was fascinated, and delighted that he even knew that Newcastle existed.

'I believe his name is Bobby Thompson.'

'Oh, fantastic. You know Bobby Thompson. I love Bobby Thompson. I know a fantastic Bobby Thompson joke – it's one of my favourite jokes of all time!' I enthused.

'Marvellous. Will you tell it for us?' he asked. I was over the moon. He was a fan of the kind of comedy that we loved, and here was my chance to tell a great joke and get the conversation off to a good start.

'Well, he's standing there on the stage, and he takes a packet of Woodbines out of his pocket. It's a packet of ten. He opens it and takes one out and puts it in his mouth, and then he looks into the box and shows it to the crowd. And he says "I bought this packet of tabs in 1948. I've only got three left ... They greed them off you.'"

Jim and Chris burst out laughing, as did I. Sanders chortled away, apparently delighted, and I felt I'd done a great job of warming up the meeting. As he laughed away a chain reaction went through all of the suits to his left and right and they all laughed appreciatively.

Sanders then took another bite of his lunch, cottage pie, which we suspected had been laid on specially for us northerners. He chewed thoughtfully before putting his knife and fork back down on the table. He looked at me across the table and asked, 'So, he bought this packet of cigarettes in 1948?'

'Yes ...' I replied tentatively.

'And he's only got three left?' he mused.

'Yes ...'

'Why is that?' he asked sincerely.

'Well ... erm ... they ... erm, greed them off you.'

There was a moment's prickly silence.

'I see,' Sanders said unconvincingly.

'Well, you see ... he thinks only having three left ... after thirty years ... is a bad thing.'

Sanders and his yes-men all laughed heartily again.

With the wisdom of hindsight I look back on this moment and think we should have known the relationship between *Viz* and IPC was doomed to failure, but the worst was yet to come.

The rest of our day at Kings Reach Tower was spent discussing quite amicably and informally the idea that John Sanders would like very much to publish *Viz*. He saw its potential to become exactly what was missing from IPC's portfolio. He asked us to produce a dummy issue – a comic like all the others we produced, but not intended for publication. The project was intended as a rather involved job interview. If Sanders and his team were to approve this dummy, then they would offer us a contract to become a minor part of their massive empire. As three young men who had struggled to earn any kind of living, the offer to earn proper wages from our own product was an amazing proposal.

Alarm bells did begin to ring, if only in muted tones, when Sanders explained that he felt something lacking in *Viz* was politics. Bob Paynter did, however, assure us afterwards that Sanders was a 'political animal' and if we managed to politicise *Viz* slightly for the dummy issue, we could be much freer to produce our own kind of writing once the publishing deal was underway. The other rather disturbing suggestion was that we should make the comic fortnightly. The best we had managed in the time leading up to this meeting was only one issue of new material in twelve months. *Viz* had been as regular as every three months when we were at our most productive, and as the stretching of time between publication dates extended, the suggestion was certainly that we couldn't produce good material to order.

I returned to Newcastle on an absolute high. I phoned Andrea immediately and blabbed out the day's events, telling her that Bob Paynter had said there was a career to be had in what I was doing and I had never felt better in my life. We went out for a meal to celebrate, still a great rarity at the time, and had our photographs taken in a photo booth to mark the occasion. I really felt at the time that things had worked out. I'd taken some knocks with being dropped into the CSE stream at school, not being able to go to university, not being accepted on to the Art Foundation Course at Bath Lane, but now I had a future for the first time. Not only that, but I had a very loving relationship. This was the happiest moment of my life so far.

Farts are funny

We spent the following weeks putting together what we hoped would be the greatest issue of *Viz* ever produced. Our main aim was to make something as funny as possible, using all of the material we had produced in the five previous years and creating some brand-new stuff aimed specifically at winning over the IPC bigwigs. There was no shortage of material that we could rehash: choosing what would be approved by the clearly differently humoured bodies in Kings Reach Tower was our challenge. We wanted to make an impact and we discussed the idea of creating the greatest-ever *Viz* character.

Jim came around with his friend Andrew Barnden, a very sharp and clever bloke. We began to discuss the idea of creating the ultimate character for the dummy issue and talked through traits that had never been used in *Viz*. The basis of all good

110

British comic characters is a trait around which their adventures are based: Billy Whizz can run very fast, Billy Bunter eats stuff, Dennis the Menace is a nuisance, Claude Hopper has big feet ... We needed to find something that was that bit more edgy, something that really represented what *Viz* was all about, something that hadn't yet been put in a comic.

Bereft of any solid ideas, we went out for a drink. Jim and Andy were great drinking friends and a night out with them was always full of lively, intelligent conversation, lots and lots of beer and loads of childish laughs. We eventually returned to Lily Crescent for coffee and smokes in the *Viz* office/Chris's room.

As we entered the room Andy stopped dramatically and bent slightly forwards to deliver the most tremendous fart. Woody, reverberant and thunderous in its robustness, its volume level and length of emission were things of wonder.

'Fartpants!' I declared, not intending to suggest I'd found our new character – it just seemed a fitting exclamation for the moment.

Needless to say, as we all cried with laughter, everyone took it I had nailed the elusive comedy trait we'd searched high and low for. Once it was in our minds it was just so obvious that it was the right way forward. We decided to make the new character as much like a proper *Beano* strip as possible – a hooped jersey, a novelty hairstyle, shorts, doughnut socks and shoes with a shiny toecap. We concluded that this little boy should have flannel shorts, like the grey scratchy ones we had been made to wear at primary school, and they would be constantly filled with gassy clouds, making them permanently lumpy in appearance. We agreed he should be about twelve and a bit fat, with his belly sticking out underneath his jumper. We had most of the ideas in only a few short minutes: a boy whose adventures were based around his own flatulence, set in the world of British comics, with parks and policemen and feasts, and, for discipline, the regulation slippering. Johnny Fartpants had arrived.

I don't think I've ever laughed quite so much in a writing session as we did that day. Probably the fact we were just speculating helped – we had not deliberately got together to write; we just began to discuss the idea and it all came flowing out. I suppose it was one of those moments where once the idea was put forward the floodgates just opened. There was an untapped market for putting the real world of what boys of that age find funny into that surreal, innocent and clean world that only exists in British comics.

More than anything, this was something that nobody had thought of before. This reminds me of something somebody told me when I said that *Viz* was not a work of genius. They explained that Schopenhauer had summed up the meaning of genius by saying 'Talent hits a target that nobody else can hit. Genius hits the target that nobody else can see.' To think of doing something that nobody has ever thought of before is real genius. Putting wheels on a suitcase, for instance, was a stroke of genius, and yet nobody thought of putting baggage and wheels together during the thousands of years in which they had the opportunity to do so. So, in this respect, I can very happily say that Schopenhauer therefore would conclude that Johnny Fartpants was a work of genius, and you can't argue with him because he's dead.

It was put to a vote: who should draw Johnny Fartpants? Jim and Andrew both suggested me, and Chris went along with them. I was absolutely beside myself. I'd always had a great admiration for Jim's drawing style. His work was unconventional and not technically brilliant, but he had a natural gift that came across in all of his work. It's very difficult to put my finger on exactly what it was, but somehow everything he ever drew made me laugh. Hearing him suggest that I should be the one to draw the ultimate *Viz* strip was a huge honour, and to have my big brother back him up in this, despite his own undeniable talent in the same department, was a dream come true.

Johnny Fartpants, when complete, did exactly what it said on the tin. It summed up what we were about. It was outrageous, but not for the sake of it, it was all brand new and it was very funny.

Unfortunately our enthusiasm for our new creation was not shared by anybody at IPC. A process began, after the dummy issue was presented to them, which was almost as entertaining as it was tragic. They put our dummy into the hands of their own humour experts, who proceeded not only to add their own work but to interfere with ours. This didn't only involve editing, a process we had never before encountered from outside forces, but also actually tampering with our cartoon artwork, changing the wording of speech balloons, and in some cases taking out our

112

endings completely and replacing them with their own punchlines. Sid the Sexist offended them. He was 'clearly a chauvinist', so his name was changed to Sid the Smooth Talker.

These changes to our work were deeply offensive to us and most worryingly showed a total lack of understanding of the way *Viz* operated. The most alarming thing was probably the complete absence of Johnny Fartpants. They hadn't even considered it worthy of editing or critique, but had simply disregarded the poor boy on the cutting room floor. I was incensed by all of this interference, but more than anything by the hatcheting of our new creation. It was almost impossible to take.

Chris wrote to Bob Paynter with a very involved breakdown of why the changes made were wrong, and tried to explain that *Viz* was maybe operating on a level that IPC's 'humour experts' were not able to grasp. He went through every change they had made meticulously, and the result was a letter from bunch-of-grapes hairdo top-man John Sanders. He wrote:

Dear Chris

Bob Paynter has shown me your report on Duffy's dummy. I do agree with a lot of the things you say.

You are right, for instance, about 'Boobs' and 'Party Lines'. The Jogger advertisement wasn't funny and nor were the Mastermind pictures. I think we truncated some of your better picture strips unnecessarily.

Having said all that, your dummy was not funny enough. Nor was it nearly sufficiently political in content. And there is still too much reliance on four-letter words for impact.

Some of your stories simply do not end. They may be noticed by some folks at college, but we have to think nationally. Paul Whicker leaves the reader hopelessly in the air in the last frame.

I think it is very good that you have defended your work so painstakingly, but if we are to work together, and I hope we can, you must be more commercial. I have asked Bob to confer with you about putting together a revised dummy. But remember:

1. All pictures strip stories must have a recognisable ending.

2. You must be more political. We are trying to put together a political strip on Maggie Thatcher, which I hope you will like.

3. Play down the four-letter words. But in Sid the Sexist, for example, they are intelligently used.

4. Stories like Sex and The Beatles will give us enormous legal problems.

Let us see if we can get this thing right. I am still very keen to do it and I am looking forward to seeing the definitive dummy.

Kind regards.

Yours sincerely

John R Sanders
Managing Director

There are so many levels on which I could bang on about the attitude of IPC. It's evident to anybody who reads this letter that the problem at the root of this awful situation was that nobody at IPC 'got' *Viz*.

For instance, Sanders says that stories like 'Sex and The Beatles' would give IPC enormous legal problems. This was a spoof tabloid news article in which we had accused each of The Beatles of having sex with his own wife in private. There was clearly no legal case to answer. The joke lay in the fact that the sensational article made a claim only that The Beatles had behaved perfectly normally and had not done anything worthy of journalistic scrutiny.

What can I say about cartoons having to have recognisable endings? As for the bit about Paul Whicker, this still makes me laugh to this day. However, were it not for the fact we went on to have great success with *Viz*, this could have been the most tragic document of my lifetime.

It offended me so greatly that Johnny Fartpants was ignored completely that I decided to put together a little bullet point list of my own in order to justify my belief that we had created a fine piece of work. I was aware that IPC probably considered Johnny Fartpants to be juvenile, and rightly so.

What makes farts funny?
1. They come out your arse.
2. They make a funny noise.
3. They smell like shit.

I've always been very proud of my childish sense of humour. I remember hearing Michael Palin interviewed in the days when the straight-laced people of the media still questioned *Monty Python*'s integrity. He was asked if he agreed that *Python* was simply postgraduate humour. He answered, 'Oh no. It's school-boy humour.'

I remember thinking at the time that this was a great position to take – that of honesty. This was a sign of a man who was unashamed of laughing at what he thought was funny, and indeed he had made a career of it, making millions of others laugh. I imagine the board of IPC in 1984 would probably have considered *Monty Python* to be rather silly.

The communication over the dummy issue dragged on for a while and became more and more strained. It was no surprise really when the day came that Bob Paynter wrote regretting to inform us that IPC's interest in publishing *Viz* was at an end.

When Chris told me the contents of the letter I was devastated. The moment when Paynter said I could have a career in comics was now a distant and painful memory. This was certainly the lowest feeling I can remember ever having in my career. I found it very difficult to tell Andrea. All of a sudden I was back to having no future, which was an all-too-familiar and horrible feeling.

Little did we know it at the time, but our saviour was not very far away at all. On Paynter's farewell letter, with which he enclosed a cheque to ease the blow, Bob added a footnote: 'Try Richard Branston.'

Viz was selling very well in Newcastle's Virgin store and Branston had over thirty shops around the UK at the time. Paynter saw Branston as being the kind of businessman who might be more inclined to allow *Viz* to flourish in its own way, rather than enforcing clashing standards on it. It was a very kind gesture from a man who saw we had potential, but not within the constraints of his dinosaur of a company.

I can look back now and say it would have been wrong to sign up to a huge corporate that would have effectively stolen some of our soul. But I have to remember, and I hope anybody reading can appreciate this: I had signed on supplementary benefit for five years after leaving school. I had no future. Just getting paid for doing a comic, even if it was butchered by arseholes in suits, was better than a life on benefits. We tried to win with IPC, but it wasn't to be.

Our saviour the public school twat

Chris wasted no time in taking Bob Paynter's advice. He packaged up the latest issue with a covering letter and off it went in the post. Branston himself never saw it, as far as we're aware, but it was directed to Virgin Vision's top man, John Brown. Public school twat Brown had seen the comic on *Sparks* and was very impressed by the statistics in Chris's letter. Chris had pointed out that *Viz* was by then selling 1,000 copies per issue in the Virgin Newcastle shop, so if this business was expanded nationally 30,000-plus copies could be sold, making *Viz* a very viable business for Virgin to have a stake in.

Brown wasted no time. He phoned the office (still Chris's bedroom), bombarded Chris with a few questions and then immediately booked himself on a flight to come and see us and discuss Chris's proposal. He got off the plane, jumped straight into a taxi and said to the driver, 'Lily Crescent, please.'

'Where's that?' asked the driver.

'Jesmond,' John explained.

'Where's that?' repeated the driver.

'Newcastle,' John protested.

'OK. I'll drive you to the railway station. This is Middlesbrough.'

Our armoury of things with which to take the piss out of John was already well stocked, and we hadn't even met him yet.

John arrived at Lily Crescent in a taxi. Not the one he got into at Middlesbrough. He was a foppish upper-middle-class man with floppy hair and a baggy linen jacket. He was very well spoken and was full of questions from the moment he arrived. We took him just up the road to a café belonging to a friend of ours. Willow Teas was a lovely little place in a converted house, frequented by Jesmond's woolly liberals, the artisan and thespian types and, like all the best cafés, lots of little old ladies. John ordered hotpot, presumably because it had Brown Ale in it, with him being in Newcastle, in a gesture remindful of IPC serving us cottage pie. He proceeded to bombard us with questions about how long it took to put *Viz* together, how we distributed it, how many of us worked on it, what the costs were, how much advertising revenue came in ... He also uttered a sentence that would change our lives forever. 'I understand that if this was to succeed I would have to leave you to your own ends. I wouldn't want to interfere with what you do at all. That simply wouldn't work.'

He understood.

He knew that *Viz* was different from other magazines in almost every respect, and if anyone was to interfere with the process by which it was made it may no longer be a success. This really was John's great moment, and he knows it. It was something he would act on and that would bring us all very successful careers.

When he left us that afternoon to fly back to London (via a train to Middlesbrough) we were on the brink of launching the comic nationally. In the next few months we would negotiate on how we could work together. John proposed the comic should be published every two months, with a view to going monthly if it were ever feasible.

Chris and I would have to produce a lot more work more regularly than we were used to, but also keep standards up, because it was only the fact that it was funny that made *Viz* sell. Any drop in quality could potentially be disastrous.

Jim was working more and more with a property developer and had been producing less and less material for *Viz*, usually managing only one page of work per issue. Many people question why he would decide to stop contributing, considering the comic's enormous success. With the wisdom of hindsight, Jim's decision to move into professional work with a property developer was a very sensible one at the time. Chris and I were the ones who were doing the silly risky stuff and potentially wasting our lives, whereas Jim was sensibly building up earnings for the rest of his life. When it came to *Viz*, Jim was slipping off the radar, and we would need all the help we could get. Unfortunately, genius cartoonists don't just arrive on your doorstep.

Dury's in

Graham Dury arrived on our doorstep dressed in a poncho and cowboy boots. Once again, good fortune shone on us at just the right time.

All the work in *Viz* up to this point had been produced either by us or by people we knew. There was always a worry that work from outside our own circle may simply be unsuitable. In our founding team of three, we'd been very lucky that our work always made others laugh, doubtless down to the fact our senses of humour had been welded together during those times listening to *Monty Python*, *The Goon Show* and *Derek and Clive*. We were always very dubious about people claiming to be cartoonists since a bloke from a band at The Gosforth Hotel had told us he was an experienced cartoonist and would like to contribute something to the first issue. Chris was so convinced by his patter that he left a space on the front cover, thinking this man's work would make our product look more professional. Unfortunately, it was hardly worthy of inclusion in the comic at all. It was instantly relegated to as small a space as possible on the inside cover. Chris then filled the gap with artwork that would set the tone for all future *Viz* covers. It showed Skinheed, Chris's seminal youth with 'social problems', threatening to shoot Colin the Amiable Crocodile if the reader didn't buy the comic. This was based on a *National Lampoon* magazine cover he had recently seen. The illustration included a picture of a creature that Jim had drawn, saying 'Geep!' He'd copied it straight from a fairground roundabout in a copy of *Shiver and Shake*. This strange little triangular creature with a combined body and head, its feet directly beneath its chin and little arms with three-fingered hands, each finger with a sucker on the end, would appear on every *Viz* cover for many years to come. Chris and I

118

even decided at one point that this creature would be called Viz, and we would, if ever asked, claim the comic was named after it. We soon forgot this promise, and at some point the *Viz* monster was forgotten from one cover, never to return.

The lesson we learned from that incident with issue 1 was never to trust the claims of people who wanted to be contributors. Instead we would ask them to show us their work, preferably when they weren't present, so we could be more honest and free from social discomfort. We'd worked this way for the first four or five years, so it surprised me when Chris announced he had invited someone round to the house to show us his work. He said, 'Listen, some cunt's coming round tomorrow, reckons he's a cartoonist. It's probably better that we're both here because that'll make it easier to tell him to fuck off.'

I duly arrived, and we waited, looking out of the office window. Bang on time, a figure approached. The house was set in the middle of a crescent, but the road was straight, so the houses in the middle had the longest gardens. Our house was bang in the centre, so we had plenty of time to watch Graham as he walked along the street and then up our lengthy garden path.

'Fuck me. He's wearing a fucking poncho,' said Chris.

Graham looked like something straight out of the *Fabulous Furry Freak Brothers*. He had a mass of long, thick, black curly hair, parted in the centre, bouncy and very bushy where it lay over his shoulders, with a Frank Zappa-style moustache and beard. Beneath his poncho he wore faded jeans and tan-coloured cowboy boots. We were horrified.

Graham was a very warm, polite and friendly person. He drank his tea black, an unusual trait that I shared, so he had one mark in my good books straight away.

His girlfriend, Karen, was a student at Newcastle University. Graham worked as a botanist at Leicester University and would come and visit her regularly from his home in Nottingham. Karen had seen *Viz* whilst in Newcastle and told Graham that it was very like the cartoons he drew. She had persuaded him, probably quite sternly, to get in touch and to present us with his portfolio.

His work, we were surprised to see, was not complete comic strips, but drawings of *Freak Brothers*-type characters and a few random pencil sketches. The first thing that struck me on looking at them all was that Graham had a style of his own. He wasn't yet a cartoonist, but I saw that this could work to our advantage.

Graham asked for our advice. How should he proceed if he wanted to be a cartoonist? Our advice was quite simple. We explained to him some of the basic rules about making artwork for reproduction. It had to be black and white, with no areas of grey. Any area appearing to be grey would have to be made using shading with very thin black line. We told him to draw out his work first in pencil and then in ink, later rubbing out the pencil when the ink had dried. We told him the size of a page and the approximate number of frames that made up the average strip on a page of the comic. We told him to look at the previous issues of *Viz* and at any other British comic he cared to lay his hands on. Once he had done this, we said, he had then to create a character of his own in the style of what he saw in *Viz* – something a bit out of the ordinary, something combining that jovial comic world with brutal reality. This was what we needed more than anything: artists who could come up with their own characters and write funny strips for them.

Graham left saying he would give it a go. I felt quite positive about the whole thing, as did Chris. I'm sure that this had an awful lot to do with Graham's attitude. He was interested in hearing what *we* wanted rather than telling us we should want something of his, and he was also confident and clearly talented. I can't say either of us knew immediately that Graham would go on to be one of the driving forces behind the comic, but we both had a good feeling about this badly dressed weirdo.

It was to be a very long time before we actually got to sign a contract with Virgin to become a nationally distributed publication. There was over a year between the rejection by IPC and the publication of the first national *Viz*.

In the meantime we continued to try and earn a living by whatever means possible. I discovered the government's Enterprise Allowance Scheme, which helped enterprising people turn their business ideas into reality by paying them £40 a week for their first year after signing off benefits. I went down to the Small Firms Centre in the Cloth Market in Newcastle and collected all of the paperwork, which I took back to Lily Crescent and gave to Chris. I proposed that he continued his work as a graphic designer, something he had been doing on the side for some time, designing posters for bands and local businesses, and that we should go into this together with him as the designer and me as the runner and apprentice. I would tout for work and make all of the necessary deliveries and collections whilst also doing artwork when needed.

I didn't hear anything back and assumed he wasn't up for it. Then, sure enough, he told me he'd concluded there wasn't enough work in the idea for two people. I was very downhearted: the idea was a write-off. I was to later hear from a friend on a bus that Chris signed up to the scheme himself. Not the greatest day of my life – communication skills have never been a strong point in our family.

However, I wasn't to be defeated, and I knew I could put my artistic talents to some use. I decided to follow in Mum's foot-steps and try my hand at making wooden toys. I had, of course, won the school woodwork prize for my cabinet. Mum had made many wooden toys in the early 1960s under the name Kaycrafts. I signed up to the Enterprise Allowance Scheme under the same name and began by making a garage in the same style as the one Mum had made for me when I was a toddler. My friends with children were impressed, and my first order was for a garage was soon placed. I was later to get work making replacement parts for council playgroup toys, but as the year progressed *Viz* was to take off and my attempts to forge a career as a toymaker quickly faded. By the end of my Enterprise Allowance year I would be trading under the Kaycrafts name but actually working as a writer and cartoonist, working on *Viz* and several other regular jobs.

3–2–1 ignition, contract

John Brown was to write a contract that would give us something that no publisher today would ever give to anyone, let alone to two men as young and unproven as ourselves. The rules of this contract were very simple. Chris and I would produce the comic; Virgin would pay for it to be printed and they would distribute it. Virgin would also sell advertising space, from which they would receive the bulk of the income, Chris and I receiving the bulk of the income from sales. We would own our work and Virgin

121

would own the right to exploit the work. It was very similar to a record contract – we were the band and we owned our songs, but the record company owned to right to sell copies of them, so one couldn't operate without the other. That part is quite normal in publishing. The unusual part was John's almost casual decision to allow us total artistic and editorial freedom. He gave us the chance to do whatever we wanted, openly and indeed legally. There was one very important rule, though: the content would be seen by a libel lawyer before going to press. Once the lawyer had ticked the box, we were the in the clear, John being covered by insurance should he be sued.

This was, without a shadow of a doubt, the most important thing that John Brown ever did for *Viz*. Without it I am absolutely sure that the comic could never have been the phenomenon it became.

During the year in which contract negotiations were moving back and forth, Graham came back to us with his first attempt at a *Viz* cartoon. 'Victor and his Boa Constrictor' was a take on 'Sid's Snake' from *Whizzer and Chips*. It was everything we had asked him to produce: it took the straightforward British comic premise of somebody with a novelty trait, in this case a pet snake, and took it to rather more brutal and realistic ends, the snake eating Victor in the final frame. At least I assume that's what happened, I can't quite remember, but let's face it, that's probably the way it ended. It went straight into the next issue. Mr Dury had entered the building.

Victor appeared in issue 12, the last copy of *Viz* to be printed at the Tyneside Free Press. Chris, Jim and I had gone down there to do the folding, collating and stitching as usual, but for some reason, possibly the quality of the paper, there was a huge amount of wastage and the floor was knee deep in rejected pages. The print run was now so big – the next issue would be 7,000 – that Chris was able to get a better quote from a big commercial printer. So issue 12A, a compilation (by popular demand) of the best parts of issues 5 and 6, was printed in a big factory somewhere and delivered in boxes to our door.

The next issue, our first bi-monthly, nationally distributed comic, would see the arrival of the next link in the chain of the backbone of the iron rod that would be the supporting structure on which the meat of *Viz* would hang. *Viz* would stride magnificently onwards into the unimaginable heights of glory and majesty and very high sales figures. And all stuff like that.

Chris had always had a fondness for *Private Eye* magazine. I could never see its appeal – it was far too political in its content for my liking. Worse for me personally, it was far too wordy – my overwhelming impression of it was masses of tightly packed small type. This was rather like kryptonite to my dyslexic brain.

In the run-up to signing the contract with John, Chris decided this would be a good place to search for new writers/cartoonists. He placed a small ad reading 'Bum rates paid by national magazine for funny cartoons.' This ad, probably not surprisingly, drew little response. In fact, it only attracted one reply, but it was from a reclusive young cartoonist who would eventually join Chris, Graham and me as the fourth member of the team who would produce the vast majority of *Viz*'s content in its heyday.

Simon Thorp was a qualified fine artist, having studied at university in Aberystwyth. He had recently returned to live at home with his family in Pontefract, West Yorkshire. Thorpy, as he quickly became known, contacted Chris by sending a very well written and polite letter, and some samples of his work. This was instantly recognisable as that of a very talented cartoonist, clearly someone with a more natural gift for this kind of artwork than any of the rest of us.

Thorpy's first contribution would appear in that milestone edition issue 13, our first national comic. 'Eric Daft: His IQ is Less Than Two' was a very simple four-frame strip in which the intrepid hero threw himself off a cliff and died. Thorpy would continue to contact us by post for the next two years, his artwork coming in thick and fast. It was always of a very high quality, and of course, more importantly, always funny. The letters that accompanied his work were almost as involved in their detail as the cartoons themselves. We knew virtually nothing about Thorpy, and we always speculated that his letter writing and anally retentive artwork was that of a man who spent a lot of time in the house alone and was probably therefore a murderer or a child molester.

The publication of issue 13 was a very special time: now it was clear that our future as comic writers and artists lay in our own hands. More people would be given a chance to see our work, and if they liked it as much as people who'd seen it previously, our future could be good. From the word go the comic attracted attention, and within days of publication I was taking a phone call from Lew Baxter of the *Sunday Mirror*. He informed me in very jolly tones that he had picked up a copy in his local Virgin store and had loved it. This was thrilling news in itself, but he went on to tell me that he wanted to run an article about *Viz* in next Sunday's edition. Amazing stuff. He asked a few simple questions: where we were based, how long we'd been going, how many of us worked on putting the comic together ... nothing pressing or heavy. I couldn't wait to tell everybody, and I rushed to the newsagents on the way from Andrea's flat to Lily Crescent on the following Sunday. I flicked through the paper as I headed for the house. I couldn't believe my eyes. Our first ever national news coverage read as follows: the headline, HEROIN COMIC BAN; the by-line, by Lou Baxter of DRUGWATCH; the sub-heading, WE GET IDIOTIC MAG PULLED OUT OF THE SHOPS.

The bottom fell out of my world. The feeling of elation drained from my body and flowed straight into the gutter to be flushed away with the rainwater and tramps' piss.

The atmosphere in the house was, to say the least, not good. I believed that our careers had been cancelled, pulled out from under us the instant they began. However, we had a lot to learn about journalism.

The basis of this news story was that Lew Baxter had been outraged by a photo romance featured in the comic. 'Too Young to Love' was the story of two kids falling in love, but their parents do not understand their romance. They run away to London and are ripped off by a slum landlord, the girl is offered a job in a seedy nightclub and a pusher offers them drugs on the street. Eventually they return to their parents, who by now have forgiven everything, and they live happily ever after. The joke in this story was simple. The kids were not teenagers, but toddlers. Baxter was supposedly outraged at the toddlers being offered heroin on the streets. They were pictured being offered a bottle of pop with the word 'heroin' on the label, plied by a dealer from an ice cream tray, which we had borrowed from the Tyneside Cinema. Baxter made no reference in his article to the fact that the children had refused the offer of drugs and had walked away, exactly per advice in government legislation at the time.

His claim that Drug Watch had managed to have *Viz* pulled would prove to be less catastrophic than it appeared. Virgin, pressured by the *Sunday Mirror*, and despite no complaint being made by any member of the public, had only withdrawn the issue from their own shops, and it would continue to be distributed to other shops. This ban did not affect *Viz* as a publication, but rather *Viz* issue 13 specifically.

Months later Chris came up with a very clever idea for clearing the backlog of comics caused by Virgin's withdrawal of the issue. He printed a back issues advertisement, using Lew Baxter's article in its entirety as the main image. It wasn't long before the entire stock had sold out. Our understanding of the expression 'There's no such thing as bad publicity' began to mature.

Too bottomy

In 1985 I eventually moved out of 116 Simonside Terrace and, officially at least, back to Lily Crescent. Unofficially I moved in with Andrea and her flatmate, Maria. The flat was on the top floor of a converted three-storey terraced house on the corner of Shield Street and Portland Road in Shieldfield. It was just over the road from Nana's new place in sheltered accommodation. Nana was great. Her Geordie working-class sense of humour was a joy. I once said, 'Nana, have you seen the new houses they're building on Milton Street? They're proper little red brick ones with gardens. They're not building those awful towers anymore, not like the ones they put you in. They look very nice.'

'Aye, pet,' she said, slightly dismissively. 'I've seen them, pet. They're very nice. Canny. But, y'knaa pet, you can put pigs in a palace and they'll still live in their own shite.'

Because of the lack of space at Andrea's I wasn't able to work there, so I decorated my old bedroom at Lily Crescent with the intention of working from it. But constant rows with Dad and his reluctance to switch on the central heating, even in the depths of

125

winter, led to me taking on a studio in the basement of a house belonging to some good friends. I'd known Bob and Soo since the very early days of *Viz* at The Gosforth Hotel, Bob having played saxophone with Arthur 2 Stroke in the beginnings of their soul band era. Their house stood on a beautiful Georgian terrace in the centre of town, close to St James' Park. Bob already had a proper drawing board set up in the basement, nothing I'd ever had before, and it took no time for me to settle into working from this new and almost professional environment.

I rode an old 1950s sit-up-and-beg pushbike between the flat in Shieldfield, the office at Lily Crescent and my studio at Bob and Soo's daily. On one journey I pulled up at some traffic lights next to a baker's van. The lettering on the back of the van made the claim 'Our buns are the best.' This got me to thinking how a claim like this would stand up to scrutiny. Would someone from some government body call round and make random inspections? What criteria would define whose buns were the best? I knew there was something in this, and before I arrived at my destination I'd created my next comic strip: 'The Bun Inspectors.' I saw them as ruthless Gestapo-like uniformed brutes, doing everything by the book and dishing out harsh punishments for unproven bun-related quality claims with cold, ruthless efficiency.

A bit further down the road, with the words 'The Bun Inspectors' spinning slowly around my head, it occurred to me that 'bun' sounded very like 'bum' and suddenly the new characters took on an altogether more sinister role of inspecting people's bums. Straight away I wrote 'The Bum Inspectors', in which officers from the Office of Bottom Inspection make random, unannounced inspections of people's arses. Anyone who has committed 'Bottom Crimes', such as wearing skid-marked underpants, is taken away to correctional facilities. Just before the strip went to print the title was changed from 'The Bum Inspectors' to 'The Bottom Inspectors', Chris and I both thinking the word 'bottom' was funnier than 'bum'.

John Brown claims to this day that 'The Bottom Inspectors' was created as a backlash to his suggestion that we put less 'bottomy' material in the comic. There's no truth in this: it was just a coincidence. Chris hadn't even told me that John had said any such thing. It's also a myth that 'The Bottom Inspectors' was a reference in any way to the Cleveland Child Abuse Scandal – it was completely unrelated.

The money from the Enterprise Allowance Scheme allowed me to take steps I'd not been able to previously. I arranged my first driving lesson for my twenty-first birthday, a date that I marked with a tea party at Lily Crescent, attended by lots of my friends, some of whom brought their babies along. It was great fun, with cakes, sandwiches and jelly. I did it really for Mum's benefit. She sat at the head of the table and loved the company, especially of the babies. It was a great day.

My driving instructor arrived in a rather disappointing brown Nissan Micra. He was a very fat little man who chain-smoked in the car throughout the lessons. He also talked at great length about his most unlikely conquests with rich and beautiful housewives. These conquests, I concluded, existed entirely within his sorry little mind. His actual teaching wasn't bad, and soon I loved driving. After a number of lessons he recommended I sit my test. As the day of the test approached he decided that I would need more practice and advised me to postpone and book more lessons instead. I thought about it and concluded that I might well learn more from a failed test than a whole bunch more smoky lessons. I sat the test and, as predicted, I failed. I booked another straight away and a few weeks later, on a glorious late-summer day, I was leaving the test centre as a qualified driver.

I later turned my driving instructor into a strip in *Viz* called 'Fatty Ballaty' about, funnily enough, an overweight chain-smoking sexist fantasist.

Things in my life were moving apace now. The years of stagnation on the dole began to melt away. My next big move was to buy a car. There really was no competition: it had to be a Mini. I'd first fallen for the Mini when I went to the toyshop on Brentwood Avenue to buy a yellow tractor. Mum gave the woman in the shop the Dinky model number, which was printed on the end of the box. There was a mistake of some kind with the number, and when we got home the model inside was the Mini Cooper from the Peter Sellers' film *A Shot in the Dark*. It was black with a red roof and yellow and black stickers on the sides, representing wickerwork. The headlights were glass and were cut like diamonds to make them reflect light in a not particularly headlight-like way. I loved it. I think I might still have it, although the last time I looked I couldn't find it, which upset me rather more than it should have done.

This love affair continued as I grew up. As a little boy I would often sit at the corner of the road at the end of Lily Crescent with my eyes closed, listening to cars coming down the street, slowing down for the bend and then accelerating away again. I got pretty good at identifying cars from the sound they made and was particularly adept at spotting the local police patrol car, a Mk1 Ford Escort. It made a slightly different sound from the other Ford Escorts. I was very proud of this achievement. Easily the easiest car to identify as it slowed to the corner was the Mini. Although I didn't know it at the time, the gearbox made the extremely distinctive whine as it slowed, and the exhaust made the throaty note as it pulled away. I fell in love with that sound, and to this day I can listen to it all day long.

Mum had been given a hand-controlled Mini 850 in 1974 by the government. She'd previously been given fibreglass-bodied invalid carriages, the distinctive light blue three wheelers, most of which were taken off the roads in the late 1970s due to their dangerous instability in high winds. Her Thundersley Invacar was known to us as the Thunderbird. Although forbidden by law, and clearly extremely dangerous, Mum would often collect me from school in it. I would have to sneak in and lie at her feet on the rubber mat, breathing in the two-stroke fumes from the scooter engine that powered it. By comparison the Mini was an absolute joy. She had to pass a driving test before she could use it: the Thundersley was officially a motor tricycle and could be driven on a provisional licence.

The day Mum passed her test I came home from West Jesmond at dinnertime as usual and she was sitting at the kitchen table beaming. I asked if she'd passed and she just smiled at me even more and nodded. I don't think I ever saw her so happy. She gave me some scissors and allowed me to cut her L plates off the car. I was very proud of her. Her Mini was her key to freedom: she could get about in it and, importantly to her, she could legally and safely take me places. When Chris and Steve were young she'd carried them on the back of her bicycle in a child seat. She was always upset that she'd never been able to take me anywhere, and the Mini gave her that chance. This little car, in its very seventies colour scheme of Teal Blue with a Limeflower interior, was very special to her.

This was a far cry from when, three years later, her car was taken away from her due to her deteriorating condition. If the truth is known, she had always been an awful driver, but she'd begun to have accidents without even knowing it. In losing her Mini, she lost a big part of her freedom. It was awful to see.

Minis were in my blood, so I proceeded to look in the local paper at some. I had no experience at all with cars, so sensibly enough I wasn't going to part with my money before the car of my choosing had been seen by someone who knew what he was looking at. I took a friend called Paul, who was living with Jane, a girl I'd gone out with for about a week when I was thirteen. They had a young daughter and Andrea and I would often spend evenings at their flat in Jesmond. Paul, importantly, was the only person we knew with a car. He was a real character, a Scouser with a fantastic sense of humour. He was to go on to become a regular figure in *Viz* photo stories, always playing the role of the driver who has run down one of the main characters, without fail delivering his one and only line: 'Sorry mate. I didn't see her/him.' Bizarrely enough, we never received a single letter from a reader who'd spotted that whenever there was a road accident in the comic the same driver was responsible.

Paul went on to become a stand-up comedian, using the stage name Anvil Springsteen. His brother Billy would break a paving slab on Paul's chest in two with a sledgehammer. Not surprisingly, Paul had to give up this particular act due to internal injuries. He's still working as a stand-up and I'm happy to say I still see him regularly.

As our car expert, Paul came with Andrea and me to see a Mini that was a bit over my budget but sounded pretty interesting. It was a fabulous little car, an orange MkII Mini fitted with an Austin 1300 GT engine and gearbox, rally harness seatbelts and a bucket seat on the driver's side. It had been in use in rallies and hill climbs. Paul fell in love with it and pretty much sold me on the idea of buying it.

Although it was a bit of a crazy machine to have as a first car, I can't say buying it is a decision I regret. Chris, seeing it for the first time at Lily Crescent, displayed his usual charm as he walked straight into the house, saying, 'It's a car. I've seen cars before.'

It wasn't long before I became preoccupied, you might say obsessed, with it. I've had a love/hate relationship with the Mini ever since. Fortunately, it's been a lot more love than hate.

After our deal was signed for national distribution with Virgin, a hefty supply of each issue would be delivered by HGV to Lily Crescent, raising a few eyebrows in the street. We continued to supply our own contacts in the Newcastle area and the orange Mini became the vehicle by which *Viz* would be delivered for the next three years, replacing the tartan shopping trolleys that Chris and I used to take into town on the number 33 bus.

When driving the Mini to work at Bob and Soo's I would park in the residents' parking area, using the permit I had for Andrea's flat. The streets were patrolled by an unforgiving trio of humourless traffic wardens, one of whom once issued Linda, Bob and Soo's neighbour, with five parking tickets in a month, despite knowing her and her car and being aware she was entitled to park there. The reason he gave for issuing the tickets was 'permit not displayed properly'. She always had to go through the rigmarole of officially querying the tickets and although she was hugely inconvenienced she never had to pay a fine. It seemed that this warden enjoyed power and was at his happiest when abusing it.

I based the three main Bottom Inspectors on these three twats. Shortly after the strip's introduction to the pages of *Viz* I learned from Bob that the one who kept issuing Linda with tickets was called Mr Leyburn, so I named the most evil Bottom Inspector Bottomdant Leyburn in his honour.

Where do you get your ideas from?

People always want to know where the characters in *Viz* come from and if they're based on real people. They always seem to have heard that Roger Mellie was based on one TV presenter or another, a friend reckoning one thing and another friend something else. 'Can you settle an argument?' is something I'm asked on a very regular basis. Is Sid the Sexist based on a friend of theirs; does he live in Walker? I've even had a reader appear devastated when told it wasn't true that Johnny Fartpants was based on his mate. I pointed out he wasn't really the type of *Viz* character based on real-life social observation.

In the simplest terms, characters in *Viz* usually came about in one of the four following ways.

Stereotypes

This is the easiest to understand. Millie Tant was one of my creations; the kind of humourless boot-faced feminist who was always to be seen in city centre pubs in the 1980s. A dying breed now, these girls were usually in further education and considered not finding anything funny to be one of life's missions. They always wore frumpy, baggy clothes in order to state that they weren't a sex object, or alternatively dressed in outrageous loud ethnic garments to display their affinity with women of other cultures. Stupid hats were a must.

Another good example of *Viz* stereotype characters would be the Fat Slags, created by Chris, me, Thorpy and Graham in 1989. These are the young ladies we knew from our own city centres – Newcastle for Chris and me, Leeds for Thorpy and Nottingham for Graham. There was some bitterness in Newcastle when they were later voiced for video in generally northern accents rather than Geordie. I often have to explain they were not specifically Geordies, unlike Sid and Biffa.

Incidents

Characters based on incidents gave us at least two of *Viz*'s all-time favourites. Sid the Sexist, as I've already explained, was based on an incident in which Graham Lines couldn't face asking a girl out. Graham is unlike the Sid in the comic strip, but his dirty Geordie wit and shyness around girls inspired the idea.

In this same way Roger Mellie was born, his inspiration being a man who didn't really bear any genuine resemblance to Roger, either in appearance or behaviour. In 1981 Chris, Jim and I were invited down to Tyne Tees Television studios to speak to a researcher called Alfie Fox. Alfie was researching for a possible item on *Viz*, which his producer chose not to use in the end. However, the meeting would produce the Roger Mellie moment.

We met Alfie in the canteen at the studios and found him to be quite a bore, lecturing us on punctuality before asking us questions that showed he didn't really understand what *Viz* was about. My mind wandered and I noticed the news anchorman Rod Griffith sitting with some crew at the next table. It was quite a thing to see someone off the telly and I tried to eavesdrop on his conversation. Before long the bomb was dropped. He had cracked a joke. I hadn't heard it properly, but I'd not mistaken his use of an expletive in the punchline. Alfie had now gone to the counter for cups of tea and I turned to Chris and Jim and whispered hurriedly, 'Did you hear that?'

In unison they both said, 'No. What?'

'Rod Griffiths. He just swore.'

We all now sat trying to tune in to what he was saying. Sure enough, he swore in his next joke too. Hearing such a familiar voice using words that would never normally come out of his mouth was a real shock and brought us out in fits of giggles, which Alfie took a stern view of.

Chris went away and gave birth to Roger Mellie by simply taking down the barrier that stops the professional presenter from swearing on TV. Thereafter, of course, Mellie's story was to reflect many real-life TV presenters, but Rod was the man who inspired the presenter who simply couldn't stop swearing on telly.

Alfie was to move away from Tyne Tees and I hear that tragically he died young. We eventually became quite friendly with Rod and he attended the *Viz* twentieth anniversary party in Newcastle as our honoured guest. He was a lovely man, also sadly no longer with us.

British comics with a twist
This is one of *Viz*'s great strengths: to take a traditional British comic scenario and add a touch of gritty realism. Somebody once described this as 'the juxtaposition between the format and what it's saying'. We laughed at this a lot at the time, but now that I understand I agree totally. We put things in *Viz* that comics usually steered well clear of, and the result was that we created a new world in which harsh street reality clashed with the harmless world in which British comic characters existed. This bizarre world of parks, adventures, hoopy jumpers, corporal punishment and feasts of bangers and mash took many names, depending on the comic it appeared in, most strips being set in fictional towns.

132

In *The Beano* all events took place in Beanotown. We created Fulchester as the *Viz* world. The name was used initially by Chris in 1983 when he created Billy the Fish, the half-man half-fish goalkeeper of Fulchester United. This was taken from a show I used to watch at Dave and Paul Rose's house when we were wagging off school: the ITV drama *Crown Court*. Broadcast mid-afternoon on weekdays in the 1970s, it was a show in which actors acted out a courtroom trial in which a jury made up of members of the public had to deliberate and pass a verdict. The trials took place at Fulchester Crown Court.

The *Viz* take on British comics gave birth to Biffa Bacon, who is Bully Beef from the *Dandy* but with genuine violence and social problems. Suicidal Syd is a typical *Beano*-style character whose comedy trait is a desire to take his own life.

In issue 1 of *Viz* there was a real *Beano*-style strip by Chris called 'Fat Sod', in which the *Viz* comic rules were laid down: the character smells the farmer's pie cooling on the window sill, he steals it, the farmer shoots him and then eats him, baked in an even bigger pie. So in proper comics Billy Whizz could run fast, Desperate Dan was extremely strong and Claude Hopper had big feet; in *Viz* Biffa Bacon dealt out relentless, extreme violence and Johnny Fartpants could do really big farts.

Real people
Characters based directly on real people have been few and far between in *Viz*, but I did create three that I can think of and two were based on my brothers.

Simon Lotion, Time and Motion Man was based directly on Chris, whose fastidious form filling, memo writing and in-depth analysis and criticism of filing systems and work practices drove us all up the walls at times, and these tendencies weren't limited to the workplace. Little imagination was needed to write the strip. The material was all around me most of the time.

Mr Logic was based directly on Steve. Once again this was far from being a leap of imagination, and many of Mr Logic's stories were based around genuine incidents.

The other most-asked question about *Viz* was 'Where do you get your ideas from?' We've enjoyed making up various stories to amuse ourselves over the years, as the boring truth – 'From our imaginations' – is usually too brief and unfathomably simple for most people.

Chris and I once decided in the very early days that we'd tell people that a mysterious old man came to our door in the middle of a storm and handed us a chest, which he asked us to guard with our lives, before he disappeared into the night, never to be seen again. Many years later we came across the chest in the attic and opened it, to discover it was full of ideas for funny cartoons.

About nine years later we – me, Chris, Thorpy and Graham – were at a comics convention in London, in our first ever formal question-and-answer session. Inevitably, the question was asked. Thorpy and Graham turned to Chris and me with 'Help us out!' written on their camera-shy faces. Chris quietly tutted his disapproval. I remembered the story about the old man and saw my opportunity, delivering the story with a totally straight face. It was so funny, watching the faces of the terminally serious comic aficionados as the penny began to drop for some, but not for others, that I was taking the piss.

The UK comic conventions were pretty freaky events, full of adolescents with BO and skin the colour of peeled potatoes and adults with BO and skin the colour of peeled potatoes. We only attended two or three of these affairs, at the suggestion of John Brown, before we concluded they weren't really for us. One of these events proved quite productive, though. One night in the hotel bar I sat with Chris and the other *Viz* contributors, joined by a mix of friends and John Brown's staff, and between us we came up with 'Famous People on the Toilet', a one-frame joke that *Viz* featured for years on end. Remarkably, in a period of about an hour or so, we came up with just about every joke that was ever used over those years. The format was very simple, hence the very quick flow of ideas. You have a picture of a toilet door, a caption declaring 'Famous People on the Toilet' and a number supposedly denoting that this is just one in an enormous series, and finally a speech balloon coming from inside the toilet containing a quote for which the person in question is famous. This, of course, had to have a lavatorial double meaning, for instance, Harold Macmillan's 'I have in my hand a piece of paper' or William Shatner's 'Captain's log …'

134

Noo Yoik!

It was an exciting period and working at Bob and Soo's was in the main a halcyon time for me. I loved the feeling of having somewhere to go to work that wasn't my parents' house. The feeling of being a grown-up and doing things properly was a big part of it: having a studio, a job that paid me wages, a car. Bob and Soo were very supportive and also offered a home away from home. There was also a social aspect of working there: they had two young daughters, Gemma and Nico, and I used to have great fun playing with them during breaks from working in my little basement hideaway. It was a world in which I was totally accepted and without the endless conflicts I was now experiencing with Chris, Dad and Andrea.

With Dad, arguments were almost constant, and I could see no way to avoid them other than spending as little time as possible at Lily Crescent. But the constant feeling I was abandoning Mum haunted me. Andrea would blame the problems we were having on the way Chris treated me, saying he didn't see me as an equal, which became more and more of an issue for her. I always felt, perhaps rather naively, that Chris was older and wiser and as such would treat me as fairly, as was right. Andrea insisted that I should stick up for myself against him, which did little but create an atmosphere of confrontation. Any problems there were between Chris and me were never resolved. It was a constant battle and looking for an acceptable resolution was not an agenda either of us had thought of: we were both far too stubborn and had been brought up in a house of unresolved arguments. Chris would always try to take the high ground by means of official, humour-free letters, posted through the Royal Mail, even though we worked together, and this is a trend he's followed throughout his life. The Bumph Club wasn't just a teenage foray into nonsense but a mission statement for life.

My personal problems grew and the fact that Mum's condition worsened as I struggled to find my feet as an adult led me into chaotic insecurity, which I would never get a chance to deal with until I was in a far worse mental state.

After a year or so Maria moved out of the flat and Gerry, Andrea's long-time friend, moved in. Life was better there, but I was hiding from all the things that troubled me and a downfall was looming large.

Andrea was invited to be a bridesmaid for an old friend who had emigrated and was getting married in Canada. It was our first opportunity to travel abroad, London being my furthest adventure and Scotland being Andrea's. She'd only once been south of the Tyne, and that was when she got on the wrong Metro at the Central Station and went 500 yards into Gateshead by mistake.

John Brown arranged for us to fly to New York as Virgin staff. I was, after all, working for Virgin Vision. We would then fly to Seattle and make our way up to Vancouver, just over the border. We were entitled to Virgin standby fares of just £25 from London to New York, and as the USA had just bombed Libya and Americans were avoiding flying, we could pretty much guarantee to fly on the date of our choice. The internal flights in America were $99, which was just £64 at the time, so we flew from London to Seattle for only £89 each.

The trip would have been the best adventure of our lives if it weren't for the tensions between us. By the time we set off for London on the brown Clipper double-decker bus we'd pretty much already agreed that we would go our separate ways on our return. The trip was to prove very difficult. Andrea's twenty-first birthday would happen when we were over there, which didn't help.

Despite the gloom in our relationship New York was absolutely amazing. Far from the gun-crime riddled, heroin-addled metropolis I'd seen on TV, I found the streets to be friendly and less overpowering than those of London. Manhattan had quite a cosy vibe to it, not at all crazy, really quite laid back.

We stayed for two nights with David Zinser, an American friend of John Brown. He lived in the top floor of a converted cheese-freezing warehouse in a stunning apartment, like something from an arthouse film. Bare brick walls were lined with bookcases, all packed with thousands upon thousands of books. Access to the flat was by one of those huge, open industrial lifts. It really was quite special, and very New York. David was a friendly middle-class eccentric; an American version of John. They'd known each other for many years, so maybe they'd rubbed off on each other quite a bit. He owned a restaurant that he drove us to in his 'van', a proper *Scooby Doo*-style affair. Like John, he bombarded people with questions, suggesting to me a slight insecurity. He continually asked if we liked his van, and each time we said yes he would ask if we thought it suited him, and this continued verbatim. His questioning was only interrupted by sudden bursts of inexplicable road rage. Stopped at a junction by traffic queuing, he wound down his window, blasted his horn and screamed at the innocent motorist across our path, 'I don't think I fucking like you!' He then slipped straight back into the previous conversation as if nothing of note had occurred.

When we arrived at David's restaurant we asked if he would order for us, as we didn't know any of the dishes listed. The menu appeared to be in Mexican Spanish. We told him we were both vegetarian and left everything else up to him.

The rice had pieces of bacon in it.

'David, I think there's been a mistake ... This seems to have meat in it,' I said.

'Oh, well, yeah ... but they're very small pieces. Is that a problem?' was his sincere reply.

Before we ventured out alone the following day, David gave us some of the best advice I've ever had as a tourist. 'If you're in a strange city, never look like you're lost. No matter how vulnerable you feel, just buy a local paper, stick it under your arm and walk like you know where you're going.'

We took time to visit the sites and went to the World Trade Center, but the observation deck was closed due to high winds. The view from indoors was still absolutely stunning. I'd borrowed a 35mm camera from Steve, who now lived in London and who we'd stayed with before flying out, and I snapped away wildly. Never having had a decent camera, and finding myself surrounded by one of the world's greatest cityscapes, I was as happy as a pig in shit.

We had planned the holiday to last an entire month, but once we arrived in Vancouver, the problems we were storing up just seemed to destroy any chance of us enjoying ourselves. In the weeks leading up to the trip I'd planned to get a whole load of extra work backed up, but my mind was in such a state I would just sit at my drawing board, staring into space, not really thinking, not really doing anything. My head was a real mess. This state of mind wasn't a new thing: it had been going on to a certain extent before I even started to work at Bob and Soo's. I had tried for a time to work at Lily Crescent, but I was wracked with insecurities and would try and put off working for some subconscious reason. I would sit and stare at Music Box, the MTV station launched in the mid-1980s. To this day, when I see music videos from this time they flash me back to those days of dark depression. I had no idea at the time what my problem was, I was only barely aware that something was wrong. I can see now that I was suffering from a deep internal struggle with my feelings. Leaving Mum behind in her hour of need, trying to be an independent adult on limited means, and the sibling rivalries, coupled with my lifelong battle with guilt over what my arrival had done to my family, were a recipe for long-term emotional problems. It would be a very long time before I finally sought help.

The rest of the North American adventure left me with little else to report: a nice wedding, a quite enjoyable and mainly dignified stag night with the groom, smoking skunkweed for the first time, a visit to the beautiful winter resort of Whistler and a lot of very unimpressive weather. We had picked the worst summer for fifty years for our first ever trip abroad. We eventually returned to New York two days earlier than planned, as it was without a doubt the highlight and we wanted to see much more of it. David had forgotten we were coming and had flown to Mexico. Fortunately Virgin put us on an earlier flight back to London, but we still ended up stuck in Newark Airport for forty-eight hours. We would have loved to have gone and stayed in a motel and seen the sights, but we were penniless. Our trip ended in a murderous sleep-deprived two days in an airport free of all comforts, from which we couldn't stray due to the amount of baggage we were lumbered with.

There was one amusing moment. A fat American woman asked us where we were from. I told her England, and she said, 'I have a friend in England. Mary Thomas. Do you know her?'

On our return, sure enough, Andrea and I went our separate ways. The split was devastating for me. I'd never felt so bad in my life, and I guess I never have since. The legend 'the first cut is the deepest' rings true. I was an absolutely lost soul without Andrea. I'd become completely dependent on her for emotional support, comfort and companionship, but now it was all gone. I'd found so much that was important in my life, and now I had nothing. That was how it felt, at least. I really thought my world would fall apart without her, and hearing that she'd started to see someone else was a blow I just wasn't ready for.

Viz, though, was in fine health and another new and significant contributor made his debut. Davey Jones began in a similar fashion to Thorpy, posting us short strips that were often a little surreal and always extremely funny. If I remember rightly his first strip was 'Vlad the Impaler', who probably not surprisingly just impaled people.

Davey lived on Anglesey, the island off Wales, and at first would communicate, like Thorpy, only by post. His artwork would always arrive in old whisky bottle tubes and we assumed he was a heavy drinker. However, we discovered many years later that he lived next door to a pub and asked the landlord to keep the tubes for him especially for posting his artwork. Coincidentally, Davey did happen to enjoy a few sherbets, invariably drinking himself into a state in which he would fall flat on his face, unable even to put his arms out to protect himself from any upcoming surfaces – floors, steps, chairs ... On one occasion he came home so drunk that he switched on the electric fire and then, needing the toilet, took down his trousers and sat on it. I have it on good authority that he has parallel buttock scars to prove it.

On the piss

After the split I found a flat in Heaton, previously the home of Davey Bruce, the Arthur 2 Stroke drummer. Living alone, I was a lost and troubled soul, and I sought solace in the bottle, or more accurately the pint glass. I went on the piss for the next five years.

Chris had recently met and started dating Dolores, an Irish nanny, and was leaning heavily towards a life of domestic normality. This created something of an extra tension as I had just lost such an existence and felt he was now looking down on my behaviour from a holier-than-thou perspective. Whether he actually was or not is another matter, but my perception affected the way I felt at the time.

My natural allies in a life of hedonism would be Jim, and Andrew Barnden. We already enjoyed nights out together, but now I was a single man the opportunity to go drinking with them whenever possible seemed like a sensible move. I have to say that I enjoyed my five-year wild weekend more than it's probably wise to admit. I was young and had a disposable income for the first time. Newcastle had brilliant nightlife. I had my own flat and my own car. The loss of Andrea was a body blow, but elsewhere my new life was starting to look up.

I enjoyed it to the maximum, but I wasn't a drunken lost cause and was aware of what I was doing. I was still able to work; indeed, during this period I probably produced the best work of my *Viz* career. It was one of the most productive and busy times I've ever known.

Although I was drinking almost every night, I still retained my fitness by swimming at least half a mile every day at Heaton pool, and I ate a pretty balanced diet. When I was out drinking I would walk everywhere and twice a week I would dance till the early hours down at Tom Caulker's nights at Rockshots in Waterloo Street. I was as fit as a lop.

I had little time for eighties' music and during my time with Andrea I'd looked backwards for something better than the dross being pumped out by the New Romantics. I'd discovered The Faces and got right into them, I *loved* them, but this seemed to be a one-man mission at the time. Through The Faces I later discovered the phenomenal Small Faces. The eighties had no answer to this. I hated the decade's music and fashion.

Tommy Caulker was a beacon in the smog of musical bilge. He ran The Trent House and put on nights at Rockshots on Tuesdays and Thursdays, and as his own resident DJ he introduced his predominantly student punters to a very nutritious diet of James Brown, Aretha Franklin and, most importantly, Curtis

Mayfield. 'Move On Up' was the soundtrack of my life at that time.

The pubs we frequented were mainly Tommy's 'World-Famous' Trent House and the legendary Strawberry, both within spitting distance of St James' Park and, on City Road, the Barley Mow and the Egypt Cottage. We occasionally drank in Jesmond at The Archer, where Chris and I were both on the pool team for a short while. We favoured seedier pubs with pool tables, as we all liked a game: the swanky chrome-and-neon 'wine bars' of Newcastle weren't for us. Chris at one time had a six-foot table in his bedroom. It was a bit shit, in particular the pockets were tiny, but at least this meant when you got to the pub the pockets there looked like buckets.

My new flat at Tosson Terrace was spacious, airy, comfortable and cheap to rent. It had a fabulous original open fire in the sitting room, with an imposing black slate surround, and there was enough room for me to set up an office in the back room, so I said goodbye to my time at Bob and Soo's. It was a very peaceful street. The flat was a bit run down in places, and like my flat on Simonside Terrace it had no central heating. But now that I was comparatively wealthy, I bought an oil-filled electric radiator, and my bedroom became a palace of opulence. Tim, guitarist in Arthur 2 Stroke, was about to emigrate to Canada with his family and he sold me his well-loved art deco three-piece suite for £15. The kitchen let the place down, but Dave Hall gave me an unwanted wall-mounted kitchen cupboard, Dick Scott sold me a new worktop for next to nothing and I got a stainless steel sink and taps from somewhere, maybe from Jim, who was working for a property developer. Jim and I tiled the wall above the new worktop and I was in business. I was now living in what felt very close to luxury.

One of the most novel things about *Viz* in those early days was that we sold it in pubs. It was Tommy Caulker who first asked if he could sell it in The Trent House and Chris and I set about building a dispenser for him to put behind the bar. It was made of plywood with a Perspex front, and its base extended out to one side where an old boiled sweet tin had been nailed as a cash box. It also had a telephone handset hanging on a hook. Tommy was told that this was a hotline for ordering new stock. He chose to use a proper phone instead.

Once Tommy began to sell *Viz*, other bohemian pubs followed suit, and before long The Strawberry, the City Hall Concert Bar, the Barley Mow, Egypt Cottage and the Free Trade Inn were all regular stockists, with their own hand-made dispensers, although The Trent House had the only hotline handset.

When the initial delivery of a new issue arrived I would drive to Lily Crescent and remove the car's passenger seat to fit more comics inside. There were bundles on the back seats, under the driving seat, in the side pockets, and not forgetting in the boot.

A typical day of work would begin with me sitting at my desk and drawing for an hour or two before driving across to Lily Crescent to collect comics for delivery. Once the deliveries were done, I would drive back to my flat and draw for another hour or two. I would then drive to the swimming baths, do my thirty-six lengths, return home to eat, a bit more drawing, and then it was time to go out and get drunk.

Tuesdays and Thursdays would usually be spent in The Trent before Rockshots and Fridays were always upstairs at the Egypt Cottage, the night *The Tube* was filmed next door at Tyne Tees Studio Five.

Looking back I can't quite believe some of the things I got up to when I was drunk. I would often be told I was 'the life and soul of the party'. I think this means my behaviour had a value akin to that of animals in a zoo: entertaining to witness, but you wouldn't want it happening in your house at Christmas.

Andrew Barnden had, like me, been trained in theatre skills. One night Jim, Andrew and I, having completed our regular mission to get comfortably drunk, were on the way back to Jim's flat to take our imbibing to another level. Andrew began to tell me he'd been teaching Jim the art of stage fighting – the way actors learn to fight dramatically, without hurting one another. So, there and then, in the street, they decided to show me what they'd managed to choreograph so far. It wasn't long before we realised that passers-by were getting quite alarmed: they thought the violence was real. We saw the potential for a bit of laugh straight away and decided to deliberately stage fights in the street when opportune moments arose. (This was always away from the town centre areas where genuine fighty-minded people tended to flock.)

We soon created a codeword for the instigation of a stage fight. One of us would recognise an opportunity – the presence of some soft-looking students nearby – and shout at the top of his voice, 'CUNT!' This was the moment in a supposed argument when things turned ugly. On one occasion Andrew began with a hefty punch to Jim's face, aided by Jim producing the impact noise with his own hands, then falling to his knees. Andrew continued with a magnificent full-bodied boot into Jim's knackers, or, to be more accurate, into Jim's discreetly placed cupped hands. Jim appeared barely able to stay conscious as he swayed, bent almost double, still on his knees. Andrew then took a run up and delivered a dropkick to Jim's face, once again actually Jim's hands.

All along a small group of wimpy students stood at a safe distance, horrified, the girls encouraging the boys to intervene, the boys not doing so.

Throughout the fight I'd been staggering around, acting very drunk, pointing at Andrew and slurring aggressively, 'The lad's had enough, man … I tell ye what … divven't bray him anymore. Ye knaa, I can see ye like a fight … but the lad's tooken a fuckin' kickin' … an' that should be the fuckin' end of it, like.'

Jim now lay in the road, motionless. Andy wandered off. I staggered over to Jim and began to speak to his stone-still body.

'Now, I tell ye whorrit is, right … I tell ye whorrit is … Ye've tooken a good hidin', right … Ye've tooken a good hidin' … but I tell ye whorrit is, right … as lang as ye've got your health, that's the main thing. Ye've took a proper kickin' here the neet, but, right, but, as lang as ye've got your health … and ya friends, that's the main thing.'

Without warning, Jim then jumped to his feet and declared loudly, 'Ta-daaah!'

The three of us then lined up and began to take bows, and as we did so I announced, 'Thangyaw laydeez an' gennlmen! Thangyaw, thangyaw! I hope you enjoyed our lidde show here donight!'

The students applauded, some more reluctantly than others.

143

Andrew wasn't the only person Jim and I spent time drinking with. Graham Lines drew our attention to an afternoon showing of the first three *Star Trek* films. Despite all being fans of the TV series as children, none of us had seen any of the films. The showing was at the ABC Westgate Road, and we spent a very pleasant afternoon there. We decided afterwards that this would be a nice way to spend an afternoon a week, so agreed to meet up the following week to do the same again. I can't remember what the film was supposed to be on this occasion, but it'd been cancelled. We talked about various other cinema options, but nowhere seemed to be showing anything we wanted to see. Eventually we decided to just sit in a pub and catch up. Graham had recently been married and we'd seen a lot less of him, hence the idea to meet regularly, so as to not lose touch. We opted for The County on Gosforth High Street, a nice pub Graham recommended, which was now his local. We drank all afternoon. Graham mentioned that he had no commitments until teatime, when he had to be home for a meal that his wife was preparing. I occasionally reminded Graham of this, but he seemed undeterred, and we continued to recharge our glasses. Eventually, he asked me what the time was, as he appeared to be having trouble reading his own watch. After the lengthy process of getting the information across was complete, he began to show some concern. He informed us that he should go and ring his wife to say he'd be a little late. It was already over an hour since he should have been home. He asked me if I knew what his phone number was, which was a little surprising. I wrote it down. Some time passed while Graham was at the payphone. He eventually returned and asked me what the number was that I'd given him. I explained it was his home phone number. He sat down and looked very carefully at the scrap of paper in his hand. 'Are you sure?' he asked.

'Oh, yes. I called you on it earlier,' I replied, trying not to laugh.

'Naah. It's not my number. Some woman told me to fuck off ... It wasn't our lass.'

We continued to drink. Graham at some point eventually returned home. We never spent any more afternoons together and funnily enough Graham's marriage didn't last.

1986 saw me throw a gauntlet down to Jim. In Rockshots, late one night, I proposed that we should have a race to see who could grow the best 'improvised jazz beard'. We each had to grow a goatee and the first to shave it off lost the challenge. It seems strange now, as so many people wear goatees, but this really was a bit of a social stigma at the time. In the mid-1980s no young people had beards, and certainly not the type sported by Jimmy Hill.

The challenge lasted about six weeks and we eventually called a truce. We celebrated the end of the jazz beard era by having a photo session with Jim's sister, in which we struck as many jazz poses as we could, trying to look as late-fifties Greenwich Village and Soho as possible.

After looking back at the photos I later decided to grow my beard back, as it seemed to suit me. I've had it most of the years since, constantly looking like a Happy Shopper beat poet.

We had another drinking partner who I shall refer to as Mr R. He developed a serious problem with alcohol and thankfully later gave it up. His ability to put beer away was legendary and he often drank in a pub called The Broken Doll, which sold a beer like no other I've ever tasted. To be honest, Slalom D's taste wasn't its attraction – that would be its unprecedented alcohol content. It was by far the strongest draft beer I'd ever touched. Its lovers were a special breed, as for most people it wasn't possible to drink the stuff in any quantity without consequences. One friend of mine, a lover of the D, who I shall call Mr W, told me he'd once woken unexpectedly one morning on the concourse of the Central Station. As he came round he realised he was lying on a bench, but the commuters bustling around him appeared to be upside down. He realised his head was hanging completely off the end of the bench. He lifted it only to discover a half-eaten kebab on his chest. On another occasion Ian Thomson, Arthur 2 Stroke bassist, was on the bus home from town one night. As it pulled into a stop he saw Mr W asleep on top of the bus shelter.

Mr R had an unusual habit of coming into town by bus from the family home in south Northumberland and spending every penny in his pocket. He would then sofa-surf until such time as his mother was in town and could give him a lift back home. On one legendary occasion he had swallowed a gallon or more of the

D and had scored a total blank in his attempts to find somewhere to sleep. In his catastrophically drunken mind he decided it would be best to walk the eighteen miles home. He felt sure he'd be able to hitch a lift at least part of the way. His navigation system as he crossed the Redheugh Bridge was to stagger into the crash barrier at one side of the road and then correct his steering again when he hit the one at the other side. I guess this explains his inability to attract a ride.

The family house stood high up, overlooking beautiful countryside, and the journey from Newcastle was entirely uphill. Mr R was soon totally exhausted and decided the wisest course of action would be to steal a car.

He duly found one, a Mini, which he knew were very easy to break into. He slipped the window and was in. He pulled the wires out from under the dash, but in his tired and emotional state was unable to work out which circuit was which. He eventually gave up. Several miles on he could face walking no longer and broke into another Mini. Once again he was unable to fathom out how to hotwire it, so again he gave up. He eventually got home and slept off the drink and the walk.

On awakening, his memories of the previous night came back to haunt him in fits and starts.

'How could I have been so stupid as to want to drive a car when I was so drunk?'

'How could I have been stupid enough to think it was a good idea to steal someone's car?'

These questions were hard enough to face, but the ones that most defied reality came next.

'How could I expect to be able to hotwire a car when I have no understanding of electrics?'

And best of all:

'How did I expect to drive the car? I don't know how to fucking drive.'

Sadly, The Broken Doll has been demolished. On the positive side, Slalom D is no longer available.

Big Log

We got our first break on national radio in the winter of 1985. We were contacted by Radio One's *Saturday Live* show and were

146

invited to be interviewed by young *Whistle Test* and *Live Aid* presenter Andy Kershaw.

Chris and I were joined by Jim, and Colin Davison, a Newcastle-based professional photographer who worked for us on *Viz* photoshoots on Sunday mornings, who was also in London with us beforehand. I remember little about the events leading up to the interview, but I vaguely recall standing on the steps of the church next door to Broadcasting House drinking Red Stripe Crucial Brew, a lethal brand of extra-strong lager that I gave a wide birth to thereafter.

Me Mark Page walked past on his way into the BBC and I shouted, 'Me Mark Page!'

He turned and waved.

I shouted, 'Wanker!'

It was going to be a good day, but in a messy kind of way.

We made our way into reception and were greeted by Andy Kershaw, who informed us we just had to wait for another guest to arrive. To our amazement, in walked Robert Plant, dressed in a Hawaiian shirt with an airline ticket poking out from the pocket.

'Hi guys,' he said softly, adding directly to Andy, 'Before we go to the studio, is there a bathroom I can use nearby?'

'Just up there, mate. We'll wait for you.'

Plant hurried across the floor of the hall, the only sound his shoes on the marble floor echoing around the walls. As he reached the steps I shouted loudly to him, 'Robert!'

He stopped and turned back. Everyone in the atrium was now looking at him.

'Yes?' he offered back, tentatively.

'Are you going for a big log?'

There was a great mix of laughter and embarrassed glances as he replied 'Erm, no ...' and continued on his way.

I had cleverly referenced his 1983 hit 'Big Log' and created an imaginative lavatory joke.

I find it hard to believe that in the mists of time I actually managed to completely forget this incident. It wasn't until more than twenty years later that I bumped into Andy at a Robert Plant gig in London and he reminded me. He told me it was one of the funniest things he'd ever seen, which was nice. It was a throwaway gag, but I guess it was a good one.

We did our interview, during which Chris took to one of his moods, presumably because I was enjoying myself too much. On leaving to catch his flight, Robert Plant turned to us and said, 'Enjoy yourselves. It's a world in which to have fun.'

Lovely advice, I thought, and easy to say when you've got a first-class air ticket to Barbados in your pocket and a chauffeur waiting to take you to the airport.

I was disappointed to discover that *Saturday Live* was not actually all live. I'd been beside myself at the chance of meeting The Ramones, who were also on the show. I'd been obsessed with them in my teens and saw them as the ultimate pop band for my generation – punk attitude and sound, but with tunes. Their piece had been pre-recorded and meeting them never happened. I was pretty deflated, but on reflection I do have a real Ramones treasure.

In January 1979 my school friend Simon Barker called at my door the day of a Ramones concert at the City Hall that we were both going to, along with pretty much all of our mates. He asked if I wanted to go to the sound check to try and get things signed. I couldn't go, but he kindly took my copy of their first album down and got it signed for me. The drummer at the time was Marky Ramone, who didn't play on the album, so said he'd rather not sign it. My album is signed by Johnny, Joey and Dee Dee, all of whom have subsequently died. My life's mission is now to meet Tommy, the original drummer, and get the set completed.

Dial D for Deadline

Drinking had to stop when deadlines approached. Working on cartoons is very intensive and requires a huge amount of concentration. Regardless of how well planned an issue was, there would always be a horrible rush up to the artwork deadline. Issues were never really 'planned' in the truest sense, but once we knew what pages we were each supposed to produce for the issue the slog would be on. This seems to be the same right across the publishing world: you can't comfortably glide up to a deadline. I think it's because you'll always use every second at your disposal to make the product the best you can. We always used to talk about how easy it would be to make a magazine that didn't have to be funny. It would certainly have taken some of the pressure off us.

Sleep deprivation was always a feature of *Viz* deadlines. Even back in the days before the publishing deal Chris and I would sometimes work right through the night just to meet our own targets. We would listen to Metro Radio: 10pm until 2am was Night Owls with James Whale, later Alan Beswick, and then 2am until 6am was the 'swing shift' DJ whose name escapes me (Dave something?) and who always sounded depressed, not surprisingly. We'd phone in and get messages read out, which wasn't difficult at that time of night. As far as we could tell, there were just us and the night shift at Greggs the bakers in Gosforth listening in. There was a café at the top of Northumberland Street that opened at some unearthly hour, 6am or so, so we'd go there for breakfast. We were always fans of greasy spoon cafés, as was Jim. When we worked down at the Free Press finishing the comics we would always spend our breaks in the Exo Café Bar on the corner of Clayton Street and Fenkle Street. This was a true star of the traditional café world, in Festival of Britain-era decor with Formica tables and pillars covered in black and multi-coloured mosaic tiles. A wonderful place, but like so many of the flawed diamonds of my youth, it's now long gone.

One particular deadline, issue 27, nearly did me in, and I have a permanent reminder of it. I had three cartoon scripts written: Johnny Fartpants, Sid the Sexist and The Bottom Inspectors. According to my calculations I had just over three days to complete each of them, as there were ten days to the deadline. This was just about right for the speed at which I could work at the time, although a bit on the tight side. I was over at Lily Crescent and in a casual conversation about when I expected to bring over my completed artwork when the penny dropped: there weren't ten days left. I had the wrong week down for the issue's delivery date and I'd lost a week. There were just three days to go. I had only one day to complete each page of work. It was an awful feeling, a nightmare that wouldn't go away.

I drove home and got my head down immediately. I drew at my desk solidly for the next three days. I never left the house, never lay down, I just worked non-stop on a diet of coffee and tabs. My brain began to play horrible tricks on me as I went through the usual highs and lows of sleep deprivation. Towards the end of the work I was a rotten state – my brain simply wouldn't work and there were no more highs.

I made some coffee and sat back down at my desk. I began to pick up my drawing board, which was just a flat piece of wood that I taped my work to. When drawing I propped it up in my lap and lay it against the desk. As I tipped it up I saw that I'd left my pen lying on it. This was my drawing pen, an old-fashioned ink pen with a pointed metal tip that you dip in a bottle of Indian ink. I went to catch it, but I missed. The point of the pen struck me on top of the ball joint of my thumb, went straight through my skin and made a horrible sound as it struck the bone just below the surface. The nib was now stuck in my skin and the pen was hanging from the side of my hand, propping up the skin where the nib had stuck in like a little wigwam. I grabbed the pen and quickly pulled it out, but as I did so I felt the cool ink as it was 'injected' under my skin. I looked down and I could see a little bulge of black ink under the skin. Instinctively, I started to suck at it. I sucked and sucked and spat out more and more tiny amounts of the ink–blood mixture. Eventually, I had to give up. I'd sucked out all I was going to manage. The black spot on my thumb eventually turned blue, as I knew it would: Indian ink is what tattoo artists use. So, I got the world's first *Viz* tattoo, although to be honest I've seen better ones since.

The X tapes

Wavis O'Shave reared his extremely weird head again when he arrived on the doorstep at Lily Crescent with a woman who claimed to be some kind of witch. I suspect they'd met through mutual use of social services. They informed Chris and me that they were on the run from some very scary people in a white van. These people had connections with the Catholic Church and the CIA and they wanted to capture Wavis because of what he knew. Wavis told us he had some tapes that contained information that could shake some people in extremely high places to the ground, and the people in the van wanted them at any cost. He needed sanctuary, just for a few days, until the dust settled.

Wavis and his mumsy-witch partner sat and drank tea and decided it wouldn't be wise to expand on their story any further, for our own safety.

We didn't know what to do. We couldn't put them up at Lily Crescent, Dad would go mental, and besides, we didn't really want the weight of the Vatican and the US Government coming down on us. Chris had a brilliant idea. We'd drop them off at a friend's house and then we'd run away.

I drove our fruity friends to Benwell, where Paul Rose was living, explained what had happened and Paul accepted them in. I then returned to Lily Crescent. Paul told Wavis and his ladyfriend that he was going out. He insisted that they waited outside for him, as he didn't know them well enough to leave them alone in the house. He walked up the street, down the back lane, climbed in the back window and then pretended to be out for the rest of the day. Wavis and Wavisetta duly returned to South Shields on the bus.

I later discovered that Wavis had hired a transit van to take his ladyfriend to Glastonbury. The previous hirers had accidentally left two Kenny Rogers tapes in the glove box. They called the hire firm, saying they could collect them if they were found. The hire shop in turn called Wavis's house, his mum took the message and relayed it to Wavis on his return from Glastonbury. 'Something about a white van. You've got tapes belonging to someone and they want them back. They say they'll come round for them.'

I assume Wavis had enjoyed the Glastonbury experience enough to knock his normally eccentric mentality right over the boundary into paranoid mentaldom.

You must be kidneying

The *Viz* reception had a brief rebirth for our twenty-fifth issue party. This was held in a club called The Jewish Mother, later to become the Hyena Comedy Café and is best remembered as the first time we met Simon Thorp. His remarkable contributions had continued via the post and he had still never had so much as a conversation with any of us. He arrived dressed all in beige, a skinny lath of a man with thick black hair and, as expected, a shy nature. He was greeted at the door of the club by Chris and

Dolores, who asked if they could look after his bag. He handed over a modestly sized holdall and said, 'Take care with that, it's got my kidney machine in it.'

Word very quickly spread around the room in hushed tones. We had all wondered what Thorpy would be like, as his work was clearly that of a remarkable artist, a man with a tremendous sense of humour and, possibly most notably, an awful lot of time on his hands in which to complete his beautifully finished products. We all agreed that it made perfect sense: his illness must have resulted in him spending an awful lot of time confined to his house. It went some way to explaining his devotion to his work.

Thorpy, we later discovered, is a very dry and sharp-witted man. It would be many months before we learned that his bag had contained nothing more than a change of clothes. He was unaware of the full-blown alarm he had caused, and we were to work with him in the same office for some time before he realised and declared in horror that his comment had been nothing more than a 'throwaway gag'. We were less sympathetic towards him afterwards.

It was in The Jewish Mother on another night that a curly haired ginger Cockney 'geezer' called Rob approached me and quietly said, 'Fack me. What on earth are you doing with the two best-looking women in the place?'

I had come to the club with two friends who were indeed very pretty young ladies, although I didn't have the key to either of their knickers. Rob continued, 'Fackin' 'ell. You mast be the silver-tongued cavalier.'

With this, he walked away. I made a mental note that one of my characters would now have a new strapline, and from the next issue onwards Sid the Sexist would become Tyneside's Silver-Tongued Cavalier.

Working on the comic proved to be a very good way of meeting women. One night in The Trent House I was introduced to a girl who worked in a newsagent that sold *Viz*. Straight away I was rather taken with her: she was tall and athletic with masses of auburn curls, dressed immaculately in the rather masculine fashion of the time with Doctor Martens' shoes and baggy jeans.

She seemed almost permanently to have a mischievous look in her eyes. She was called Catherine and would be my partner in a very much off-and-then-on-and-then-off-again relationship for the next few years.

Although I had spent some time in the company of other women, Catherine was really the first girl I had anything serious with since the breakup of my relationship with Andrea. Catherine couldn't have been any more different from Andrea, both physically and personality-wise. She was adventurous, ambitious, competitive, sporty, and had a fantastic sense of humour. She was always mildly irritated by my childishness and was able to make me laugh hysterically at will by simply burping out loud and then dismissing my belief that it had in any way been funny.

We had some great times, clubbing, drinking and going on adventures, like camping at the Edinburgh Fringe, and seeing some great shows – Jerry Sadowitz and John Hegley spring to mind. Her mother would lend Catherine her brand-new VW Polo and we'd drive to London to see her old school friend Alison, who was working for John Brown, and Steve, who, having forged his own path into the world of special effects, was working for Jim Henson. We would go with a load of friends to the Notting Hill Carnival.

I really enjoyed my time with Catherine, although our relationship wasn't romantic in the same way as my time with Andrea. Catherine was much more reserved about her feelings, and I found that quite hard to live with, but her vibrancy, humour and love of music and film added a lot to my life, for which I was very grateful.

I was heartbroken when she moved to Leicester to study medicine, but surprisingly we carried on making things work for a while. I would drive down most weekends, setting off after work on Friday and sometimes staying right up to Monday morning. She lived in a lovely little house and I helped her move in and decorate. Our relationship even stayed afloat somehow when she moved to Germany on a work placement.

During Catherine's stay in Germany she wrote to me nearly every day, which I didn't really appreciate until many years later when I was clearing a load of stuff out and saw the sheer quantity of correspondence she'd sent me.

I went out to visit her in Germany and had a great time. Later she invited Steve to stay and over he went from London, driving, on his first trip abroad. After two weeks or more staying at Catherine's flat, despite many heavy-handed hints from Catherine and her flatmates, implying that it might be time for him to move on or go home, he stayed put, immune to all mentions of how long he'd been around. Hints, no matter how brutal, never worked with Steve, because by their nature they aren't literal; they aren't logical.

Steve's very logical, and at times very irritating, behaviour was always considered to be the workings of an eccentric mind. Chris even believed he'd modelled himself on Mr Spock from *Star Trek*. The truth didn't come out until, having watched a TV documentary, Steve himself concluded that he may have Asperger's Syndrome, a condition on the autism spectrum. He took himself off to be tested and sure enough he was right. It answered so many questions and made it much easier for everyone to understand him, and was especially helpful for Steve himself.

Catherine was still in Germany on the momentous night when the Berlin Wall came down. She drove there with friends and, equipped with what tools they could lay their hands on, they broke away what they could from the reinforced concrete structure. She brought me a piece of it back: it was about the size of a peach stone, with remnants of red and blue graffiti on its flat side. It stayed in my china cabinet for years until my cleaner threw it away, thinking it was a piece of rubble from building works in the house. I never told her what she'd done: I knew it would upset her terribly. However, it is quite a funny story, so I had to tell it. I really hope she doesn't read this, but I fear she will.

Photo stories

When I was still a single man, photo stories had proved to be a great way to meet girls. In a nightclub, remarkably cheesy as it sounds, offering a girl a starring role as a model in a national magazine was a great way to break the ice. We almost always had photo story ideas at the last minute before the weekend we would have to shoot them. The result would be going for a night

154

out on a Saturday knowing we had to get up to shoot a photo story the next morning, but not yet having a full cast of characters. The search would be on from the moment we arrived in a pub. Having said it was a great way to meet women, it was also quite a difficult and high-pressure situation. Colin, our photographer, would be booked, we had a script, we had a deadline, but we had no models.

A number of people actually met their life partners when we were shooting photo stories. Colin himself met his wife Rashida as he shot her in one; our friends Billy and Amanda married after being paired as lovers in a photo story; and I met Julie, my partner of fourteen years, when she fell for a space alien in one of my photo romances. More about that later.

Photo stories were often a messy affair. I would be rushing around Jesmond knocking on doors, getting old friends out of bed and pleading with them to spend four hours standing around on street corners getting either bored or frozen to death. Many times it would get so desperate that I would approach total strangers on the street and ask them if they wanted to appear in the comic for no reward. They were often taken aback when, on asking when they were expected to fulfil this commitment, I said, 'Now. That's the photographer waiting for you on the other side of the street.'

I always laugh when I look back through old copies of the comic and see the faces of people who were persuaded to appear on the spur of the moment.

So, the photos were always shot on Sunday mornings with Colin and me and most of the cast suffering from hangovers. Despite having to drag ourselves out of bed out to do them, the shoots were almost always great fun, unlike much of the cartoon work, which was intricate and involved and tied me to a desk. Getting out and about was always a bonus.

We always produced the stories as cheaply as possible. The models were always volunteers and locations were almost always our office or one of our houses. My house was used time and time again. Each time I would use a different room, and when all the rooms had been used I simply started again. As well as being used as homes, rooms also doubled as restaurants, nightclubs, offices, garages and shops. One of the saving graces of working on *Viz* was that sometimes the less convincing something looked

155

the funnier it became. We did one story called 'The Hand from Outer Space' in which we used the ticket hall of Jesmond Metro Station as the inside of an alien spacecraft. We just walked in, carrying cardboard ray-guns, and started taking pictures. We never asked permission and only once did this lead to trouble. Chris and Colin were shooting a story outside St George's Church, also the location for the youth club and most of our family's weddings, when the vicar came out to ask what was going on. Ever the true professional, Chris instructed his cast to run away. They moved to another church and finished the story there. The appearance of an entirely different church without explanation wasn't a problem in *Viz*. Far from it.

'The Hand from Outer Space' appeared in three parts and starred my old mate Phil Smith in the first two. In the fine *Viz* tradition of organisation I simply called at his door on the morning we were shooting. He'd gone away on holiday. I hastily went on a mission to try and find someone living nearby, available at very short notice, and of course he needed to be a double for Phil. A few streets away I eventually found Kevin Harper, who was up for it. He bore no resemblance to Phil, but given the circumstances, two out of three was fine. Needless to say, the model in the story changed appearance completely without explanation.

A footnote on St George's Church. Andy Storey married Gillian, a girl he met at the youth club. The wedding was at St George's on 4 July 1987. I was an usher, along with Phil Smith, alongside other old friends Ali McClean and David 'Pleb' Appleby. We stood together in a pew at the very back of the church, dressed in the full morning suit regalia. It was a glorious day and the heat was absolutely stifling, and the doors immediately behind us were left open to allow some air to flow. At the pivotal moment in the service, as hush descended on the congregation, the couple softly spoke their vows. All of a sudden the perfect mood was dealt a hammer blow as an ice-cream van slowly drove past. The distorted, tinny sound blaring out from its tannoy was 'Yankee Doodle Dandy'.

156

The last resort

As 1987 drew to a close our sales overtook those of Britain's most established and longest-running humour magazine, *Punch*, and this was big news. *Punch* had been around since 1841, and it felt that way. By the mid 1980s it survived almost entirely on subscriptions for dentists' waiting rooms. As *Punch* was the fuddled old guard of British humour, it was historically significant that the snotty young punks of *Viz* had passed it by. Chris and I got our first invite to appear on live national TV.

Back in 1985 we'd been contacted by a London-based comic fan who had recently made a successful pitch to produce a late-night talk show for the infant Channel 4. Jonathan Ross had been early to discover *Viz*. As a long-time lover of both comics and British humour, he became a big fan as soon as he laid his hands on it. He invited us both to the Soho offices of Channel X, his little production company. He informed us that his show was to be '*anything but* the Jonathan Ross show'. It was to be a knock-about magazine show with musical guests, interviews and comedy routines all blended together, called *The Last Resort*. He gave us the pilot episode on VHS. He wanted us to write for the show, saying he thought we were the hottest property in new British comedy. I thought it sounded really good and at the time Chris seemed to think so too. However, we got home and sat down to watch the pilot that had won Ross the series. It was *awful*. We wouldn't be working with this twat.

I think Chris's decision not to work with Jonathan was mainly about us needing to devote our time to our new *Viz* contract. To be fair, Jonathan had told us he knew the pilot was flawed and things would be better by the time the series was made. The pilot VHS tape marked 'Return to Channel X' is still in my possession. I don't think it's ever been shown, not even on any of those awful *Before They Were Famous* shows. The bidding starts now.

Despite not having the Donalds writing for him, by 1987 Jonathan had established *The Last Resort* as one of Channel 4's flagship shows for young people. It was essential viewing for students and when we were offered a chance of being interviewed on it this had to be seen as an immense opportunity. It's difficult to put into a comparable modern context. There was no internet and only the four TV channels, and young people watching telly late at night would almost certainly watch Channel 4. We were about to introduce *Viz* to a generation of TV viewers in the age group our comic sold to the best.

We had a big office outing to the London studios with Thorpy and Graham coming along to watch, along with Steve. The other guests on the show included Barbara Windsor, with music from Mick Hucknall out of Simply Red and French novelty act Monsieur Mangetout, assisted by hoity Eurovision Song Contest legend Katie Boyle acting as his translator.

Monsieur Mangetout's special ability, for which he had international notoriety, was to eat 'undigestibles' – glass, rubber, metal – and claim to suffer no ill effects. He'd famously eaten a light aircraft over a period of time, although for what reason I have no clue. During the show he was to eat a drinking glass and a vinyl record.

Rehearsals involved a full-length run through followed by a meal in the studio canteen. At the meal it amused us all that Monsieur Mangetout ate a normal dinner after having eaten the glass and the record in the rehearsal. After the meal he returned to his dressing room. Suddenly, Jonathan excitedly ushered everyone he could get hold of from the canteen into the gents' toilets. He showed us all into the cubicle Monsieur Mangetout had just used. After flushing the toilet, the water was clear, but the heavy pieces of the record had remained in the bottom of the pan. As this was only fifteen minutes after he'd eaten them, it was evident the suffering Monsieur Mangetout's mouth regularly went through was spared his ringpiece.

The Last Resort was an all-round brilliant experience, although I have to say the one thing that let it down was our interview. We were inexperienced at TV and Chris, awkward at the best of times, never seemed comfortable when we were interviewed together. The pressure of the fact we were going out live to millions didn't help. We both looked and sounded nervous. That wasn't the biggest problem we faced, though – that was trying to get a word in when our interviewer was Jonathan Ross.

I was chewing gum backstage and I forgot to get rid of it before we walked out for the interview. During one of Jonathan's lengthy questions I realised I was chewing gum, so thinking the camera would be on Jonathan, I took it out of my mouth and stuck it under his desk. The viewers were actually getting a shot of all three of us at the time and the studio audience all laughed. It looked to everyone like I'd done it as a joke. Result.

Barbara Windsor was absolutely lovely to me backstage. I got her autograph and she told me, 'I 'ope you sell a lot more, darlin'!'

It really was a special night. Before this I'd never stayed in a hotel in my life. Channel X paid for me to stay in one. It was great. I even had breakfast in bed, although that was a bit disappointing. To this day I still get excited about hotels. Even shit ones.

6

John Brown Publishing

In 1987 the Virgin empire decided to sell off a number of its subsidiaries, including Virgin Vision, the part John Brown was running. As Virgin didn't really do magazine publishing, they considered *Viz* and *Hot Air*, the in-flight magazine of Virgin's infant airline, to be obvious targets for offloading. John, however, had seen how *Viz* was building nationally and was prepared to take the risk of setting up a new company on the back of it. He created John Brown Publishing and took with him both us and *Hot Air*.

John isn't known for his great decisions in publishing, being most famous for taking on readership-free *Wisden*, some sort of funds-haemorrhaging cricket pamphlet, and for buying the Soviet airline Aeroflot's in-flight magazine two days before the fall of the Iron Curtain. The multiple disasters for which we get many laughs out of John are very much a genuine part of his business fingerprint, but that said, John's decision to take *Viz* on through JBP was a godsend. He appears to have made two good decisions in his life, and fortunately for me, and everyone at the comic, they both involved *Viz*: total editorial control in our contract and his devotion to our cause from 1987 onward.

Once JBP was up and running we were soon in the thick of a tour promoting our book *The Big Hard Number Two*. *The Big Hard One* had been our first book, and was published by Virgin: it featured all the best bits of the twelve issues that had been released before national distribution. It proved a great success and John wanted to capitalise on this by making sure the world was aware of the launch of our second such venture, featuring highlights of the following few issues.

Publicity tours would take us on remarkable adventures around the world of local radio stations based on soulless industrial estates in the heart of nowhere in particular. I loved touring. I always loved being out of the office.

Our PR agency was based in London and they usually put us together with Eddie Blower, a genial Brummie who would drive us all around the country in a Range Rover that wasn't quite big enough to seat us all in comfort. We had to rotate turns in the middle back seat, which had no proper seatbelt and involved a constant battle between your knees and the trinket box betwixt the front seats. He took us to the offices of newspapers and radio stations, and often the tours would also involve book signings at shops in major town and city centres.

Our first taste of book signings had happened at Christmas on home territory. Newcastle's only comic shop was called Timeslip and was run by a lovely and colourful fella called Chris Moir. He'd been selling *Viz* and advertising in it since the very early days and he proposed we did an in-store signing at the launch of *The Big Hard One*. Graham and Thorpy were recruited, so the whole team was available to personalise people's books. There was a huge turnout, really quite overwhelming. Chris Moir was kind enough to furnish us with a crate of Red Stripe and no time limit was put on the event. We rolled out of the shop many hours later, completely shitfaced, having descended into defacing people's books with phalluses and expletives. Timeslip signings became a great annual event.

The first publicity tour saw us focusing on London's media, being based there for a whole week. John and our publicity agents, Eugene Beer and Gareth Davies, were all members of the recently formed Groucho Club in Soho. The club offered bijou and gem-like (small) bedrooms to members and their guests at very good rates for central London, so they opted to put us all up there for the duration of our stay. The club, we soon discovered, is the haunt of both media types and celebrities seeking a quiet drink away from the hurly burly of poor people and autograph hunters.

Mum at work, Fenwicks c1951

Mum & Dad, wedding & honeymoon 1956

Mum's family c1955

Mum with Dad's family 1956

20 Sunbury Avenue 1956

Pregnant with me, Isle of Arran 1963

Bathtime 1964

Third birthday 1967

Lake District 1965

Experimenting with art 1967

Me, Chris & Steve
perambulating 1966

Big bird 1966

Bedtime 196

Mum with her 'Thunderbird', Sunbury Avenue 1967

Lily Crescent dressed up for FA Cup final 1974

PUPIL'S PROGRESS

Name...... *Simon Donald*......

Our one & only family portrait 1971

Barns Lane House

Summer holidays 1974

Social Attitude		B	*Cheerful and helpful.*		
A. Excellent	— B. Very Good	— C. Average	— D. Below Average	— E. Poor	

Remarks *Simon shows a refreshing originality in his approach to his work. Should do well at his new school as long as he is able to keep his sense of humour within acceptable limits.*

Class Teacher...... *G. Cutson*......   Head Teacher...... *I. Houlder*......

School report 1975

Steve with some of his special effects work 1984

Newcastle Festival
CITY HALL
Newcastle upon Tyne

Sponsored by Alcan (U.K.) Limited

Eric Morecambe and Ernie Wise
AND FULL COMPANY

SATURDAY 25th JUNE 1977
at 6.00 pm

AREA £1.00   SEAT   Z 39

BOX OFFICE CITY HALL   Tel 012806
This Portion to be retained

With Andrea 1982

PLAYHOUSE
THEATRE

Greenside Place
Edinburgh

Adult

World Trade
Center
Observation
Deck

Sunday
24 August 1980
at 7 30 pm
Doors Open 7 00 pm

REGULAR MUSIC
presents
for
THE EDINBURGH ROCK FESTIVAL

THE RAMONES
PLUS SUPPORT

£12   STALLS £3.50
INC VAT

With Catherine
Notting Hill Carnival 198

Steve with Frank
1990

Merry Christmas
from Go! Discs
You Groovy Fucker!

SECTION:

WEST - 'A' WING

KEVIN KEEGAN'S FAREWELL
NEWCASTLE UNITED
V
LIVERPOOL

THURSDAY 17TH MAY 1984
KICK-OFF 7:30PM

STANDING
ONLY

FOR TIC
MATCH
TELEPHO
NEWC

SECRETARY

ADULT

IN THE EVENT OF A POSTPONE
MENT THIS TICKET WILL BE VALID
FOR THE RE-ARRANGED MATCH.
NO REFUND FOR AN ABANDONED
MATCH.

£ 2.50 inc VAT

JUV. & SEN. CITIZEN

£ 1.00 inc VAT   No.

NEWCASTLE UNITED F.C. LTD.   TO BE
ST. JAMES' PARK, NEWCASTLE UPON TYNE   RETAI

Chris weds Dolores 198

Mum with my aunts Muriel, Cynthia, Thea, Marie & Ann 1991

My niece Jamie as mascot for Shearer's 12-minute hat-trick 1997

LYNX

My first nephew Dale 1989

Anne, Tom & Rachael 1992

Newcastle upon Tyne
CITY HALL

Phil McIntyre Pres
THE SMELL OF REEVES & 8th
MORTIMER - On Stage 7.45pmt

TUE   Evening
8 March   7.45 pm

STALLS   T   13

0.00 (inc. VAT)   (P)

COMPS   240294JS0074T 13
         NO CAMERAS/RECORDERS ALLOWED
CONDITIONS OF SALE ARE DISPLAYED IN BOX OFFICE

Goddaughter Rebecca 1998

Julie 2004

The Gosforth Hotel

King's Cross
Station 1989

★ DAVID BOWIE "He is an incredibly well-read and
intelligent man, so it creased me up when I caught him
reading Viz. The magazine even began a regular David Bowie
column after they'd seen my picture. David is one of the
world's greatest rock stars, but he's happiest when he is just
part of the gang. He's nervous of flying, so on this Canadian
trip from Quebec to Montreal we'd taken the train. He was so
relaxed, none of the passengers even noticed it was David
Bowie! He was just so happy not to be travelling by plane."

Jim, London 1981

ACCESS
ALL
AREAS

ONE
HOUR
WITH
JONATHAN
ROSS

CITY HALL
Northumberland Road, Newcastle upon Tyne 1

Thursday, 11th January, 1979, at 7.30 p.m.

STRAIGHT MUSIC
presents

ELVIS COSTELLO
and The Attractions
IN CONCERT

BALCONY £2.00   SEAT F 90

Booking Agents: City Hall Box Office
Northumberland Road, Newcastle upon Tyne (Tel 20007)
This Portion to be retained.

FULCHESTER
AXE
MURDERER
STRIKES AGAIN
PLUS £5,000 BINGO
and TITS!

Photo shoot 1988

Colin, Chris, Jim & me,
Radio 1 1985

Thorpy, Chris, me & Graham,
Magazine Awards disgrace 1989

Millionth Viz,
Liverpool 1989

Bomb scare party 1994

Giving it some Dracula 1995

Miles Ross,
Stick Bongo champ
1991

With Alex, Teenage Cancer Trust
fridge 2003

As Sid, Sunday for Sammy 2002

WHITLEY BAY
ICE RINK
& Ten Pin Bowling Centre

PAUL WELLER

TO CELEBRATE OUR 25th ISSUE
YOU ARE INVITED TO THE
Viz
Silver Jubilee Ball
AND CONTINENTAL BUFFET
With
Top Group FANTASTIC and a galaxy of stars!

THE JEWISH MOTHER
Monday 27th July 1987

Tip Top Trumps
MODERNIST GEEZERS
Paul Weller

SURREAL HAIRY GEORDIE COMICS
Ross Noble

Celebrity alph...	...bet position	C List
In-street reco...	...nisability factor	57%
Simon's spec...	...cle angle	0°
Brake hors...	...wer	6
Mod	...ciency	Bronze

GUITAR LEG... ...ayall

Tip Top Trumps
KNACKERS-OUT COMEDY LEGENDS
Barry Cryer

Celebrity alphabet...

Tip Top Trumps
SHOUTY-CRACKERS ACTORS
BRIAN BLESSED!!!

Celebrity alphabet position	
In-street recognisability fact...	
Simon's spectacle angle	
Brake horse power	
Loonatron factor	

Tip Top Trumps
BANDY-LEGGED FOOTBALL GODS
Malcolm MacDonald

...ECCENTRICS
...ber

Celebrity alphabet position	H List
In-street recognisability factor	39%
Simon's spectacle angle	N/A
Brake horse power	603
Goals against Cyprus in one game	5

...sition	N/A
...ty factor	0%
...gle	0°
	0
...ships	1

TipTopTrumps
PINT-SIZED ROCK FRONTMEN
Roger Daltrey

TipTopTrumps
RUBBER-FACED FUNNYMEN
Lee Evans

TipToptrumps
...ACING ICONS
...kirk

TipToptrumps
FOOTBALLING LEGEND TV PUNDITS
Alan Shearer

TipToptrumps
FLASH-IN-THE-PAN ROCK STARS
Justin Hawkins

TipToptrumps
HEAVILY-EYEBROWED MANCUNIANS
Noel Gallagher

Celebrity alphabet position	B List
In-street recognisability factor	79%
Simon's spectacle angle	31°
Brake horse power	213
Friends named after Sid the Sexist	1

TipToptrumps
HIGHEST QUALITY FLUFF
Jodie Kidd

Celeb...
In-str...
Simo...
Brak...
Drug...

Sim...
Bra...
ug...

Celebrity alphabet position	B List
In-street recognisability factor	59%
Simon's spectacle angle	0°
Brake horse power	766
Leslie Phillips 'I SAY!' factor	99

Crazy sales...
Viz mountain,
Newcastle Airport,
Easter 1992

Me & my mate
Catboy... oh, & Pel
2003

ALRIGHT SIMON-
HOPE YOU LIKE
THIS !
Paul W.

Bollocks
TO
Alton Towers

The late great
Screaming Lord Sutch
1993

BALTIC CHAMBERS

Movement Machine,
Quayside 1981

Mr Suggs, Angie & me 200

ECIALS THE SPECIALS THE SPECIALS

Weller recording *As Is Now*,
RAK Studios, London 2005

New Jersey Airport
1986

The Who
GUEST

'we're zipping up our boots'

Viz
COMICS

2004

A Quato-Centennial Viz Reception
The Gosforth Hotel · 10th December 2004 · 8.00pm

1988

100% PEAR

Aug 15th 01

Dear Simon
        Many thanks
for the C.D. and the
letters. I've used some
of the letters already.
    work is going
well. I'll be working
on the portrait of
Ricky Hatton today
for Sports-relief.
    Thanks again
    Best wishes
    Peter.

Jim & me,
improvised jazz beards
1987

Viz office, Milburn House 2003

TWAT

Shieldfield Wednesday 1999

Stan the mental cat 1987

Blyth Spartans 2002

VIP
ARTIST WELLER
AP
VENUE
5/12
DATE
3a

Portrait by Vic Reeves 1996

Kilkenny 1999

THE CLASH

Soccer Sixes, St James' Park 2003

THIS IS SIMON
BY
Vic Reeves
x.

Soccer Sixes, Goodison Park 2004

CHAMPIONS

raceland 1998

Premier League All Stars 2007

GUEST
1 3 JUL
OASIS
TOUR 2005

distilled in 1971

Get Carter
11.06.99

directed by Mike Hodges
starring Michael Caine

re-released nationwide

blended & bottled by

bfi

Viz inflammable bus, Newcastle 2001

Mini Countryman 1990

Lambretta &
Mini Cooper S 2002

MFL 159H

'Tart's boudoir'
1992

MGF in *Viz*
photo shoot with
Huw & Julie 1996

Scooter habit 2003

My second
nephew Josey
in my Lotus
2000

MG Midget 2008

Colin shoots Mini Cooper S, *Viz* love story 1990

Stu, Oxy, Iain & James, Ibiza 2008

HUNGOVER STUNTMEN

With original member Martin, Ibiza 2006

Blame the BBC

With Carl Barât, Ibiza Rocks 2008

IBIZA ROCKS HOTEL

The Sage, Gateshead 2006

Movement Machine 1981

Resident band 2008

Barry Twyford 2009

2005

THE STAND COMEDY CLUB

Junior Simpson
Simon Donald
Woody
Henry Ginsberg
host - Susan Morrison
Doors - 7pm   £10/9/5
Show - 9pm

Bingo from Benton 2009

LEE EVANS

Vintage presents.......
Gavin Webster
28 Feb 2004 at
Seat: 25

UNRESERVED SEATING
18 OCT 2013 12.50

DUREX PRESENTS
DANIEL KITSON
DUREX PERFORMA COMEDY
NEWCASTLE
SAT 18 OCT 2003
£7.00 PM

Me & Ross Noble
wrestle Johnny Vegas
off stage 2006

My 5 characters
Edinburgh 2010

Friday 13th August
Edinburgh Preview Show
Swearing Is Both Big And Clever
at The Red Lion,
Market Place, Wirksworth

With Alex 200-

By
Geoff Laws
2010

3 BAND STAND

PAUL WELLER
JOOLS HOLLAND
ROSS NOBLE
JOHNNY VEGAS
JILL HALFPENNY
STEWART LEE
AVA VIDAL

AAA

FRENCH
HENRY

CAPTAIN
SCREECH

GORDON
TREEHOUSE

BOB
CHEESE

BRIAN
TREACLE

OLIVER
PORK PIE

The Sage, Gateshead 2006

Acting like a primary school headmaster, John issued stern instructions: we must observe the rules of the club strictly, and this meant under no circumstances should we approach any celebrities. Instead, like the star-struck kids we were, we sat in a corner of the bar and Thorpy secretly totted up a star count. The range was vast, although I can only currently trawl two up from the depths of my mind: Matt Dillon, because he was a huge star at the time, and Arthur Mullard, because he was a proper British comedy legend. I'd spotted a man I thought could be Mullard just outside the club. I was about to tell Thorpy, but I wasn't sure. We'd always play a 'Look, there's someone or other!' game whenever we spotted lookalikes in the street, and this bloke's outfit was perfect, with mac and flat cap. As he got closer I realised it actually was him. Despite his years, he was still a huge man, and I just managed to catch him speaking to a friend as he passed. His voice was so deep it was like a little earthquake.

During our time in the club we decided the easiest thing to do was to put all food items on one room number. As John was paying the bill, this seemed a sensible way to simplify things for him. We also thought it would be apparent that we'd done this.

John, though, had, at some stage in his life, developed a habit of always questioning bills: in cafés, hotels, restaurants, pubs, theatres ... wherever. As a businessman, it's a clever thing to do: by showing scrutiny you let the retailer know you're not a soft target. However, it can't be said that it's a great way of making friends. On receiving his Groucho Club bill for our stay he looked at the charges to Graham's room and without looking any further rang the *Viz* office and demanded to speak to Graham.

We all sat around tittering as John boomed out a vitriolic list of queries in Graham's ear.

'What's this? Bowl of chips?! And what's this ... Peach tart!? ... Mozzarella sandwich?'

Without hearing the whole conversation we all knew what the misunderstanding would be and listened sympathetically as Graham attempted to defend his corner.

'But John ... But John ... Yes, I know it's on my room ... Yes, but ...'

We all began to egg Graham on to hang up the phone, knowing we could afford to have a laugh about it, as before long John would spot his own error.

Graham dutifully slammed down the phone. We hastily made a plan. We knew John would call straight back, so we instructed Ann, our secretary, to tell John that Graham had stormed out of the building. Sure enough, the call came straight back. Ann was fantastic. She deserved an Oscar. In the meantime we called Graham's girlfriend Karen and told her that in the event of John calling she should say Graham had come home and refused to speak, leaving the house in a dark mood. On receiving John's nervous call, Karen's performance was also commendable. John, having now realised his misunderstanding, was in a blind panic. He rang the office back and this time I answered. I told him I'd been out of the room and didn't understand what had happened, and now everyone had left the building in a hurry without explanation. He rung off immediately and called Graham's house again. We'd predicted this and under instruction Karen didn't answer. He rang the office again and I answered.

'Simon?' He sounded pretty shaken.

There was a short silence, after which I held the phone handset aloft and amidst the shrieks and howls of laughter everyone in the office bawled: 'Wanker!' 'Sucker!' 'Public school twat!' And other such tributes.

I always enjoyed taking the piss out of John.

I loved our week in The Groucho Club. It seemed now that every day something else would happen that said, 'You've made it, you've escaped!' Signing on was too distant a memory to haunt me too much.

Chris and I later both joined The Groucho and I occasionally hang around there, like an out-of-touch new-money traitor to the Geordie nation. Liam Gallagher was famously barred for breaking a snooker cue and throwing one of the red balls through the window. It was front-page news in the tabloids: 'LIAM BARRED FROM POSH CLUB' or some such headline. Chris and I went in to play snooker a few days later and there was fresh putty in one of the window frames, one of the red balls was missing and the two halves of the broken queue had been put back in the rack. I decided this would be a nice souvenir and slipped the smaller half inside my coat before leaving. Chris and an anonymous other went back later that night to get the other half, which I'd secreted under a sofa. Unfortunately, by this time talentless cabaret entertainer Robbie Williams was sitting on the sofa. Regardless, they ploughed on and rummaged under the seats as discretely as possible. Williams was none the wiser to the fiendish plot, about which he doubtless couldn't have cared less, his only comment being, 'Have you lost your lighter?'

The two halves were later reunited in my china cabinet. Now I've told this story for the first time I'm keeping my fingers crossed I don't get banned myself for the theft of a national treasure. I can always return it. Or perhaps a similar one.

The best piece of press ever to come out of a publicity tour was in the *London Evening Standard*. The paper had the 'great' idea of taking us for high tea at The Savoy to do the interview. We really were rather down on the idea, thinking it was a silly novelty. When we arrived we were told it was compulsory to wear a jacket. Graham didn't have one with him. The cloakroom provided him with a bright blue one, at least two sizes too small. We sat down at a table with the journalist, a very quiet and unassuming bloke. He didn't really speak a lot. By the time the tea and sandwiches were served, we'd taken to talking amongst ourselves about the surroundings.

'Look at the big daft chandeliers,' Graham said. 'Ridiculous. Just there to impress the fat Yanks.'

We'd spotted Adam Faith sitting nearby.

'Well, he's not as tall as you'd expect from an actor-turned-financial-advisor, is he?' Thorpy suggested.

Chris was quite disgruntled about the contents of the sandwiches.

'This is smoked salmon, is it? It's not even bloody cooked. The tinned stuff's loads nicer than this.'

We played pop trivia questions.

'Name The Sweet's first three top ten singles in chronological order,' I said.

We began to play 'How Much To ...?', a game in which participants have to name the lowest cash sum they would accept for performing an unsavoury task.

'How much to cut the waiter's tie off when he's pouring your tea?' I asked.

Throughout the conversation the journalist said nothing. We ate our sandwiches and cakes, drank our tea and, having said goodbye, wandered back to The Groucho and pondered what his article might comprise of. We all concluded he'd probably just print the press release verbatim.

What he actually did was print pretty much everything you've just read. He'd simply observed us four northern lads being dropped into an unfamiliar and uncomfortable situation and descend into taking the piss out of everything, which was, of course, what we did for a living. It was one of only three interviews that I can think of that really captured what we were like together.

Goodbye to the house of *Viz*

As *Viz* progressed into a slightly more professional organisation, so the Lily Crescent office became less of a bedroom and more of a business hub. Much to my surprise, on arriving one day I found Graham Dury had become a resident office worker. Chris hadn't mentioned he was taking Graham on – those silky communication skills were evident once again. Graham's unannounced arrival rather put me on edge. I felt my position was in some way under threat, although I didn't know in exactly *what* way. It was just my imagination seeking out worst-case scenarios, but I was rather thrown by it, clearly as a direct result of the subject not having been discussed.

Chris's attitude towards communication has always been weird to say the least. When he decided *finally* to have a separate office phone line fitted he neither asked our parents' permission nor told them. It was only when the engineer appeared at the door that they first got wind of it. This followed in the wake of him not really telling them *Viz* existed until the BBC crew from London turned up to film *Something Else*.

As I say, things were a getting a bit more professional, but everything was still touched with a dysfunctional madness. I think *Viz* itself probably has a lot to thank for that. Graham's residency at Lily Crescent, occasionally bolstered by spells with Thorpy, wasn't to last long, as we were soon to move into a 'proper' office. Surprisingly, Chris did manage to tell me about this before it happened.

He didn't, however, manage to tell me about his plans to hand *Viz*'s local distribution over to Andy Pop. That I found out about on returning from seeing Catherine in Germany. I was more than a little put out, as this was something I'd been in charge of for some time. From a business perspective it made perfect sense, as with ever-increasing circulation it was getting to the stage where too much of my time was devoted to deliveries, although I really enjoyed getting out in the car and seeing the people in the shops and pubs. I would sorely miss that part. Andy was a good businessman, too, which I'm not. So yes, I had issues with the decision, but they lay only in the way it was handled. This was a constant problem when dealing with my brother. He could have done with a public relations manager.

Our move into the world of big business (a proper office) happened in the spring of 1988. After three years of production from our old bedroom it was finally time to move on. The offices were on the first floor of an old Victorian townhouse conversion on the outskirts of the city centre. Portland Terrace must have once been a very posh residential address, but in the 1980s the street was entirely in use as offices. Our office wasn't anything special: the windows faced some accountants' offices and a bus garage, and our next-door neighbours were, entertainingly enough, the offices of the Conservative and Unionist Association.

The whole building had until recently been owner-occupied by a local advertising agency, whose top man had fallen into ill health, possibly not helped by the myriad empty vodka bottles we found in his office when he moved out.

The plans were ambitious. Graham and Thorpy had moved to Newcastle and we would all work together for the first time. With a typewriter and a professional secretary three days a week, everything was now in place for the joint forces of British toilet humour to rise to the top of the publishing world.

Ann Hedley had previously worked at the Newcastle University Print Shop and prior to that at Prontaprint, so she'd been responsible for much of *Viz*'s repro work and typesetting for

167

many years. Chris offered her the post of *Viz* secretary and she started work as soon as we took up residence at Portland Terrace.

Ann was a hilarious person to have around. She was effervescent, to say the least. She was forever crying with laughter when she read our work and could always be heard exclaiming 'EEEEEE!' and 'D'you mind?!' from pretty much anywhere in the building.

Her mum would come at the end of the day to drop off Ann's little son Adam and there was something of a family atmosphere in *Viz*'s new home.

We initially only had three rooms – a drawing studio, a writing room and a reception area. We all had drawing boards in the studio; there was one big conference table and four chairs in the writing room; and in reception were the secretary's desk and some not particularly comfy chairs around a coffee table.

The atmosphere was great and it wasn't long before the fruits of us writing together as a team began to show. Sales of *Viz* had been on the rise from day one back in 1979, but post our moving into one office, things went ballistic.

Chris also announced around this time that he was to marry Dolores. I was informed by telephone the night before the service that I could collect my buttonhole from Lily Crescent the following morning. Great honour as it was, this was the first I'd heard that I would be an usher at the ceremony.

The weather on the day was fabulous and it was lovely to see Mum so happy. I'd imagined in my time with Andrea that I might be the first son to marry, and I'd often imagined how happy it would make her. Sad as it was for me that things went pear-shaped there, it was great that Mum got a day in the sun seeing one of her boys happily married.

The reception took place in the Imperial Hotel on Jesmond Road, Colin was Chris's best man, and to my shame I made a couple of cheeky heckles during his speech. Colin, like a true professional, turned the tables on me in quite brilliant style. He finished his prepared speech and then added a footnote: 'Chris's brother Simon has made a special request to say a few words of his own.' With this he gestured towards me with an open palm and sat down.

Fortunately, I am gifted with an ability to speak endlessly, and even invented a theme to my speech as I spoke. I suggested that I hoped, as we hadn't really met Dolores' family before, the marriage would represent the coming together not just of two people, but of two families. I just about got away with it. Thanks, Colin.

Spirits continued on a high at *Viz* and as we all got to know each other the fun really began. Since the days of The Bumph Club Chris had had a passion for stealing headed notepaper whenever he could and using it for practical jokes. He managed to get his hands on some Newcastle City Council paper and used it to write a letter to Graham at the house he had only just moved into, on which he'd taken out his first mortgage.

The house stood on Warwick Street in Heaton, a bus route and quite a busy access road in and out of the neighbourhood. Graham's house was a traditional Victorian terrace and had a front garden that was probably only two yards deep.

Chris's council letter explained that Graham's garden was subject to a compulsory purchase order as the street was to be widened to increase traffic flow. His door would in future open directly on to the pavement and car owners would be asked to park half on the pavement to allow buses to pass at higher speed. The letter later became extremely silly, revealing itself to be an obvious joke.

It was posted to Graham on a Thursday and on the Friday, all in on the joke, we eagerly awaited his arrival. He came in as normal and nothing was said. We assumed the letter hadn't arrived, but doubtless he'd get it on Saturday or Monday and we could all laugh about it then.

On Monday Graham, rarely one to swear or raise his voice, marched into the office and shouted, 'You BASTARDS!'

The post had arrived late on Friday, so he'd picked the letter up when he'd got home from work. He was about to set off to Nottingham to spend the weekend with his family and he'd only read the first few lines of the letter before dropping it back on the mat in disgust. He'd driven south in the foulest of moods, spending the whole weekend distraught over the impending loss of his garden. Only on his return home had he read further on and spotted the joke.

In the summer of 1988, with sales ever on the rise, I realised I was now in a position to buy a flat of my own. I found a pretty plain little Tyneside flat on Warton Terrace, a couple of streets away from the one I was renting. It wasn't in a good state, but it had all of its original doors, sash windows and fireplaces, so I saw it had potential to be a lovely little home. I planned to move in and do it up whilst living there. I jumped the gun and gave up my tenancy on the flat I'd been so happy in on Tosson Terrace. Soon I found my new flat would have to have most of its floors replaced due to rising damp and dry rot, so I couldn't move there yet.

Thorpy came to the rescue and offered to put me up in his flat for the predicted two weeks' work on the floors. He was living only a couple of streets away in a flat on Simonside Terrace, where I'd first lived when I left home. The flat belonged to Colin and Rashida, who lived above. As the work got underway on my flat the wiring was condemned, so as I was planning to re-jig the kitchen and bathroom I had to start pulling walls down before I could get the place re-wired. Two weeks dragged on into a ten-month renovation.

Thorpy and I lived an *Odd Couple* existence with my slightly mental cat, Stan. We spent Friday nights at the Egypt Cottage and moved on to the Riverside, Newcastle's best nightclub and venue at the time and the venue for a *Viz*-sponsored club night. The management had been very keen to have a *Viz*-branded event, which in sponsorship terms only involved us paying for a few posters. We could choose a name for it, but there was one stipulation: it had to have 'Big Fun' in it. This was a marketing ploy. The night had previously been called the Big Fun Club, and would in reality remain the same, so in order not to lose regulars they wanted to keep the name. We went with Shaky's Big Fun Club, as Shakin' Stevens was very much a leitmotif with *Viz* at the time.

The Riverside was later made infamous when Noel Gallagher, performing on stage with Oasis, was punched in the face by a stage invader and a riot ensued. It's no longer with us. RIP.

Writing development and sales success was only one side of the new office-based *Viz* coin. Working together with Chris was never really a totally smooth ride. Despite the increased and improved quality, the upped productivity and enjoyable banter, it wasn't long before he decided to isolate himself from the rest of us. Unannounced, a joiner arrived and began to erect a timber and glass partition between our drawing boards and his.

1988 closed with a rather unexpected and quite mad Christmas party. John Brown had secretly sent a video camera to us all as a gift, in the hope we would further line his public school pockets with masterpieces of filmmaking. He'd given the camera to Andy, along with a vanload of champagne, a crate for each person in the office. Andy had invited Phil to be the presenter of the gifts and they hatched a brilliant plan.

Starting at 9am, they loaded the champagne into Andy's van, all along Andy recording Phil doing TV-presenter style pieces to camera, effectively making a documentary about John's gifts being delivered. To add to the colour of the piece, delivering his lines like a true professional presenter, Phil opened one of the crates on camera, popped a cork and took a swig from the bottle.

They then drove all around Jesmond and Gosforth, filming a surreal mini-documentary, which they made up as they went. For every piece to camera Phil delivered, he took another swig from the bottle.

At around noon they arrived at the *Viz* office, still filming. Andy filmed Phil as he gathered us all together in the reception area and announced that the camera and the champagne were ours. He was absolutely mortal by this point and could hardly stand or speak. Then the VHS tape was loaded into a player and we all sat down to watch the documentary. It was a tremendous piece of work that could never be replicated: it just captured a moment perfectly.

The funniest moment was when Phil interviewed an elderly lady on a park bench on Northumberland Street about the success of *Viz*. She'd never heard of it and had little understanding of the interview's purpose. Phil, realising this, told her he was from a big TV company and gestured to the camera. 'You see him? The cameraman. He's on £100 a day.'

The old dear moved seamlessly into, 'Eeee. Never.' She looked the unseen Andy up and down in disbelief and horror. 'Do you know how much pensioners get?'

Phil quietly sympathised. 'I know. It's terrible isn't it?'

It was blissful. Television gold.

Far from John's imaginings of groundbreaking DIY video comedies, the next thing the camera was used for was to document a raid on a T-shirt factory.

Viz distribution had now moved into an adjoining vacant office behind our reception area and Andy was shifting a huge amount of *Viz* T-shirts. (By this point, brand *Viz* had started selling a load of official merchandise too.) A customer alerted him to a distributor that was undercutting his prices. Investigations pointed to a warehouse in Middlesbrough, distributing and possibly also producing the entire range of *Viz* shirts, all counterfeit.

John Brown knew that in the event of such a discovery the best course of action is to come down swiftly and hard, and to do it publically. By being seen to be ruthless, word would quickly spread amongst counterfeiters that this was a brand worth avoiding.

We had a daredevil time of it, collecting together a team of very big lads, who in truth served no purpose other than to be present, as we had right to enter but no right to use force. We would gain access to the building accompanied by the local police.

John flew up from London first thing in the morning, accompanied by his solicitor. When the solicitor went to the toilet in our office, John told us in a puppy-like frenzy that he was paying for every minute of the man's time. 'It costs me £9 every time he has a facking piss!'

We proceeded to Middlesbrough in convoy, John driving a hire car, me accompanying him. I'd sold my beloved orange Mini some months earlier and had never seen it again since. As we drove through Gateshead we approached a red traffic light. As we began to slow down, John asked me, 'Whatever happened to that orange Mini you used to drive?'

As the last of his words left his mouth we came alongside a street to our left. The first car parked on it was my orange Mini.

'There it is!' was my stunned reply.

I've never got over how unimpressed John was by this staggering coincidence.

The T-shirt raid itself was nothing to write home about, really. The police knocked and entered, with Andy filming, we were

172

eventually all allowed in and I stood around with the heavies while embarrassed workers looked at the floor as John's solicitor did a stock take of the fake goods. The stock was confiscated and later destroyed and no further *Viz* fakes have ever surfaced.

It was a great day out of the office though, and quite a thrill. Excitement was not common when working on *Viz*. Disappointing as it may sound to readers, once a piece had been written, the task of turning it into a finished cartoon, photo strip, feature or news page was every bit as dull as working on a magazine without arse jokes in it.

The completely uninteresting footage, comprising of nothing more than a few seconds of two policemen knocking on a warehouse door, was later accidentally taped over. Not really the magic John had expected from his video camera.

You're going home in a fucking ambulance

Our rise from the shackles of dole scumdom was gathering pace and *Viz*'s sales were beginning to look like some kind of administrative error. Every quarter the per-issue sales figure would come in from the official records body, the Audit Bureau of Circulations (ABC). It was always staggering. Since overtaking the legendary *Punch* in 1987 we'd charged on, and upon overtaking *Private Eye* we became the biggest-selling humour title in Britain. We celebrated our astonishing jump to over half a million sales per issue in the sumptuous surroundings of the office. To mark the event, Thorpy took a Polaroid photograph of the rest of us enjoying a cup of tea and a packet of Fig Rolls. We kicked major arse.

This unbelievable figure was by no means the last huge shock we were to get, as in the following months sales continued unabated, seeming to almost double every time a comic hit the streets.

In 1986 I'd taken a photo of Steve at a comics stall on the Portobello Road, which marked the first time I'd seen *Viz* on sale anywhere in London since seeing the poster in Rough Trade's window in 1981. Now, when I arrived on London visits, the newspaper seller at King's Cross had a massive homemade display screaming 'NEW *VIZ* OUT NOW!' with more than half his stall devoted to rows of our comic.

173

When we launched the fourth *Viz* annual we debated for a while whether we should use the title *The Dog's Bollocks* or not, as we thought it would limit our chances of shelf displays in some of the bigger shops. We threw caution to the wind. We were on a roll. 'Who cares? We'll still sell plenty' was our collective thought. Our attitude had always been that we'd make what we wanted to make, and if people wanted to buy it, that was a bonus. Now seemed a good time to celebrate this.

The next thing I knew, I was standing outside WHSmiths in Newcastle Central Station, staring in disbelief at the display of *The Dog's Bollocks* occupying the entire window. It seemed that it was now us calling the shots and that life was some kind of unrealistic Disney-style dream sequence. Although Disney wouldn't have used the word 'bollocks', obviously.

Naturally, the next amazing step would be a giant awards ceremony at a luxurious London hotel.

We were invited to attend the Magazine Advertising Awards Ceremony 1989 at the Grosvenor House Hotel. All four '*Viz* boys', as we had become known by John, would attend, along with John himself, a handful of his staff and Andy. *Viz* was nominated for the Magazine Circulation Award, as we'd broken just about every record in magazine sales history in the previous twelve months. It was little more than a formality that we'd receive the honour.

The tickets specified 'black tie'. I literally thought this meant you had to wear a black tie. Dress in anything, as long as you wear a black tie. Apparently not. On being told we needed dinner suits, Thorpy and I took a trip to Newcastle's Haymarket, where junk and knick-knack shops shared run-down shop frontage with low-budget jewellers and kebab vendors. We climbed the dark, narrow stairs to a 'retro outfitters' selling musty second-hand clothes. We each found an ill-fitting tuxedo and headed for our big night in London.

Like being taken to the BBC Television Centre, seeing The Groucho Club for the first time, or having tea at the Savoy, this was another surreal experience. We posed for photos and excitedly discussed what 'crazy gags' we could crack when we went to collect the award. John Brown was eager to impress on us that we mustn't make fools of ourselves. We in turn told him he wouldn't be allowed to join us on the stage.

We discovered that at these kinds of events – for which someone pays an absolute fortune for your seat, in our case John – there is oodles of 'free' booze. Apart from a few cans of Red Stripe at Timeslip, none of us had ever experienced free booze before. We went mental, drinking everything the waiters put on the table. The ceremony began on the stage and we soon realised this would be one of the most tedious and drawn-out events we'd ever had to sit through. The list of upcoming awards in the evening's programme never seemed to get any shorter as a constant stream of company names and gushing praise for the 'creatives' at various 'agencies' was read out by a shower of cunts. We continued to drink heavily.

What seemed like days later, but was probably a couple of hours or so, our award approached. We were now hammered. A frenzied circuit of 'Shhhhh!' chased itself around the table and eventually all eyes and ears were on the stage as our award was read out. We all heard the word '*Viz*' and went mad. Cheers, whistles and screams of 'Get in!' filled the air as we all leapt to our feet.

John had kittens. 'Sit down! Sit down, for God's sake!' he shouted.

'Cheer up, John, we fuckin' won!' I replied.

'It's just the facking nominations! Sit down!'

Sure enough, it was only the nomination we'd heard. We all sat back down impatiently, just in time to hear our name read out for the second time. This was it. We went beserk. I could see John through the mad celebrations, and once again he was ushering us to sit down. He looked like he was about to have a stroke.

'Sit down, for fack's sake! For *fack's sake!* Sit *down!*'

Through all the confusion it became apparent that what we'd won was a high commendation, not the award. As angry queries and explanations were bandied back and forth across our table, the announcement was made that *Auto Express* magazine, a new tabloid motoring paper, had won the award for 'breathing new life into a stagnant marketplace'.

Still on our feet, we all began to jeer and boo loudly. John looked mortified. I had a sudden realisation and shouted to everyone at our table, 'They sponsored one of the awards!'

More confusion.

'They sponsored one of the awards!' I repeated. 'Earlier to-night! *Auto Express* sponsored one of the fucking awards!'

All hell broke loose around our table and just as the *Auto Express* team arrived at the stage we began our barrage.

'Fix! … Fucking fix!' I blared.

'Cheats! You fucking bought that!' Chris shouted.

Even the extremely mild-mannered Thorpy and Graham were angry and jeering. The feeling of injustice was unbearable for us all.

John was ready to pass out.

'Shut up, for fack's sake! Shut *up!* This is so embarrassing. We'll be thrown out!'

I wasn't ready to sit and be shafted like this.

'We've been fuckin' shat on, John! This is fuckin' wrong and we should be heard to say it's wrong!'

John began to plead, saying his reputation was on the line. We cautiously began to calm down, but this wasn't over.

Everybody was in agreement that this was a disgrace, an in-sult. How dare they invite us here and put us through this charade? All we now wanted to do was to get out of this pit of tossers and go and find a normal pub to forget about it all in. John pleaded with us not to walk out.

We continued fizzing. Suggestions for revenge began to do the circuit. We all agreed that our best course of action would be to wait for the ceremony to finish and then charge the *Auto Express* table, chanting, 'You're going home in a fucking ambulance!'

By the end of the show, despite the passage of time, we were still angry and drunk enough to carry out our plan. I led the party and Thorpy, Graham, Chris and Andy followed. As we ap-proached the table, some people stood aside nervously; some rose from their chairs, alarmed. The *Auto Express* journalists sat, in the main, smiling. I introduced myself with the words, 'You cheating bastards!'

Amongst some, there was initial confusion about who we were; from others, a bit of concern about our threatening behav-iour. Some knew why we'd come and some even agreed with our complaint. Before we knew it we were sitting down having a drink with them all. A bit disappointing, really. Not that the cheerful mutual congratulations would make the headlines. The chanting of 'You're going to get your fuckin' head kicked in' while we made our way over would.

After the dust settled, a couple of posh young journalists from the *Mail on Sunday* or some such shite decided to come and 'network' with us. They insisted that we had a drink together. The wine had run out at our table and they asked the waiter to fetch a crate of beer. The beer came, we drank it, and then the waiter gave them the bill for it. Their jaws hit the floor and they flapped, telling him they believed all the drink was free. They tried to charge it to John's table.

'That's not going to happen,' I assured them.

I quietly enjoyed their discomfort as I walked away.

At some point in the evening, and I have absolutely no recollection why, Thorpy was chased out of the Grosvenor House kitchens by a chef brandishing a meat cleaver. This harked back to my similar ejection from Mark Toney's on Percy Street. Eeeeee. You stand around waiting for a cartoon cliché to happen in real life, and then two come along only ten years apart.

Tenth anniversary

We celebrated ten years of producing *Viz* with a big party at Newcastle's Mayfair Ballroom. Andy, who had many years' experience of organising events, was put in charge. We at the office would simply invite our friends and families and turn up.

The Mayfair was a Mecca Ballroom with a capacity of 3,000 or so for music gigs. It was a place that everyone in Newcastle knew well, being most famous for its heavy rock nights every Friday for decades. It wasn't my favourite place – the beer was expensive, poorly kept and served in crazed plastic glasses, the door staff were infamous due to rumours of brutality, and it was inextricably linked with the music–fashion disaster that was new wave heavy metal – but if you were going to throw a massive party in Newcastle, this was the place.

There was a certain amount of trepidation regarding what was in store for us as guests at a party being thrown in our honour. I was feeling nervous, but excited about what the evening had in store.

Thorpy and I arrived with Colin and Rashida. It was all a bit surreal. This cavernous place was full of people, but every face was familiar. We'd invited everyone who'd ever been involved in *Viz*'s ten-year rise to the dizzy heights at which it now stood. Every cartoonist, writer, printer, photographer, shopkeeper, advertiser, the journalists who'd interviewed us, the TV crews who'd filmed us, the people who'd been dragged out of bed on Sunday mornings to be in photo stories – pretty much the *Viz* world and his wife.

There was a huge, glittering *Viz* tenth-anniversary logo above the stage, which was dressed in some style, and it wasn't long before the entertainment got underway.

On a giant screen over the stage we were treated to a genuinely breathtaking array of anniversary video messages from Michael Palin (with a sheep on his head), ginger chanteur Mick Hucknall out of Simply Red, and none other than the great shaking one himself, Shakin' Stevens. The Shakester's message was an audio recording only, but was edited together with a still photo of his face with Terry Gilliam-style comedy animated mouth move-ments. It was all fantastic. Well, I could have done without Mick Hucknall, but all the same.

There was live music from local hotshots of the time The Kane Gang, Arthur 2 Stroke's comedy alter ego Tony O'Diamond and his Top Group Fantastic, who had all been tailored especially for the event in seventies glam outfits.

There was some sort of 'comedy' performance by those two blokes off the Carling Black Label adverts and an anniversary cake presentation. Well, there was supposed to be an anniversary cake presentation. Chris, Thorpy and Graham had all refused to get up from their tables, in front of hundreds of people. There were mutterings and shaking of heads. When I was halfway across the stage floor Phil, as Tony O'Diamond, threw the cake and I just about caught it. The comedy of his improvised action just about saved the moment. I sometimes felt I was the only person on the *Viz* creative team with any social skills at all.

The cake moment was embarrassing, but there was worse in store. Phil and Andy had made a number of short films for the party, to be shown on a giant screen on the stage. The films were all based around *Viz* characters. The final film saw an SAS-style assault on our house in Lily Crescent, balaclava-wearing commandos doing shoulder rolls across the lawn, under cover of stun grenades, to a soundtrack of dramatic music. They arrived at the front door and rang the bell. My Dad answered. The commandos, then unmasked, turned out to be Bottom Inspectors, Phil playing their leader, the Bottomdant.

Watching this all unfold on the giant screen in front of hundreds of friends and family was agony. In what I can only describe as the most painful moment of my life, Phil told my Dad he was there to inspect his bottom. My Dad then acted very badly, delivering the line, 'No, not that, not the bottom inspection, no, not that.' He then dropped his trousers, revealing Paisley-patterned underpants. Phil probably then acted out an inspection. I don't know, as I was hiding my head in my hands.

We didn't ever have a better anniversary party, though. Chris had one to celebrate *Viz* turning thirty that came close, but I think the tenth was all about the moment. In ten years we'd gone from the quagmire of benefits to the solid ground of earning and owning houses and cars, and we seemed to be breaking circulation records in publishing every other day. That was ten years worth celebrating.

Mellie vision

Viz's ventures into the world of television were never wholly satisfactory, and in certain respects all had failings, albeit to different extents. The first *Viz* TV project, *Billy the Fish*, was a triumph, and remains a joy to watch to this day. Harry Enfield, who Chris had worked with previously, provided all the voices. Harry had earlier approached Chris and asked him to write something for a new character he was creating for *Saturday Live*. Buggerallmoney would be a Geordie character directly opposing his unloveable Cockney, Loadsamoney. I wasn't a fan of Loadsamoney and I didn't much like Harry's Geordie. To me, the character had no real value. The accent was absolutely awful and it seemed most of what he said had previously been done better on *The Tube* by Wavis as The Hard. I felt somewhat vindicated in my disapproval when on tour, performing the new character at Newcastle City Hall, Enfield was roundly heckled with calls of

'Biffa Bacon! Biffa fuckin' Bacon!' and 'You've stole it off the *Viz*!'

My unease with Enfield wasn't helped when visiting his London flat. A group of us had been out drinking and I was trying to explain to him the importance of football in the lives of people in the north east. I was explaining how I'd idolised Malcolm MacDonald from the terraces as a boy and how seeing him play up close, the raw power, the Olympian speed and the fierce way he struck the ball, all combined to make him a god-like hero to a young boy.

Enfield agreed. 'Yes. It sounds just like the first time my father took me to the opera in Venice.'

I was about to laugh, but looking him in the eye I realised he was serious.

But Harry's performance as all the characters' voices on the *Billy the Fish* series was brilliant. Billy the Fish really lent itself to the short animation TV format. The cartoon in *Viz* was a parody of British football comic strips like Roy of the Rovers and Billy's Boots and merely exaggerated further their already larger-than-life storylines, characters and clunky plot explanations from anonymous crowd members. As an average *Viz* cartoon page runs to approximately five minutes' animation, turning each Billy the Fish episode into a Captain Pugwash-style cartoon was a pretty logical and straightforward move. A bonus factor in using Billy the Fish was, unlike most of *Viz*'s content, it's free from swearing, so it could be shown on television without any problems.

Once Harry had recorded the soundtrack the animation was provided by a Welshman by the name of Tony Barnes. The production was low budget, which was good because Tony was a low-rent animator, and that was just what was needed for *Billy the Fish*.

My memory is unclear, but according to Wikipedia, in a section on *Billy the Fish* not surprisingly riddled with inaccuracies, Channel 4 initially showed the series all in one go as a film and then later showed it as four episodes broadcast weekly on Saturdays at 5pm.

The highs of *Billy the Fish* were really never reached again with our TV ventures. However, with the success of *Billy* now recognised by Channel 4, a Roger Mellie series was commissioned. It was made very much in the style of Billy's animation, with, unbelievably, Peter Cook voicing Roger and Enfield doing the rest of the voices.

Cook was, of course, one of my all-time comedy heroes. Chris met him, but sadly I never did. Chris tells a very funny story from the day the sound was recorded for the Roger Mellie series. Peter walked into the recording studio and the receptionist greeted him in a very warm, somewhat disingenuous fashion: 'Peter, darling! You're looking marvellous!'

Cook, sadly, was certainly not looking his best. A very heavy drinker and constant smoker for decades on end, he would live only four more years. He replied, just as the receptionist was out of earshot, 'Yes, dear. Another bottle of vodka and I'll be a sex symbol again.'

When all's said and done, *Roger Mellie* isn't a bad cartoon, but this time around Tony Barnes' weaknesses were not the cartoon's strengths, as they had been for *Billy the Fish*. The killer problem wasn't the low quality of the animation but the awful timing created by the poor sound editing. Even the most useless hack comic will tell you that in comedy timing is everything. It might be the oldest cliché, but it's undeniable.

Viz was now the hottest property in the world of yoof media. We'd now had many more TV interviews, including one for a late-night show called *Night Network*. The crew interviewed us in what they described as a production meeting at the Free Trade Inn over a number of pints. The truth was that we never did any work in the pub, we very rarely all drank or socialised together, and we usually found that ideas produced during drinking sessions were worthless in the cold light of day. There were exceptions to this – ideas can come at any time – but specifically going to the pub to work was a fiction created by the TV crew for their own ends. This said, what they managed to get out of the interview was the closest thing ever captured on film to us in our natural state, knocking jokes and surreal ideas around and constantly taking the piss out of each other. It was a bit like the *Evening Standard* interview captured on film.

The director was a young Irishman called Phil Morrow and he did a very clever thing – he also interviewed us all individually. By doing this he brought out aspects of our behaviour that didn't

181

show in the group interview. Thorpy and Graham would rarely say a word under the constant barrage of surreal ramblings that came from Chris, and even I would struggle to get words in, but when alone they were given the time and space to show their interesting and funny personalities. I was able to talk about my work on a more serious level, something of which the others would never approve.

It all made for a really colourful and interesting interview, with plenty of laughs. Its success led to Phil Morrow and his partner Peter Ward proposing a fly-on-the-wall documentary about *Viz*. I thought this was a great idea and knowing the director was also behind the interview for *Night Network* made me confident. I thought it would be a great record of an amazing period in our lives, but it wasn't to work out that way.

A fatal flaw in the show's construction soon began to show. The makers wanted to make a funny documentary, but if you're covering a funny subject, funny journalism is, in my opinion, a no-go area. I believe that if you're making a programme about people who are a bit weird, and I think it's fair to say we all are to differing degrees, the straighter the presentation, the more extreme the eccentricities of the subjects become. Think Louis Theroux.

Phil and Peter began looking for our input and we suggested Phil (Arthur 2 Stroke) Branston would make a great presenter. We showed them the film of Phil interviewing the old lady on Northumberland Street on the day he presented us with the champagne and camera. They liked Phil and he was hired. Now they wanted us to have some fun with our own interviews in the show, and I suggested an interview in and around my 1965 Mini Cooper S, my pride and joy. This was arranged. Graham was interviewed in his greenhouse, his great love being plants. It was arranged for Chris to pretend he owned a railway locomotive, and he was interviewed on one at the Central Station. Thorpy didn't really have a hobby to speak of and it was decided he would pretend he drove a vintage bus to work every day. The problem lay in the mix of reality and jokes. No one watching would know what was a joke and what wasn't. It was all going off at half-cock.

To make things worse, my interview was inaudible due to the noise of the car, and a reshoot had to be shoehorned into the schedule. I had a stotting headache the second time around and it has to be the worst interview I've ever given.

To be fair to Phil Morrow and Pete Ward, who've gone on to good careers in programme making, the finished show has some decent moments in it, especially a wonderful interview with Keith Chegwin that brought me to tears laughing. I have to say, though, that I think it was a mistake to make a joke-on-joke programme. A straight documentary, a record of what life was like for us at that time, would have been a lovely thing to have now.

The show was broadcast on Channel 4 and released on Polygram Video, as the two cartoons had been. It was rightly panned by most who reviewed it.

The main problem with our TV work, as I see it, was a lack of cohesion from all involved, especially at our end. I think we all had differing opinions about our involvement in projects outside of the comic itself, resulting in us all pulling in different directions. Without total commitment and agreement from all on board, any project undertaken is bound to end up half-baked.

Another factor playing against us was having to work with other people, allowing them to 'touch our baby'. Cooperation was not something we did a lot of in creating *Viz*. We worked ok with JBP, but confrontation and stand offs were not uncommon, especially between Chris and John, Chris usually confronting, by means of letter, or later email, and John usually giving in.

Roger Mellie was considered successful enough that two more *Viz* series were eagerly proposed by a young high-flying executive at Channel 4 (whose name thankfully escapes me) who wanted to commission Sid the Sexist and The Fat Slags. We were to script them and then, on approval, they'd be commissioned for broadcast. Channel 4's funds would pay for much of the production.

The Fat Slags was to be animated using stop motion animation and plasticine. Thorpy and Graham had really taken on San and Tray as their own since they'd been jointly created by all four of us a couple of years earlier. Chris would work on the TV script with them. Sid the Sexist was to be turned into a straightforward animated cartoon, like *Billy the Fish* and *Roger Mellie*, and I'd work on the script alone, with the producer, Miles Ross, in control of the project.

In time we heard the young high-flying executive from Channel 4 had issues with a large number of 'words and phrases' used in our new scripts. Quite how he imagined it could be possible to commission shows under the titles *Sid the Sexist* and *The Fat Slags* without use of language likely to cause offence, fuck only knows.

Without Channel 4's financial input the shows could still be made, but they would go straight to release on video. We were able to turn our backs on Channel 4, but at a cost: it meant losing virtually all chance of any profit, but we were happier doing that than making compromises on content. We had some clout, which was a nice feeling. The queue at Box 5 at Swan House Department of Employment was fading away.

The Sid the Sexist animation had come about after a rather more exciting proposal fell through. The suggestion was made in a surprise visit to our office by Jimmy Nail. He arrived unannounced, with a nasty-looking facial wound to his brow. We got well into the conversation before he thought to mention he was filming *Spender* and it was actually prosthetic make-up.

None of us had met Jimmy before and, in an excited yet very casual and friendly manner, he put it to us that he'd like to play Sid the Sexist in a live-action TV production. This was fantastic news. I'd always seen Sid as lending itself to real actors: it wasn't based on comics, like Billy the Fish. Sid was about real situations in pubs and on the streets. In my mind's eye I'd always seen any TV or film idea for Sid being like a Mike Leigh film – realistic yet outrageous, socially awkward, gritty, emotionally difficult and belly-laugh funny. I was flattered that Jimmy wanted to play such a loser as Sid. My only worry, and it wasn't a great one, was that he was too tall.

We discussed the potential for making the series over a few weeks and Jimmy and I got close enough that he even proposed ... that we did the RAC Classic Rally together in a Mini Cooper S. However, Jimmy's success with *Spender* was to bring the curtain down on the Sid live-action project before it really got started. He had a second series and now had to put a load of time aside for writing. Sid was the first casualty.

I'd been watching *Spender* and I'd actually thought that Jimmy's sidekick in the show, Stick, would make a perfect Sid. Stick was played by Ronnie Johnson, who I had a drink with occasionally in the Newcastle Arms. He also shared a flat with a friend of mine. His stage name was Sammy, as the name Ronnie Johnson had already been used by another Equity member.

When the live-action idea was snubbed out it was proposed that we make Sid into a cartoon. For the John Browns of this world, it was vital that we got big names in to play the characters. I wanted to do all the voices myself, I knew I was more than capable, but the money men said we needed names.

Miles, a hilarious and very loveable brother of Jonathan Ross and, unsurprisingly, also a Londoner, was the producer for all the *Viz* videos. He proposed asking Vic Reeves and Bob Mortimer to play Sid and his friend-cum-rival Baz. Vic and Bob were flying high at the time with *Big Night Out* on Channel 4. They were TV gold. Rather alarmed at this suggestion, I pointed out that Bob was from Middlesbrough and Vic from Darlington. Unperturbed, in fact not really understanding my gist at all, Miles approached them both and Bob agreed to take part.

I love Bob – he's possibly one of the funniest people to come out of Middlesbrough since Mavis Wilton – but I explained that Sid should be played by a Geordie. It would be fine for Bob to play Baz, though: the different accents could add to the animosity between them.

I stuck to my guns and persuaded Miles that Sammy Johnson was the man for the job. I also edged my way in to play Sid's oval-headed friend Bob, and I also provided the voice of Sid's mother. Jenny Eclair, Simon Day, Geordie comic Mike Milligan and actress Denise Bryson played the remaining characters.

I wanted to take Tony the animator to some places in and around Newcastle that he could use to base the animation's backgrounds on. Miles came up with him and we used a video camera to film the exterior of a lovely old pub building in Walker, along with the terraced Tyneside flats opposite. These would be Sid's local and the home where he lived with his mother. We also filmed in the Bigg Market, for Sid's big night out, and Miles filmed me doing the walks of each of the characters. I felt this was important.

One of the scenes in the video would feature a montage of Sid using his infamous chat-up lines, which never fail to fail. These too actually came from the streets of Newcastle. I rarely invented a disastrous chat-up line for him – more often than not I simply heard them used. Friends would always report to me the worst ones they'd heard, and girls, on hearing I wrote Sid, always had two or three abominations up their sleeves.

As long as I live I shall never forget the day of the Sid recording sessions. I met up with Miles at the sound studio in central London and the rest of the crew began to arrive. I was bowled over to have such great actors and comedians working on my scripts. I was especially a great fan of Bob Mortimer. He and Vic had given me some of the biggest laughs I'd ever had. Meeting him was a treat. He was a lot shorter than I imagined and a very polite and friendly man. After some brief introductions we got straight down to business. There were two microphones, shared by everyone. I ended up right next to Bob, with Ronnie to my other side.

Throughout the recordings Bob continually added swear words into the script in an attempt to get me to laugh, and it worked, time and time again. His delivery was done with such commitment and childishness that I couldn't help but admire his lack of professionalism. This was the kind of moment I'd dreamed of when I was hiding behind the sofa watching *Monty Python*, when I was making pretend radio programmes on my cassette player, and when I was writing comedy sketches with Gordon at school. Here I was, with my own script, featuring my own characters that were already a success, and I was recording voices with a comedy legend. Not only that, but he kept cracking up too. This was as good as a day's work could get.

My memories of that day are tainted by the loss of Ronnie. He died in 1998 while jogging near his Spanish home. He was a friendly and down-to-earth man with a great passion for acting and music and a fantastic sense of humour. RIP. Following Ronnie's death, his friends and fellow actors, including Tim Healy and Jimmy Nail, set up the Sammy Johnson Memorial Fund and hold a series of concerts called Sunday for Sammy every other year to raise funds to support young people's careers in the performing arts, as well as keep Sammy's memory alive.

The *Sid the Sexist* video is still popular to this day. In a recent DVD re-release, astonishingly, I'm told it outsold the Peter Cook-voiced *Roger Mellie* by twenty-seven to one. It seems to have something of a cult status. I've heard wonderful stories of it being enjoyed in all sorts of places. Steve McManaman told me it was never off the TV in the Liverpool FC coach. Peter Beardsley told me the same story and added this was also true at Everton. I was also told by another ex-Newcastle player that it was watched repeatedly on their away trip to Barcelona in 1997, some of the foreign players learning Sid's chat-up lines parrot fashion and then trying them on girls in the legendary Julie's nightclub on the Quayside, with varying results. I also have it on good authority that Philippe Albert bought the boxed set of *Viz* videos before returning to Belgium. 'We have nozzing like zeez in Belgium!' he's reported to have said as he walked out of HMV.

Despite the popularity of *Sid the Sexist*, I can't watch it without cringing. Like the *Roger Mellie* animation, it's ruined by bad timing at the editing stage. The making of it was nevertheless one of the absolute highlights in my time at *Viz*.

Millionth-comic Liverpool

With sales having been on a crazy upwards rise ever since the founding of JBP, it was inevitable that we would soon reach the magic figure of a million sales per issue. Through pre-orders from retailers we hit this mark for the first time in 1990.

To capitalise on publicity marking this monumental event we hatched a plan to give away a ton of money with the millionth copy off the presses. We discovered that one ton of either 1p or 2p pieces has a value of £2000. We decided to present the money to the lucky winner by ambushing them as they left the shop where they bought the comic and presenting them with a barrow-load of 2p pieces in front of the waiting media.

Logistically, we faced quite a problem: how to ensure we were present when the millionth comic was bought. It was calculated precisely where the millionth copy would be sold by using the time it came off the press to work out which distributor it would go to. In turn, the distributor worked out which outlet the copy would go to. Well, that's what we told the press. The truth was it would have been impossible to calculate this, so an outlet was picked at random. The real solution was simple. We cheated.

A voucher was printed, something like the golden ticket from *Charlie and the Chocolate Factory*, only shitter, and we took it with us to the prearranged outlet, slipping it into the top *Viz* on the newsagent's display. All we then had to do was hide in the back of the shop until a customer bought it.

We were based in London immediately before the big day, staying at The Groucho and being photographed with the mountain of coins that would be presented to the unsuspecting reader. John insisted that we skip breakfast at The Groucho, about which I was most disgruntled, as it was one of the best aspects of staying there. He assured us that by buying us breakfast on the train and paying for us to travel first class we would be more than happy. We arrived at Euston at some unearthly hour of the morning and boarded the train to Liverpool, where the Ton of Money stunt had been arranged for a newsagent close to the station. The prize would be handed over by Phil dressed as another alter ego, Mr Moneybags, in a gold lame suit, as per Elvis in the 1950s.

It was absolutely freezing as we boarded our train and sat waiting for it to pull away. The due departure time passed. We waited, and waited ... and waited. The train carriage was extremely cold and still there had been no announcement about the delay. After half an hour a curt message came over the tannoy: 'Due to a technical problem this train will travel without heat.'

We sat in disbelief for another half an hour. The train still hadn't moved. Eventually, another announcement was made. 'Due to no boiler, there will be no hot food on this service.'

After what seemed like an entire Russian winter the train pulled away. We were treated to a number of equally short and apology-free announcements. 'We have partial boiler operation. There will be limited hot drinks.' A bad-tempered waiter then came through the carriage, putting out cups and sandwich plates. Then another announcement. 'The boiler is no longer working. There will be no hot drinks.' Eventually there was an apology, albeit a deflection of blame: 'We apologise for the late running of this service and the lack of heat. This is the fault of maintenance contractors at Euston.'

The waiter appeared again, collecting the cups back in, throwing them angrily into his trolley. 'Service with a smile,' I offered sarcastically.

'There's no need to be rude,' he barked back venomously, blind to the irony. I explained my dissatisfaction.

'Mate, we've been sitting here for hours freezing our nuts off, we're hungry and late and all we're getting from this very expensive service is rudeness.'

He was quick to pacify my anger with a few professional words.

'You think it's bad for you? We're losing commission here!'

Eventually cold drinks were unceremoniously dumped in front of us, and prawn sandwiches, cut into halves to make them stretch further, were thrown on to our plates. Flabbergasted, we eventually arrived in Liverpool cold, hungry and unhappy.

We met with Phil and the PR team and headed for the newsagent's. We readied ourselves, hiding in the back room of the shop, and the golden ticket was placed into the top comic on his display shelves. We realised we might have to sit for hours, but *Viz* was selling so well it was almost like a newspaper: a huge percentage of customers bought it. The probability was someone would buy one pretty soon. Sure enough, a young woman came in, had a look at a few titles for a while and eventually picked up *Viz*. Moments later, outside the shop, she was stopped Mr Moneybags and surrounded by film crews and cameras. A security guard appeared with a huge cage full of bags of 2p pieces and a photo call scrum developed. When interviewed, the girl said she'd never bought *Viz* before and was unable to explain exactly why she'd randomly picked it up on this fateful day.

After the media feeding frenzy was over, she headed home, telling the newsagent she'd see him later. We suspect we might not have been the only people guilty of rigging this particular giveaway. No one was bothered either way: we got our publicity, although we never got our breakfast.

Railway turns tables

I think it's fair to say that we all remained fairly grounded, despite the runaway success of our work, but not everything remained the same. Chris, as most *Viz* fans will know, is a lifelong railway enthusiast, or trainspotter as he prefers to be called. His love of trains and all things trainy led him to search for a converted railway station to live in. Dolores had recently given birth to their first son, Dale, and Chris's plans to move to a rural, idyllic, railway-centred life were put in motion. He found an old station that had been in use as a residence since the Dr Beeching branch line closures of the 1960s. It was about fifty miles north of Newcastle, so would mean a two-hour daily round trip by car. Chris's inability to drive didn't seem to put him off at all. Dolores had learned to drive and she'd bought a second-hand VW Golf, which she proudly brought to the office. Chris didn't go outside to see it: 'It's a car. I've seen cars before.'

Soon after, Chris passed his driving test, and before long he was making the daily commute. Days in the office didn't really change too much: Chris just arrived a bit later. He'd now taken on a second secretary-cum-receptionist to work the two days in the week Ann wasn't in. Susan was a very bright and friendly young woman from Whitley Bay who, like Ann, was often to be found in the office in kinks of laughter. He also took on an office manager or personal assistant (I'm not really sure of the job title – we just used to make them up). Maddie was from Gateshead, had previously worked for JBP in London, and was bubbly and efficient. She was the first person to turn my attention to *Vic Reeves Big Night Out*.

Our writing sessions weren't really affected by Chris's move. They just took place during the hours he was in the building. We spent most of our time drawing, so the new setup worked perfectly well.

Then in the office things did start to get a bit crazy. Chris began taking on more and more rooms in the sprawling building. In fact, I'm now a bit lost as to how many we had to start with. We had one floor, then in the studio Chris had his Mr and Mrs-style isolation booth built. Then he got Maddie in and she shared the isolation booth with him. Then he took on the floor immediately above and the studio moved there, with Maddie getting the isolation booth to herself. Then he took the floor above the new one, which was a pretty grim attic. At some point we all had drawing boards in there … Or did we? I can't even remember. It was like musical drawing boards. What had been our writing room, I think, was handed over to Andy and *Viz* distribution. I think the room that had been the original drawing studio was just fallow. We even ended up with a room for the storage of pornography. We had declared a porn amnesty in the comic, saying all would be forgiven if you simply sent your art pamphlets and jazz magazines to us. We were inundated with skud. We often used the faces of the 'stars' of these publications as our correspondents in columns and news articles.

Chris then decided that outside of writing sessions I should work on my own. Typically enough, he told me this in a letter, which was sent in the post. It said that Thorpy and Graham had complained about my constant talking, saying it disturbed them. Years later I mentioned this to them and they were both horrified. They thought the move had been my idea. Work it out yourselves, if you can. I really struggle to excuse some of Chris's behaviour towards me. I was effectively removed from all contact with everyone in the office, except on writing days and during breaks.

I soon slipped into depression. I began to struggle with the idea of even turning up to work and became less and less productive. I began to believe that *Viz* was the last place on earth where I was appreciated and contemplated walking out on the comic, but I wasn't even confident enough to do that. *Viz* was all I knew. I'd always wanted to be a comedian, have a sketch show, but I didn't feel I had a way into that world and felt isolated.

Not for the first time, my struggles in trying to work with Chris had led to problems in my relationships with women. Catherine didn't like seeing how unhappy it all made me and complained that I forever talked about leaving, but never did. My at times troubled relationship with the girl I'd got on so well with eventually petered out.

Things continued to be rather mental at work. While working in my solo studio I heard a commotion going on on the floor below. I came downstairs to the 'fallow' room to find Chris, Graham and Thorpy smashing things with a golf club. The Altar of Destruction had been born, and over time we were to put everything that we thought would be fun to smash on it. Over the following months an object would be held aloft and a cry of 'Altar of Destruction!' would go up. We'd all charge into the disused room to see it smashed to fuck with the golf club. Andy

191

Inman once did a bottle of Tipex, which wasn't the best idea he ever had.

Huntsham Court

As ever, work that got me out of the office was always the most enjoyable. Certainly one of the most laughter-punctuated weeks I ever had in my life was the one we spent working with Miles at a place called Huntsham Court in Devon. It was a beautiful, slightly decayed Victorian gothic grand country house, standing in amazing grounds overlooking rolling hills, inhabited by mature deciduous trees and grazing cattle. It was used as a sort of informal hotel, almost like the world's poshest B&B. The couple that ran it, Mogens and Andrea Bolwig, were lovely, somewhat eccentric, very accommodating and hospitable.

Our journey began at Newcastle Central Station where we boarded the train for Plymouth. When the guard came to inspect our tickets we asked him if he knew what time the train got in to Tiverton Parkway, where we were to be picked up by Mogens and Andrea.

'Tiverton Parkway?' he queried. 'There's no such station.'

'There'd better be, we've bought tickets to it!' Graham said.

'I can assure you there's no station at Tiverton Parkway,' he informed us very confidently, whilst rooting through a train timetable of biblical proportions. After a few moments, he announced, '18.56.'

'At Tiverton Parkway?' I questioned.

'Yes,' he replied, busying himself with other travellers.

The trip was planned and paid for by John Brown. He wanted us *Viz* boys to get together with Miles and write him a groundbreaking film script in order that he could conquer the world by means of film and television. John had imagined we could work like the *Monty Python* team, getting around a table in some idyllic location in order to write a new project. But he failed to see that we worked together every day, writing in our dull office. He'd now put us in this amazing location, and we were the only guests. There was a full-size snooker table and a giant lawn, footballs, a cricket set, a croquet set, golf clubs, sunshine and a serve-yourself honesty bar. Although we wanted to write during our first time together away from the confines of the office, there were far too many distractions. I'm sure that in time we might have learned to work this way, but this week would prove to be one long, hilarious jolly up.

Miles was a constant source of machine-gun wit and nonsense. He told us some frankly ludicrous stories, but he did it with such conviction that they developed an air of credibility that in the cold light of day they clearly didn't deserve.

He told us that the reason why Cliff Richard wears a colostomy bag (which he doesn't, although it's such a rampant rumour that one top lecturer on incontinence actually cites Cliff in his presentations – Cliff openly denied it in an interview many years ago, even laughing about it) was due to being raped by the Kray Twins at Mile End tube station. He also told us that Daley Thompson believed he'd been abducted by aliens, who had replaced his spine with an alien one.

Miles wasn't just funny with his stories. When we were all stotting drunk in the bar one night he began to do impressions of Chet Baker playing the trumpet. The hotel was full of musical instruments, mainly pianos, but Miles found a trumpet hanging on the wall and it was showtime. The impression was completely silent, revolving entirely around the facial expressions and bodily movements leading up to a passage of play. You had to be there – I was – and it was so funny I thought I'd suffocate laughing.

Miles's greatest manoeuvre of the week came at the dinner table. He began a conversation with hotel owners over their wine cellar (Mogens and Andrea had dispensed with their staff and were serving us themselves). The husband was something of a wine expert and also acted as a merchant. Miles asked what the most expensive bottle of wine he stocked was. The answer was something outrageous: £250 or so. Once Mogens had left the room we excitedly hatched a plot. Miles had to order the most expensive bottle of wine the Mogens owned for us to drink with our meal without raising his suspicions that the only purpose was to hit John Brown with the biggest bill possible.

His rise to the challenge was something to behold. He asked so many questions, appearing fascinated by the reasoning behind paying so much for something so seemingly unimpressive. Could he possibly taste the difference? Would he be capable of appreciating such a thing? He slipped almost unnoticed into the order. It was genius. We were laughing so much every time Mogens and Andrea were out of the room that we could hardly eat.

Eating also proved a problem when smoked salmon was served as a starter. Nobody was really a fan of it but we were being waited on hand and foot and we didn't want to cause offence by not eating it. I chose to throw mine out of the window, in the knowledge that I could deal with it later on a walk in the garden. I waited for the all clear and I quickly flung the fish outside. Moments later we saw the house cat run past the open door, carrying the fish in its mouth. It was straight out of *Fawlty Towers*. We couldn't stop laughing. It was painful.

The most expensive wine necked, the smoked salmon thrown to the cat, Miles decided to ask what was for dessert. Continuing with the questioning line he'd used so well to spring the wine order, he made numerous queries about the puddings Andrea was attempting to describe to him. Eventually she left the room, returning with a trolley on which she'd placed everything the hotel had to offer from the sweet menu. She said she'd give him time to decide and walked out again. Miles sat back in his chair and pointed at the trolley. 'Look at that. That's got "Miles Ross is a cunt" written all over it.'

The sun shone and the fun and games continued on the house's magnificent lawn. We created a football game that we called Stick Bongo. We each stood behind a single cricket stump, in a circle about twelve yards across. The object of the game was to score points from opponents by hitting their stump with the football. You got extra points if you only made one touch to return the ball and once your stick was struck three times you were out. There were various other rules that time has eroded. Miles was crowned the Stick Bongo Champion.

We switched to golf. Miles taught us how to 'fizz' a drive, and we shot the balls into a field from the lawn and later went to collect them. I managed to walk into a very solid tree branch when searching for mine and ended up concussed, having my head X-rayed the following day.

John Brown arrived to spend the final two days with us. In the hours leading up to his arrival, we'd hastily written out the few ideas we'd had for his groundbreaking blockbuster. It came to about half a sheet of A4. The Pondmakers was the story of two rival families, both in the landscape garden trade in a small rural village, that fought ruthlessly over contracts for local garden ponds. It was *Dallas*/*Dynasty* on a small scale. That was pretty much it.

John was unable to hide his disappointment, and he hadn't even seen his bill yet. But we taught him how to play Stick Bongo and all was well again. Great, great memories.

7

Farts Bought Me A Mansion

Tom Caulker had gone on from DJing nights at Rockshots to found his own vibrant nightlife venue, Club Africa. On a night there with Colin and Rashida I met Anne, a tall, slim, pretty woman with a kind face and a very engaging personality. Straight away we got on like a house on fire. Anne had two small children and was in the process of going through separation from her husband, with whom she still lived in the marital home. I wasn't put off by her clearly difficult situation, or by the fact she had kids – all I was looking for was a friend. Anne was exceptional as a listener, to the extent that she put dealing with her friends' problems above all else but her children.

The situation at the office was affecting my mental health to the extent that I was hardly able to function: I couldn't face going to bed at night and then I couldn't get up in the morning. I would turn up to work in the middle of the day and sit in my isolated room, staring at a blank piece of paper. I could find no motivation. A cartoon that should have taken two or three days to complete would take me ten days or even a fortnight.

Mum's condition was worsening and Dad was having trouble coping. He was struggling and his lifelong attempt to push on without help was taking a heavy toll on his mind.

It was all too much for me to deal with, and without knowing it I was heading for a fall. It was a time of great emotional need for me, but despite her own problems Anne would always help.

She would be my companion and guide through some very dark times indeed.

Her children, Rachael and Tom, were a delight to have around. Rachael was three and Tom was two, and their company was the greatest tonic I could wish for. Anne was a brilliant mother to them, and she made it her mission in life to ensure they were always happy and as unaffected as possible by her separation and eventual divorce from their father.

Anne moved out of her marital home just outside of Whitley Bay when she found a flat to let in High West Jesmond. It was only a few minutes' drive from my flat, and with arrangements in place for the children to be with their father at weekends, Anne settled into a new life in Newcastle. It wasn't long before she and I were pretty much inseparable. She was the kindest and gentlest person I'd ever known, a phenomenal cook and she really liked a laugh.

We'd watch *Vic Reeves Big Night Out* together and video it so the children could watch it the next day. It wasn't long before three-year-old Rachael was gently easing herself to the floor and saying, 'I've fallen!' She was a slightly quirky girl, with the loving nature of her mother and a cautious leaning towards adventure. She was something of a tomboy, but always had an eye for the mirror, and chose her own clothes every day from a very early age. Tom was a bundle of fun, never cautious, but big, boisterous, adventurous, kind and gentle in equal measures. He was huge for his age, standing head and shoulders above his nursery classmates.

Jumpy Jack attack

I was lying in bed one afternoon, recovering from a migraine. I suffered with these from the age of eleven until I was thirty. There was a knock at my front door, so I looked through the security viewer, or spy-hole as Dad always called it. Outside was a young man in fairly scruffy clothes with a little black woollen hat on the back of his head. My first thought was that this looked just like my own black woolly hat. He was pacing relentlessly from side to side in the restricted space of my path, which was only a couple of feet wide. I thought he looked well dodgy. I cautiously spoke through the door.

'Hello?'

'Mate, hi, how are you? How are you? Are you all right? ... Sorry to trouble you, like. Is that your car, mate? The Mini? Is that your Mini? The green one? The Mini Estate? The Mini Traveller, is that yours? Is that yours, is it? Lovely car that, lovely car, man!'

He didn't seem to ever stop for breath. Like a radio DJ, he wouldn't allow there to be 'dead air' during his shift.

'Erm, yes ... it's mine. Why do you ask?'

I kept the door closed.

'It's a lovely car that, man. It's a lovely car. It's mint. I've got one myself the same. I've got one myself. Mine's not as good as yours. I say it's the same, it's not the same, it's not an estate, but it's green, it's the same green is yours, it's Almond green, that's what yours is isn't it? Almond green? Mine's a 1964, yours is '67 is that right, is that right, '67?'

Although I was concerned that he seemed to be off his head, the more he spoke, which was a lot, the more I realised he was knowledgeable about Minis. He hadn't yet stopped talking.

'I guessed it was your car, what I did was I put the car and the front door together. Are you a graphic artist? I looked at the door and I thought "That door belongs to a graphic artist." My sister is a graphic artist, she would have a door like that if she could.'

He was referring to the Victorian front door on my flat that I'd painstakingly renovated and refitted with original brass hardware. It was the only one like it in the street; almost every other had been replaced with a Kentucky- or Carolina-style door, the ones that look like the windows from *Play School*, which were all the rage at the time. I was impressed with his ingenuity in looking for the kind of door that would belong to the person with that kind of car. He might be a bit eccentric, to say the least, but he was clever.

I eventually let him in. He introduced himself as Huw Evans, and he is one of my closest friends to this day. I'm still waiting for him to stop talking. It turned out he wasn't on drugs – he just talks a lot, and very quickly.

Housey housey

Viz's success was starting to pay, and to pay quite handsomely. I decided that a house would be the order of the day, as despite the endless hours of work I'd put into renovating my flat, it only had one bedroom. I was now also renting two garages for my growing collection of 1960s Minis.

I'd bought a beautifully restored red 970cc 1965 Mini Cooper S, the 1967 Austin Mini Countryman estate that grabbed Huw's attention, a 1275cc 1967 Mini Cooper S and a black Mini Mayfair from 1988, which I couldn't stop modifying.

I thought with Anne and the children being so close to me it would make a lot of sense to have more room, as I hoped that eventually we could live together. Like my brother, although not driven by railway enthusiasm, I began to look at houses in rural Northumberland and the Tyne Valley in particular. Then, on a night out with Colin, he gave me some advice for which I shall forever be grateful.

'What do you want a house in the country for?'

I thought it was obvious.

'The peace and quiet, the space, the country walks, that kind of stuff.'

I thought this was a good answer.

'You can get all of that by going into the country on holiday. You like camping, go camping in the country. You're a city lad. Think about what you do in your life: you like cinemas, restaurants, pubs, theatres, takeaways, live music, you socialise a lot. You can't do any of that in the country, not like you do in the city.'

He was so right. I'd never even thought about finding a nice house in the city, but now the search was on, and it wasn't long before I found my dream home.

The estate agent's brochure was given to me by Dolores. Apparently Chris and she had been interested in it some time earlier, but they'd never been to look.

The house stood only about a hundred yards from Anne's flat. It was on a street corner, facing the Metro line to one side: this was the same railway line that passed at the top of Sunbury Avenue and faced our house in Lily Crescent. It was a nice-looking house, not audacious, but with some beautiful features. I discovered later that it was built just before the First World War, although most people thought it much later. The architect had been well ahead of his time.

I made my appointment with the agent but it was the owner who I met to show me around. She was an elderly lady, quite refined and very proud of the house, in which she'd lived since 1962. She and her husband had bought it from the family who built it, and the good news was that they'd done very little to change it. As I walked around with her, every room I entered screamed: 'This is the one! Buy it! Buy it! *Buy it!*' If the reception rooms weren't enough, I was bowled over by the games room, with a full-size Burroughs and Watts snooker table standing on a parquet floor and a window overlooking a rockery to the front. But there was so much more to come.

Mrs Regnart had spared no expense when having the bathroom and kitchen refitted when she'd moved in. The kitchen was huge and its style was so far up my street it was up the hall and out the back door. Built by Dainty Maid of Tipton, it was an early fitted kitchen with sliding glass-fronted cabinets on the walls and Formica-topped units on the floor. All the cupboards were made with concealed piano hinges, and the drawer sides were of solid mahogany, despite never being seen. The quality was like no kitchen I'd seen before, and I've seen none better to this day. The floor was lino, cut in a Mondrian design – bright block colours with bold black dividing lines. The entire room was stunning.

If the games room and kitchen had taken my breath away, the garage launched a haymaker into my solar plexus. Its heavy timber panelled doors led to the street at the side of the house; at the back was an up-and-over door into the back yard; and the space was vast at over thirty-two feet long and about eighteen feet wide. Not only was it massive, with doors at each end, but it had a mezzanine loft for storage, a rock-solid timber workbench and an inspection pit. I was like a pig in shit (meaning I was happy, as opposed to smelly).

I put in an offer pretty much straight away. Mrs Regnart had already received an offer from someone else, but knowing I wanted to keep her beloved bathroom and kitchen, and the others wanted to tear them out, she decided to sell to me. I have never been as excited as I was in the days leading up to getting the keys. I would occasionally tell the agent I needed access for measuring for curtains or some such thing in order to get them so I could just wander around the house, taking it all in.

The house proved to be a great place for parties. Every time a Newcastle or England game was live on TV, I'd have a big football party. I'd go out and buy in samosas, pizzas, posh crisps and beer, and my friends and I would all get bladdered and after the match have a game of snooker, or retire to the pub.

There were lots of big family parties too, the first of which was to celebrate Mum's fifty-eighth birthday. Dad was really struggling with her care, and despite volunteers and nurses helping regularly he was never going to be able to cope with her increasing needs at home. She'd been having respite visits to a grand old country house called Matfen Hall in Northumberland, which was at the time a Leonard Cheshire care home. Mum would stay there for a few days while Dad rested, although he went to visit her every day. Mum liked Matfen, but it was the hardest thing for everyone, especially her, knowing we would see her go there permanently before too long.

With this in mind I thought it would be good to remind Mum of how important she was to so many people. The last thing I wanted was for her to feel she would be sent away and forgotten. I decided, with much help from Anne, to arrange a big party for her and to make sure absolutely everyone was there. On top of that, we decided to make it a surprise, and the only way we could stop Dad from letting the secret out was to make it a secret from him too.

It was a fantastic success, and it's a great memory for me. It proved to be the last time she saw many of the people who came, some of whom she hadn't seen for years, so I'm very glad we arranged it. I also made a big step in inviting both of my Dad's sisters. He'd had a mysterious falling out with them years earlier and I decided that enough was enough. In light of Mum's worsening health I felt that life was too short for such tragic spats and I was sick of living my life not seeing two of my favourite aunts. It was lovely to see them together with the whole family again and Mum smiling through it all.

Massive Mini move

As well as allowing me to throw big parties, this grand house allowed me to engross myself in my other passions: 1960s cars, property restoration, twentieth-century design and nick-nackery.

My love of the Mini soon took over the enormous garage and it wasn't long before I fell foul to the curse of having more space – you fill it up. My collection of four Minis grew by the months and I soon had two red Cooper S types, the green Countryman, the black Mayfair, a 1960 van, a 1978 pick-up, a 1965 Riley Elf for Anne (the Elf was one of the posh Minis with a long boot and tail fins) and a 1971 Mini van conversion we called the Creepy Coup. The Creepy Coup was a wheelchair transporter that I happened to see for sale at around the time Mum lost her ability to transfer from one chair to another, meaning to ride as a passenger she needed a vehicle in which her wheelchair could be accommodated. It was a great little thing, and having previously had a Mini herself, Mum loved it.

I had two in the back yard, four in the garage, one on the drive, one on the front street and the Creepy Coup stayed at Matfen. Huw and I spent many hours working on Minis in the garage. He would often bring his over – he also had several, though not all at the same time.

I never lost my love of the Mini, but I eventually kicked the habit of owning more things than it's possible to enjoy. But my love of cars and friendship with Andy Wilman of *Auto Express* would lead to one of the most amazing days of my life.

Andy wrote a feature for *Auto Express* on my Mini collection and this led to similar, even bigger features in both *Mini World* and *Classic Cars*. Andy always kept me in mind whenever *Auto Express* did anything with the Mini and he called me one day to ask if I'd like to be a guest at the opening of the contents of Sir Alec Issigonis's personal office.

Issigonis had designed the Mini, along with the Morris Minor, Austin/Morris 1100 and many more. After his death he left the contents of his office to the British Motor Industry Heritage Trust and they had put everything into storage without touching it. Andy was going to be present when they found out what exactly they'd got for the museum and archive, and was kind enough to think I might want to be there.

I drove down to Birmingham and met Andy, who was accompanied by a photographer. When we got to the storage facility we were met by the archivist of BMIHT. He walked us into the room where Issigonis's possessions were stored and I was rather shocked to see no one else present. *Auto Express* had exclusive access to this event, and they'd invited along only one person: me, the man who'd charged their table screaming abuse months earlier.

When Anders, the archivist, began to look through the drawers of Sir Alec's chest he found some artists' renditions of some Issigonis designs, but nothing of any huge significance. Then he found a very small notebook, with handwritten entries in pencil. He flicked through it and his eyes were drawn to the same page as mine – we'd both spotted the codename ADO15, as the Mini was known as during pre-production. I remember exactly what the entry said. Dated 17 July 1957, it read: 'Took Mr Herriman and Mr Lord around the track in ADO15 today. Some problems with final drive, but generally good. PRODUCTION APPROVED!'

We'd stumbled on Issigonis's private diary, and were the first people ever to see his own record of what was without doubt one of the most significant moments in British motoring history.

In my new house, renovation had begun pretty much straight away, but sympathetically restoring and upgrading, mainly in my spare time, would take fifteen years to complete. I had contractors in early on to do some major roof work and the heating system was replaced by a family business, but the vast majority of work was undertaken by me and friends. For the first few years I was joined each weekend by Brian, a joiner I met through Colin the photographer. Brian worked at the photography studio where Colin did most of his commercial jobs, building the sets.

Brian and I would work long days at weekends and some evenings, always singing songs in the club style as we laboured. We'd often be joined by Huw: as an electronic engineer, he would undertake the electrical jobs, and he also soon became a good plasterer, woodworker and plumber.

Working on the house and the cars was the time I loved the most. I've never been good at doing nothing in my spare time, and having a desk-based job it was great to have hobbies that required hard, physical labour, especially outdoors. Brian and I have stayed great friends and I'm godfather to Rebecca, one of his granddaughters, something of which I'm very proud.

Arthur 2 Stroke, aka Phil, also spent many long hours working on my house, mainly labouring for Bob the Hippy Brickie, who did lots of brickwork, including turning my design for intersecting circular brick flower beds at many different levels into reality. He also laid the entire yard with handmade bricks in my design of concentric circles.

One summer Phil, Bob the Hippy Brickie, a mate called Jason and I undertook the unenviable task of upending an old cast iron GPO phone kiosk that I'd bought. Phil and I had transported it on a car trailer, and just loading and offloading it in its horizontal state, with the help of a winch, had been a nightmare. Now we faced the task of standing it up, and it was a seriously dangerous undertaking. Bob the Hippy Brickie had been an engineer in the pits and was confident and fearless. With the aid of a block and tackle, three scaffold poles, two oak beams, lots of rope, a galvanised dustbin, gallons of tea and four hours' hard graft in which both life and limb were at times genuinely under threat, we got my K6 Jubilee red phone box standing. That was a great day's work.

Huw later installed a light that came on automatically at sundown and a working phone that could be switched off from the house. It was a great thing to have and children loved making calls from it. It was used in a number of photo stories, as was every single room in the house, many times. The phone box even appeared in a documentary about the Yorkshire Ripper hoax calls, an actor playing the hoaxer making the infamous 'I am Jack' calls from the bottom of my garden.

Archbold Terrace

Sales of the comic reached a quite frankly silly high at 1.2 million in 1989. A chart was created months earlier for the office wall, mapping the insane rise in increments, and we added another point each time the official ABC sales figure was announced. A line was then drawn, joining the points, creating a line that only ever went up. The constant rise was extremely sharp and the image of our success in such graphic terms made for great morale around the office. We weren't naive and we knew sales would have to reach a peak sometime, and a continual rise would have seen us overtake the only two magazines for sale in newsagents that still outsold us: the *Radio Times* and *TV Times*. Bizarre as it may seem, we did see them in our sights for a short while. It's incredible looking back now to realise that the TV listings were still governed by legislation preventing the broadcasters from publishing each other's programme times. As a result, many households bought both, so had that legislation not been in place we could well have outsold the biggest of the big.

The ABC sales figures, it must be said, although the official record of how many copies a title sells, are a little misleading. They refer to per-issue sales, so any weekly publication with the same ABC figure as us would in fact be selling eight times as many magazines, as *Viz* was only published every eight weeks.

The day came, not as significant at the time as it appears now, when the first lower ABC sales figure in our history appeared. It wasn't down a lot, we were still over a million, but it would prove in time to be a downward trend, and although much less steep than the upward one it was almost as constant. We began to have fun with the wall chart, which was renamed 'The Chart of Doom', also charting momentous imagined future occasions at lower and lower heights. Graham, the great worrier amongst us, was the butt of most of The Chart of Doom's predictions. For instance, 'Graham sells house and buys Caravan' was one of the lower marks.

I was still trying to work in the studio I'd been sent to alone, and it wasn't going well. My spirit was extremely low and things in the office were getting quite bleak. To say I wasn't coping well would be a polite exaggeration. One morning, while staying at Anne's flat, the day arrived that I simply couldn't face. Years of pent-up problems, issues over Mum's condition both in the past and in the horribly impending present, my troubled relationships with Dad and Chris and my stoic attempts to keep going despite it all exploded. I cried for hours on end. I couldn't get out of bed, get dressed or face speaking to anybody. Anne was wonderful to me; she held me and comforted me; she rang the office and told them I wasn't well and may be off work for some time.

Without Anne in my life at that time I have no idea what might have happened. She persuaded me to go to the doctor and accompanied me. Her patience was limitless. To walk into a doctor's surgery and try to explain that you've got problems that you've hidden from for years is difficult enough; to admit you believe those problems to be mental illness is another ball game, and not a very nice one. It was doubtless the bravest and most rewarding move I would ever make.

My doctor was very understanding and knowing the family and my circumstances very well he referred me to see a psycho-analyst. I was terrified at the prospect, but I was suffering and just couldn't face daily life. I knew it was the right thing to do, but that didn't make it any easier. I felt constantly self-conscious and began to experience some rather scary incidences of unpro-voked panic. The first appointment was months away, and as the weeks crawled past eventually I was begging the time to pass quicker, as I needed professional help. It's difficult to think about what it felt like, as unlike so much of my life that I've committed to this book, these memories are less clear. I suspect either my mind was fogged at the time, or part of me just doesn't want to remember.

Anne explained as best she could to Maddie, our office man-ager, about the problems I was having and how the imposition of isolation on me at work had certainly not helped. There was a lot of understanding shown and it was agreed that things were better when we all worked in a room together.

It so happened that plans were underway to move to a new office, just around the corner. Some months earlier John Brown had bought the Portland Terrace building from its owner, becoming our landlord. Chris felt it wasn't good to have John in a position of such power over us and decided it was time to move on. John's ownership wasn't the only reason for change: we all felt that the labyrinthian and warren-like Victorian terrace wasn't best suited to what we did. An airy, open-plan studio would be a much better environment to write and draw in.

Looking back, none of us liked our workspace that much. Any chance we got, we would go on missions to escape for an hour or two. We would drive to the coast and sit in the Rendezvous Café,

a virtually unspoilt 1950s Formica-tabled affair on the prome-
nade at Whitley Bay. Its expansive arched windows overlooked
the usually fearsome North Sea, and after frothy Italian coffee
and Viscount biscuits we would walk along the ageing and
unloved prom, where Graham would dare us to attempt the 'Run
of Doom'. This never-before-attempted game involved descending a set of steps built into the sea wall, waiting two or three
steps from the sand at the bottom for a wave to come in, and as
soon as the wave hit the sea wall and began to recede you had to
jump off the stairs on to the beach and run straight along it,
parallel to the sea wall, in an attempt to reach an opposing set of
steps before the next wave flooded the sand. The course covered
a distance of about thirty yards.

We watched time and time again as wave after wave came in,
trying to establish if the challenge could actually be done. Was it
just a crazy dream? Graham, like Dustin Hoffman in *Papillion*,
was ever thoughtful and quietly observant. After a number of
visits over a period of months, without ceremony and unannounced, Graham descended the steps. We watched on, the sea
air filled with tangible suspense. People had descended before,
but had always returned, getting cold feet without ever braving
an attempt. For a few moments he silently watched the waves,
then, the instant one wave struck, he launched into his desperate
sprint. As he leapt for sanctuary seconds later, his final foot lifted
into the air as the second wave rushed under it. It was like
watching Jackie Chan versus Spiderman and seeing Jesus win a
coconut at the shooting gallery all in one. Graham remains the
only person to complete a successful Run of Doom.

Other favourite distractions included going to play pitch and putt
at Gosforth Park Golf Club, a game at which we were all pretty
shit. Cars in the car park were occasionally wounded. During
writing sessions that fell flat we would all sit, thinking. The hope
was a thought from someone would reignite our imaginations and
lead to a frenzy of biro scribbling. Often, in the event of failure
on all our parts to come up with a single idea, the inevitable test
of the recreational waters would go up: 'Pitch and putt?'

Just like an idea put forward for a cartoon or an article, the
response of the others would determine whether the suggestion
was taken seriously or not. No reaction: shit idea.

207

I'm often asked how writing on *Viz* worked, and that sums it up, really. We would sit around and each suggest ideas to the group, usually from the top of our heads. Most would be ignored or hummed and hah-ed at, but eventually one person's idea would spark a good reaction and then we would all begin to chip in different thoughts. Some days it was a slow and tedious process; other days it was like lightening. Some ideas would be developed by only one or two of us, while the others either gave no suggestions, or their ideas were not well received. There was no place for ego in this process: you just had to take it on the chin if your idea didn't get a reaction. The best days would see us all firing on all cylinders. These were fairly common, but not a daily occurrence. A usual day would see two or more of us on form and the others playable, but not fully match fit. The worst days, and they rarely happened, but when they did they were depressing, would be those when no one could think of anything even half decent. It took us a long time of working together to learn to give up on attempting to write on days like this. On these occasions a cry of 'Pitch and putt?' would be received with relief.

The person who usually drew a character would hold the editing role: he would write the ideas, and eventually the script, down, having the final say-so in which of the better suggestions were used and which weren't. The person who almost always drew a character had almost invariably created the character in the first place.

Interestingly, it's worth pointing out when talking about our working process that Chris, although choosing the job title 'Editor' for himself, wasn't an editor in the established sense, in so far as he didn't edit our work. It was his say-so if work was printed in *Viz*, but he didn't reject or edit the work produced by the Editorial Cabinet (Me, Thorpy and Graham). From the day we all began work in an office together we worked on almost all writing decisions as a team. There were a few exceptions, but as a rule that's the way it was.

The search for a new office was on and after looking at various places from the sublime to the ridiculous we ended up just two streets away from our home of the last four years. Crestina House was an early sixties low-rise office block on Archbold Terrace, a street that been half residential until the mid 1970s, when the row of Victorian houses that made up the opposite side to our new office was demolished and replaced with a hideous, prefabricated concrete structure called Scottish Life House. This building also spanned the street at both ends, offices on stilts standing out over the road, blocking out the sunlight and causing mini tornados of litter even on days that didn't seem particularly windy.

It was just on the outskirts of the town centre and despite the stark, desolate view of Scottish Life House from the front windows the layout of the place was spot on for us. Everything was on one floor, with a huge studio room at either end of a corridor that opened out into a reception area, a kitchen with a Michaelwave oven, a darkroom, and two further small offices.

Andy and the *Viz* distribution team would take the big room at one end and we would take the other studio as one big workspace for writing, drawing and layout. Chris and Maddie would have an office each.

A great healing was taking place for me. The new office space offered me a feeling of a new start working together properly with the others. My sessions with the psychoanalyst had finally begun and progress was really difficult, but hugely rewarding. I found out things about myself with virtually no help from the analyst – he just sort of moved my thoughts in the right direction. I have to say the sessions genuinely changed my life. This seems like a very simple way of summing up what happened, but I think in truth it represents the gist of it. I felt the way I did – confused, upset, lacking in confidence and angry, to name but a few of the unpleasant emotions – because quite a lot of shit stuff had happened to me in my life. That realisation, that my inability to cope could be corrected by simply understanding what had caused it, saved me from a life of God knows what. I know that taking the whole painful journey of discovery was what freed me from my mental prison. I don't think for a minute that anti-depressants could have done the job that I needed doing.

Everything suddenly made sense when I took a step back and saw what my life had thrown at me from when I was very small. I still have problems from time to time, but I'm equipped to deal with them now. I can approach them without the fear and the confusion and the lack of self-belief that once ruled my whole world.

It was a good job I started lessons in coping with my own life, because it was about to take me down again.

Despite the office move and the respite from Chris's moods that came with the new building, things were still not entirely comfortable. He began a very curious practice of engaging in business pursuits that he didn't seem to enjoy. He became a landlord, letting a handful of flats in Jesmond. Maddie acted for him in most of these matters, but his frustration and annoyance with most aspects of the venture were made very public in vocal rants at the office, along with lengthy and graphic descriptions of his bowel movements.

My success and consequent wealth had led to the purchase of a dream home and a vast and virtually insane car collection, both of which proved a great drain on my time and energy. Chris went down a similar route, but on a grander scale: he began to collect railway stations. I guess when the opportunity to do something you've dreamed of arises, you take it without question. Chris dreamed of railways, and before long he had three disused stations, having bought one either side of the one he lived in. He rented one out to Cynthia, one of Mum's younger sisters, and the other he decided he would renovate and open as a restaurant.

One thing I can say about Chris, without fear of contradiction, is that he's never been a great lover of food. When we were kids Steve disliked fruit to the extent that he admitted it was a phobia. He happily ate most other foods. I ate anything, usually with gusto. I later became a vegetarian, but that was a lifestyle decision, not a fad or a fear of any foodstuff. Chris was, to put it simply and bluntly, the faddiest eater I've ever known. He would only eat peas if they were frozen, and then only if they were from Findus or Birds Eye. He recoiled at the mere mention of butter, margarine, salad cream and especially mayonnaise. He would study every item on his plate, turning it over with his knife, prodding it with his fork, gingerly examining its every detail. I never saw him eat a complete meal, always leaving a good percentage of it untouched, but well examined. His ideal restaurant food was Kentucky Fried Chicken, the predictability and dryness of the food both being attractions for him. He had no problem with biscuits and could eat entire packets in one sitting.

I once saw a documentary about an autistic boy whose favour-ite food was Pringles. His mum said that this was because they were very predictable and familiar, every one looking the same, tasting the same, having the same texture. In a packet of Pringles there's nothing unpredictable, no surprises.

I can't help thinking there's an element of that autistic trait in Chris. It fits well with his obsessiveness, his preoccupation with numbers and ordering of things and his communication troubles.

On a publicity tour, we were about to do a signing in a big bookstore in Bristol. The manageress had arranged a bells-and-whistles buffet for us, every Marks & Spencer sandwich under the sun, fruit, samosas, bhajis, quiche, and so on. We'd been on the road all morning and were ravenous by the time we were presented with this grand party spread. Graham, Thorpy and I tucked into the grub like we were in a Three Bears comic strip. In the meantime, Chris sat alone, muttering incomprehensibly under his breath and casting accusing glances at food items from across the room. The manageress became concerned that he wasn't eating and asked if anything was the matter. He assured her that all was well and that he was on a diet, which raised a few eyebrows amongst us, as it wasn't anything he'd mentioned previously. The manageress tried to make conversation about the nature of his diet, but no conversation was forthcoming.

We'd finished eating by the time Chris approached the table and after some quietly verbalised displeasure he singled out an item for his attention. In full view of the horrified shop staff he gingerly dismantled the sandwich, removing all items of salad one at a time, then attempted to painstakingly remove all traces of mayonnaise from the remaining slices of chicken and bread with a rudimentary tool he'd fashioned from a piece of discarded cardboard. At the end of his work he was left with two slices of white bread and a slice of chicken. He took one bite that he then spat into a piece of paper. He didn't touch the sandwich again.

Taking all of this into account, I would personally have said that a restaurant wasn't the kind of business he would be likely to run with a passion. However, my opinion was not required, and those who offered opinions – most notably his accountant – were rejected out of hand.

Shortly after we moved into Crestina House, Ann, who'd been with us now since we first started at Portland Terrace, left *Viz* and moved to Scotland where her husband, Nick, had been offered a better job. Her jovial, loud and at times outrageous personality was greatly missed, but the void would later be filled in an extraordinary fashion.

In the meantime, Maddie was packed off to Northumberland to oversee the completion of Chris's restaurant project. Susan became office manager and PA to Chris, and Stevie, a woman of the lady female variety, a friend who originally helped us out as a cleaner, began to work as receptionist.

No *Blue Peter* badge

Around the time of the move, the *Viz* boys were invited to take part in a charity football match at Gateshead International Stadium. Thorpy, being a Yorkshire softy with no interest in football, didn't take part, but Graham, Chris and I jumped at the chance.

I hadn't played football since damaging a ligament in my left knee at the age of fourteen, when playing unsupervised on a frozen pitch at school. I'd been terrified of playing all these years as the physio who'd looked after me told me never to run or play sport in the cold again. It having been close to freezing when the damage was done, and my ligament had snapped, as opposed to torn, so rather than knitting back together it relied on a thin area of scar tissue, and this could easily snap again and leave me with a limp.

Enticed by the thought of playing at such a famous stadium, I told myself that one game would surely be ok and I risked it. Although pretty unfit, I got through the game and I've never looked back, playing at least once a week thereafter (with the aid of a Neoprene knee support) until breaking my ankle in an unrelated non-football accident in 2008. I'm running again now and I aim to be back to football later this year.

The game at Gateshead was a strange affair, really poorly promoted, and the crowd comprised only about 200 people. The match was between local and national celebrities. Our team comprised a couple of Sunderland footballers, some young lad

212

off *Byker Grove* who no one in the dressing room recognised but most of the punters had come to see, and Eddie the Eagle Edwards, who wasn't local. The national team comprised lanky Scottish ex-*Blue Peter* presenter John Leslie, and ... erm ... I don't remember anyone else, except their goalkeeper, ex-Newcastle star Kevin Carr. There was a definite regional disparity in the picking of the keepers. The 'Nationals' were the fancied team, and Leslie was their captain.

Our kits, a fetching orange, were far too small and the shirt chaffed my nipples before the game had even got underway. We were pretty awful, and not having kicked a ball for twelve years, that went double for me, but remarkably Michael Gray put in a great cross and our Chris nicked it in past Carr at the far post. Before the break we managed to steal another and as we walked to the changing rooms we were stunned to realise we were two goals ahead. As we got into the tunnel I found myself alongside John Leslie, who was looking pretty annoyed. I turned to Chris and said in my best robotic punditry, 'Well, after the first forty-five-minute period, as we enter the half-time break, I think we can say we've managed to achieve as much as was expected of us.'

Leslie went apeshit and, red-faced, he shouted angrily at me, 'You've done a damn sight better than anyone could have expected of you!'

We proceeded to our dressing room, where as soon as the door was closed we all fell on to the benches, laughing like drains. The second half was significantly less fun and, out of steam, we came away 3–2 losers.

However, we did win in a way. Leslie had recently split with Catherine Zeta Jones and Chris made a sticker in black marker pen on a piece of white paper reading 'I'VE SHAGGED CATHERINE ZETA JONES'. In the car park I volunteered to be the one to tape it on the boot of his car, while Chris 'kept toot'. It was funny enough to see Leslie set off for London after the game, the sticker still attached to his hired Ford Escort, but the biggest laugh came at the *Viz* office some time later. A letter came, addressed to the Celebrity Cunts section of the Letterbocks page, from a reader in London, claiming he'd seen John Leslie, the ex-*Blue Peter* presenter, driving in central London with a sticker on his car reading 'I'VE SHAGGED CATHERINE

213

ZETA JONES'. I assume Leslie had just not noticed the impro-vised bumper sticker. I'm pretty sure he hadn't left it there 'for the craic', as our conversation in the tunnel appeared to show he was a man who'd be ill advised to put 'GSOH' in a lonely hearts ad.

Sheila starts

For many years our typesetting had been outsourced to a handful of local repro houses. This involved sending the text typed out on a standard typewriter and marked with measurements such as column width and type size. It would be taken by hand to typesetters' offices and then collected, or in later years delivered, a day or two later.

In very early issues there was no typesetting at all. Articles were typed out and then the size of the type was decreased using a photocopier. The move into using a professional typesetter had been a great step forward – we always wanted *Viz* to be more 'proper'. With hindsight, the more professional our production became, the more of *Viz*'s original 1970s independent feel was lost.

By the early 1990s the days of the professional typesetter were numbered. Ann had suggested for some time that we should get our own Apple Mac in order to do our typesetting in-house. In around 1989 I tried one out for myself down at the Students' Union Print Shop and I was sold on it. It seemed to make perfect sense. Chris was initially resistant and we pushed on with repro house typesetting for a few more years.

Eventually, the inevitable passage of time prompted the deci-sion not only to get a Mac for the office, but also to employ a production manager to run all of our typesetting and layout. For the first time in our professional lives we would actually have a proper interview for someone to work on the comic with us. Thorpy and Graham had both found us almost by accident, and the other people who'd worked in the office had not been involved directly with magazine production – their roles were mainly administrative.

Sheila Thompson stuck out like a sore thumb at the interviews. She seemed a little less professionally minded than the other applicants, casually mentioning that her husband 'looked like a

214

smack addict', but Chris rightly pointed out that she was clearly the person with whom we would most easily get on, which was a huge factor.

I've never in my life met anyone quite like Sheila. Even Ann's constant laughter, incessant talking and ever-present screeches of 'EEEEEEE!' couldn't hold a forty-watt lightbulb to Sheila's personality. An ex-punk Cumbrian living in Gateshead, Sheila had once been involved in putting on a gig in Silloth, one of the less salubrious towns of Cumbria, as part of the John Peel Roadshow. There was a fundamental error in selling tickets for the show, as besides a hundred or so indie kids and goths baying for The Sisters of Mercy the room was packed with pissed-up factory girls baying for 'The Birdie Song', and subsequently for Peel's blood. He was barricaded in the manager's office and had to be escorted to safety by the police.

Peel later said in piece he wrote for a broadsheet paper, around the time of his sixtieth birthday, that he had had few bad experiences in his lifetime in music, but Sheila's gig had been the worst of his professional career. He claimed that, lying in bed at night, he sometimes woke in a sweat, hearing the wind crying, 'Silloth! Silloth! Silloth!'

Sheila's workstation was set up in our studio and soon the air was filled with whole new barrages of 'EEEEEEE!' Her company was difficult to ignore at the best of times, but about twice a day she would let her presence be truly felt when she did her rounds. This comprised of wandering from one drawing board to another, repeatedly announcing, 'I'm stalkin', I'm stalkin' … aih?'

The 'aih?' is a Cumbrian trait. It's like 'eh?' but is used as punctuation. It's pronounced sort of half in questioning intonation and half as a statement of fact, almost like a rhetorical question. It's a bit weird until you're used to it, unlike Sheila, who remains a bit weird even when you are used to her. Her ability to talk was unbelievable, once staying on the phone for a single personal call for two hours in the morning and another for three hours in the afternoon.

With Sheila's arrival in our drawing studio, which had previously doubled for writing, we'd converted Maddie's old office into a writing room. When Sheila was on the phone we would shut the door quietly to protect our ears and her feelings at the same time.

We entered a great window of opportunity at this time, as Stevie and Sheila as a pairing were a dream come true for practical jokers, both believing almost anything that we told them. Stevie was great fun to joke around with, but Sheila's gullibility was in a league of its own. We had new vertical blinds fitted in the studio on a day when she wasn't at work. The blind fitter left some waste to go out with our rubbish, including a metre-long off-cut of clear plastic rod, used to open and close the blinds. We were fascinated to notice that this plastic tubing, hexagonal with a hollow centre, was identical to the outer part of a Bic disposable pen. Within minutes we'd taken a Bic pen apart and slipped the nib and ink tube part into the metre-long plastic off-cut, putting the little domed stopper from the pen in the other end. We then put our metre-long pen in Sheila's desk tidy, along with her other pens and pencils. It looked hilarious, reaching upwards from the corner of her desk, bending slightly under its own weight and almost reaching the office's low ceiling.

On Sheila's arrival she was instantly curious, asking where we'd got the long pen. We told her it was just a normal pen from her desk tidy, but we'd put it in hot water and stretched it. Some molecular physics was casually thrown in by Thorpy to add authenticity. Throughout the rest of the day she kept casting glances at the giant pen towering over her desk. The magic moment arrived about halfway through the afternoon when she dipped a pen in her tea and, like a potter working clay, attempted to gently lengthen it.

A penny for your thoughts

There was a rejuvenated spirit of fun in this new office, but my private life was suffering again. Anne had stayed in her rented flat, not wanting to move into my spacious house for reasons best known to her. She would occasionally bring the children over to stay the night, but it was infrequent and involved endless hours of seemingly meaningless negotiation. When it happened it was wonderful fun: Rachael and Tom were lovely, happy children and their company was never less than a joy. However, getting on with Anne was rarely less than a challenge; arguments were

216

regular and always seemed to cover the same ground. I think her marriage had left her questioning trust in relationships, and she seemed determined to test my resolve to destruction.

The good side of the relationship was wonderful. Anne had such a lovely nature and could see the positive side of anything. As we were both lovers of outdoor life, I bought a beautifully fitted camper van and we began to take the children away on great adventures in it. Our first trip was to Cornwall, a nine-hour drive. As we got to the first roundabout, a hundred yards from home, Rachael asked, 'Are we nearly there yet?'

We also took the camper to North Berwick, close to Edinburgh, when Mum was being looked after at an MS Society holiday respite home nearby called Leuchie House, where she could share a room with her sister, Thea, which was wonderful for them both.

As far as I'm aware Mum never talked to anyone about her suffering, and everyone wondered about her feelings. One day at Leuchie Thea observed Mum looking out of the window from her bed for a very long time. Thea wondered what was going through her head. Mum's communication had slowed a lot in recent times, and although she could still speak quite well, she regularly forgot where she was and what people had said to her.

Thea chanced a question. 'A penny for your thoughts, Kay?'

Mum's answer was immediate and defied her situation entirely. 'Are we talking real money, Thea?'

Dealing with troubled times through humour ran right through our family.

Thea had taken Mum on holiday many times over the years but as her condition worsened it was becoming a struggle. It was a relief when Leuchie was suggested. The nuns who ran the home did all of the nursing care, allowing Thea to enjoy a proper holiday with her sister again. Lots of the extended family stayed nearby, camping or in B&Bs, and we all visited Leuchie daily, taking Mum on day trips and spending evenings in the gardens of the house.

Leuchie House was a great place for us as a family to enjoy time with Mum without the pressure of her daily care. I'm very grateful, as is the whole family, for the loving care the sisters gave her during her stays there.

Keegan wonderland

In 1992 my love of watching football was reignited by the reappearance of Kevin Keegan at St James' Park. His return as manager at Newcastle came when the changes of the Taylor Report (the inquiry into the Hillsborough disaster) were really beginning to show and St James' was well on its way to becoming a stadium for the twenty-first century. Keegan's arrival had seemingly rejuvenated the entire club to such an extent that the team was now moving through an amazing season towards the second-tier title, having the previous season been one kick of the ball from the third level. For the non-football lovers amongst those reading, I'm trying to avoid terms such as 'First Division', as it's just too confusing due to the formation of the Premier League during our last season in the Second, becoming First, Division. Confused? You should be.

Chris and I both bought season tickets. Unfortunately, the two men who sat behind me in my new seat, nice as they were, bore an uncanny resemblance to Waldorf and Statler in *The Muppet Show* (the two old gentlemen who sit in the box and complain endlessly about the entertainment). I had to tolerate their complaints on a fortnightly basis, despite the quality of football being consistently the best that any living fan could have seen. During one game we were 4–0 up against Coventry City when Ruel Fox attempted a back-heel pass. He made a poor contact with the ball and it went out of play. Outrage from behind: 'Euuugghhh! He's tryin' bloody fancy stuff now!'

Eventually, in around 1994, during a game against Blackburn Rovers, I finally flew out of control. I'd sat, holding my tongue about their constant and abject misery, for years on end. On hearing yet another moan about players singled out seemingly at random for imagined atrocities against football, I completely flipped. Standing up in my seat and turning to them, I screamed at the top of my voice, 'I come here to support the fucking team! I come here to enjoy myself! All I've heard buzzing in my ear for years on end is fucking complaints from you two, you fucking miserable pair of bastards!'

Unfortunately, the moment at which the camel's back violently broke, I was accompanying Tom, who was five or six at the time. He was quite surprised to say the least at witnessing my outburst and was very curious as to the reason for it. The old fellas were very apologetic, for which I felt guilty in turn, and we've always got on very well since. That said, one of them passed away a few years back and the remaining one has brought a series of younger members of his family and seems to be grooming them as potential replacements for his old pal, egging them on into finding the negative in any positive situation.

During the Keegan years I began to go to a great deal of away games. Away games were simply something I'd never done before the Taylor Report. Chris had been to a few in the 1970s and the tales of cattle trains, police brutality and the constant threat of hooliganism had put me off somewhat. I felt the 1990s' spirit of football was so much more positive and friendly. I began by driving to the more exciting away ties, the likes of Liverpool and Leeds, and fell in love with the whole experience. Soon I was going whenever I possibly could.

I was lucky enough to be at both of Newcastle's famous 4–3 games at Anfield. I went with Jim to the first one, and we stopped at the Hillsborough Memorial before the game to pay our respects, then walked unsuspectingly into what is now accepted by most pundits as one of *the* best games of football ever played in the English Leagues. It must feel good for Liverpool fans to have been there and come away with a win: either way, I know I was privileged to have attended. I would often go to away games with my old mate Micky Davidson, and we had some amazing times. One that sticks in my mind was an away game at Bolton Wanderers in the 1980s, when a popular terrace song was 'You Only Sing When You're Winning', usually used to goad 'arm-chair' or 'prawn sandwich' supporters. Bolton had suffered financial troubles and had sold off half the terracing at one end of the ground to a supermarket chain. Where the terracing would normally slope back from the pitch, there stood the sheer brick wall of the Normid Co-Op supermarket. From the terracing next to the shop the views were restricted to say the least, leading to a giant wedge of empty terracing adjacent to it.

During Bolton's last season at this historic Burnden Park ground, Newcastle were ahead, the mood was buoyant, and the United fans all began to point at the supermarket, singing to the

Bolton support, 'You only sing when you're shopping, Sing when you're shopping, You only sing when you're shopping!'

The Bolton fans were great sports and when they came to St James' later in the season they were doomed to relegation. They made the absolute most of their day out and happily sang, 'We are bottom of the league! We are bottom of the league!' adding to the spirit of the moment with, 'We're going down with the Mackems!' There was something very special about a crowd of thousands whose team was going down managing to make it funny.

Possibly *the* funniest moment I ever witnessed at a football ground was away to Tottenham. A very large Rastafarian steward walked past the front of the Newcastle section of the crowd, who, in the moments it took him to walk those few yards, all began to sing, 'No woman, No pies! ... No woman, No pies!' Cruel, but very funny.

Up the five hitter

Graham Dury's *Fabulous Furry Freak Brothers* appearance sadly faded over time. The hair was cut, the beard shaved, the cowboy boots replaced with Birkenstocks, the poncho exchanged for an M&S jumper. But the legend lived on – he was still the hippy in the mould of the creators of underground comics of the sixties, the intellectual rebel, the stoner. 'Myth' would really be a more fitting term than legend, as every stereotypical view anyone had about Graham was based on his appearance and his trade, and not on his behaviour. Graham is in truth as straight a man as you can possibly imagine, law abiding to the extent of frowning on anyone doing seventy-one on a motorway, as far from being a stoner as George Best was from being a vicar – basically as close to being an old man as you can get without actually smelling of piss. Graham is very much a sensible family man, which made it all the funnier when he fell foul of an 'administrative error' at the *Viz* office.

In 1992, before the days of personal computers, Photoshop and six year olds digitally re-touching photographs in seconds, we needed a photo for the letters page of *Viz* that revolved around readers' pictures of 'funny' car number plates. The idea was that 'a reader' would send in a photo with a comedy number plate and a letter asking 'Do I win £5?' The registration number in the picture was to be 'B16 T1T5' (which would, of course, very cleverly appear to read 'big tits'). It was to be my job to make it and photograph it.

I put the thing together by buying a blank self-adhesive rear number plate, the kind that used to be put on caravans and trailers, and all the necessary self-adhesive letters and digits. I made up the plate in the *Viz* office and stuck it directly over the back number plate of Graham's car in the car park at the back of the building. I proceeded straight to Boots to have the film developed overnight.

When I arrived back at work the following morning the usually placid and polite Graham greeted me with, 'You bastard. You absolute *bastard*.'

It seemed I'd left B16 T1T5 on his car.

While I was at Boots, 5pm came around and Graham, being a punctual man, walked straight into the car park, jumped in his car and drove straight home. He collected his wife and family and drove them to Sainsbury's to do the weekly shop. When they came out, Graham trooped around the car park several times looking for his car. He couldn't see it anywhere. There was one just like it, but it had the wrong registration number. When it finally dawned, he wasn't well pleased that he'd driven the eight-mile journey up the A1058 Coast Road to his very nice Victorian house in a very nice street in the very nice neighbourhood of Whitley Bay with the legend 'big tits' emblazoned on his car boot. When he called me an absolute bastard I thought he must have been arrested for it, but no, the embarrassment was horror enough for poor old Gray-bags.

The story doesn't end there, though. Many years later a friend of mine who knew this story well was in a pub and overheard a row at the bar between a group of lads. One was saying, 'Nah man, I'm telling yuz, I seen a one once that said "big tits", man!'

His friends were adamant this wasn't possible.

'It cannat have said that man, yu cannat have that on a number plate!'

But he continued, 'I'm fuckin' tellin' yuz, man, I seen it, it was on the Coast Road, it was a Golf, it said B16 T1 ...'

'Nah man,' he was interrupted, 'if ye have B16 then a T it'd be just letters after that, ye cannat have a number after the T, man!'

221

My mate walked off laughing as the row got into the depths of the vehicle registration numbering system.

But the story doesn't end there. I told the 'big tits' number plate anecdote as part of a talk on the history of *Viz* that I presented together with Alex Collier at the Edinburgh Fringe in 2004. When I was visiting my mate Huw in Italy I told him about the story's inclusion and he asked me, 'Do you tell the Charlie Browns story?'

It took ages for the penny to drop, but how could I ever have forgotten? The number plate photo in *Viz* had been one of a pair. The 'reader' had had the 'big tits' photo published and his letter had asked 'Do I win £5?' The editor's reply was no, so in the same issue the reader had another published, asking, 'How about this, then?' In the second photo there are two cars parked next to one another, the number plates spelling out a more outrageous message. I made these two plates up on white card because they were too long for a normal number plate, but I used the same type of adhesive numbers and letters that I'd used for the 'B16 T1T5' plate. I bought all of the letters from Charlie Browns Autocentre on Chillingham Road. I went in with a note of all the letters I needed and began reading them out to the man behind the counter. 'Two Bs please, four Ss, four Is …'

At first he was writing them down, but before long he downed his pen. 'Just give me the paper, man.'

I tried to continue.

'Erm, no, that's five Is, one H …'

'Just give me the paper, man,' he repeated.

'No, two Hs …'

'Just give me the paper, man. It'll be easier.'

There was now no escape. Before reluctantly handing it over, I looked down. Boldly written on a plain piece of white paper were the words 'B16 T1T5' and '1 5HAG B1RD5 UP THE 5H1TTER'.

After his initial shock, and my hasty and embarrassed explanation, my note was handed around every member of staff. Even the tyre fitters were called out of the workshop for a good laugh.

Bomb-per Book of Shite

In 1993 we launched a book of all-new material entitled *The Bumper Book of Shite*. It was themed around boys' adventure books and designed to look like one. As far as I can remember, it was the first time we'd launched a project of all-new material since the hugely successful *Viz Holiday Special* of 1988. This being the case, we decided to throw a big party. John Brown wanted to make a media impact with the launch, so insisted it should be in London. As we felt it was important to recognise the efforts of the people of our home town who'd done so much to help launch *Viz* in the first place, we put on a bus from the office, and half of Newcastle was on it. Well, Chris wasn't. He got the train.

The party itself took place in the rather grand Porchester Hall, in Bayswater. In the lead-up to the party John Brown had been in a panic that the huge venue would be wasted, as we hardly knew any people in London. The idea somehow got out that Andy should invite his London contacts, the people who distributed *Viz* to record shops and other independent retailers. I suspect there may have been an overreaction on the invite front, as when walking through his office one day, I noticed a ticket addressed to someone with 'PLUS 9' on it.

As our bus approached the venue we saw an airship displaying a giant *Viz* logo on the side, plus an announcement of the *Bumper Book of Shite* release. We all piled into the party, which was themed as a Night of a Thousand Stars. Celebrities would be allowed in free, and would be paid a fee, dependent on how famous they were. They would then have to wear a huge badge declaring 'I'm a £50/£100/£250 celebrity.'

At the front desk, vacuous showbiz cunt Piers Morgan was hanging around uninvited, trying to get in on the act of deciding how much celebrities were worth. Not that many turned up, unsurprisingly. Viv Stanshall and Lionel Blair were the only ones of any note, although there were some E-listers around: Jeremy Clarkson, who was significantly less famous at the time, Quentin Wilson, Keith Allen, Emma Freud and erm … erm …

Before long the place was getting ridiculously busy. Then it got busier and busier. Then it started to get crammed, and it wasn't really any fun anymore. Then an alarm went off and

223

everyone was sent on to the streets, the staff and police informing us that there was a bomb scare. The party was ruined, and many people wandered off to find somewhere else to get a drink. When – eventually – the doors were reopened, no bomb forthcoming, notably the door staff were meticulous in checking tickets and counting the numbers of those coming in.

After the bomb scare, all of the wine, paid for by John, was missing. The only people who had access to the building were the police. As our American friends would say, you do the math.

One scenario in my mind that I've not been able to get rid of is that the bomb hoax was invented to evacuate the building without consequence to the management. They could lose their licence for overcrowding, but not for a bomb threat – that would be out of their hands.

Many of the bar staff never reappeared. Perhaps they were away somewhere with the stolen booze. A clutch of JBP staff were grabbed by John and drafted in to man the bar, and another was sent to an off licence to stock it. The cloakroom staff had also disappeared, so it was run by Ronnie and Bev from JBP and Neil Murray from Whitesnake. You couldn't make it up. Well, you could, but it wouldn't really be worth the effort. Apparently, Jools Holland played at the party. I never even saw the stage, let alone the band.

So, I had a shit time at that party, but it was ok – I had a rock 'n' roll hotel to go back to. Everyone from the Newcastle coach was staying there and we'd drink until the early hours. Well, that was the plan. Unfortunately, the barman saw fit to short change Michael, Susan's husband, by £10. Michael, a giant bricklayer, hauled him over the bar and suggested that he might like to give him the rest of his change. The barman accepted that there had been an error and handed Michael a £10 note. He then proceeded to close the bar and refused to open it again. Not the best party night we ever had.

Currying favour

We started to receive rather strange correspondence from a man called Abdul Latif, looking to get some coverage in *Viz* for his restaurant, The Rupali, 6 Bigg Market, Newcastle upon Tyne, NE1 1UW. We liked Mr Latif – his attitude of allowing us free reign to say what we wanted about his restaurant, and indeed about him, fitted perfectly with *Viz*'s remit.

He was better known as Lord of Harpole, a title that he'd bought in a shameless publicity stunt, publicity stunts being his stock in trade. He was a true giant in Newcastle culture for over thirty years, setting up his restaurant in the Bigg Market in the late 1970s and becoming an icon of the good-humoured side of Newcastle's character. Mr Latif was an absolute gentleman and became a good friend to all of us at *Viz*, not least for many years of personally delivering takeaway curries to our offices when we were up against deadlines. Our relationship with him was always very casual, and his gentlemanly, genial nature always made doing business with him seem like a friendly conversation.

As possibly his greatest publicity move he decided to create the world's hottest curry. He then threw down the gauntlet to idiots everywhere: eat it all and you don't pay. The Curry Hell Challenge would attract some of the world's most prominent fuckwits, most notably Garry Bushell.

When it all started, a businessman from Birmingham said he would give a substantial sum of money to charity if a member of his staff could finish the Curry Hell. The dare was accepted and the date was set for a young man to be the first to try the killer curry. Mr Latif asked if we at *Viz* would act as independent adjudicators and bear witness to his attempt. The offer was a free meal for all from our office who turned up. We arrived six-strong: I took Anne; Susan and Sheila took their husbands. What we witnessed was both one of the most tragic and yet one of the funniest things I've ever seen. We sat at a table with the young man and his boss, who'd driven up specially and would return immediately after the 'meal', facing the lad who was about to undertake the challenge. On our side of the table we all looked though the menu and chose our favourite dishes. It turned out that the poor sod was a huge fan of *Viz*, with an encyclopaedic knowledge of the comic, and was keen to ask as many questions as time would allow.

Things were fairly relaxed, and eventually our meals were delivered to the table, followed by the ceremonious arrival of the Curry Hell in a highly decorated and ominously large gold-plated serving dish. When the lid was removed the meal appeared to comprise a few pieces of chicken swimming in a mass of chilli seeds.

The lad told us he'd been eating phall, the hottest Indian dish, for breakfast in an attempt to 'train'. In the middle of a question about which artist was responsible for which character, he gingerly took his first mouthful of food. At first there was little reaction, more apprehension than anything. Then the Curry Hell hit home. Tears were quickly followed by hiccups, in turn followed by a pint of water, reddening of the face, violent dry gagging, and eventually a strangled attempt to talk again. He took another tentative forkful, and this time his gagging became more violent. He jumped from his seat and rushed to the nearby toilet.

For the next forty minutes or so he tried desperately to ask questions about his favourite things in *Viz*, punctuated by more eventful mouthfuls of this appalling 'food' and numerous trips to the toilet to 'vacate the sluices at both ends'.

As official independent adjudicators, we were so moved by this poor bastard's plight that we began to surreptitiously hide some of his food in napkins, cigarette boxes, and under pieces of naan on our own plates. He was in a frightful state by the time Lord Harpole announced he had successfully completed the challenge.

The next day, his boss telephoned to say that on the 205-mile journey back to Birmingham he had had to stop the car every few minutes to allow the Curry Hell champ/victim to shit and/or vomit into roadside bushes.

Lord Harpole was a true eccentric and worked every hour his God sent him. Not only was he the restaurateur who entered *Guinness World Records* for the longest takeaway delivery (Newcastle upon Tyne to Australia) and the producer of the world's hottest curry, but many of the hours he spent working went to charity and local politics. A vibrant and colourful man of the people, it was a very sad day for the city, and especially for his family, when he died in 2008 at only fifty-two.

The Rupali lives on in the hands of Mr Latif's son Rukon, perhaps less of a self-publicist than his late, great father, but not afraid of seeing the restaurant's shameless placement in *Viz* and elsewhere continue. Speaking of which, I note with interest that The Rupali is still situated at 6 Bigg Market, Newcastle upon

Tyne, NE1 1UW, and the menu is packed with flavours from many areas of India, prepared from the freshest ingredients sourced from local suppliers. I also notice they serve halal food and their chef will be happy to prepare any dish of your choice.

The saddest homecoming

Now in a virtually constant state of argument, but determined to try and save our relationship, Anne and I sought counselling from Relate. This exposed weaknesses in both of us, in my case revolving especially around my difficult relationship with Mum, who was now very poorly and confined to bed most of the time, and also with Dad, who was not in a great state mentally.

I found I was better able to speak with the Relate counsellor than I was to my psychoanalyst. This, I think, was due to her being a her. The analyst had brought a lot out of me, but I found speaking from my heart was easier with a woman, perhaps because when I was small I'd found my Dad difficult to speak to when I was troubled.

Mum had, of course, been ill since I was born, but the trouble with MS is that in most cases, the longer you've had it for, the faster the condition accelerates. So in Mum's case she was fairly stable for twenty years, but her condition began to deteriorate more quickly thereafter as time passed. By the time she was living at Matfen she was severely disabled, but could still eat and would spend daytimes in the grand communal hallway, with its giant stone fireplace and coats of arms. Matfen was a beautiful village and we'd take her for walks into it, stopping in the beer garden of the pretty little pub for Schweppes Bitter Lemon, her favourite drink.

One night I got a call to say Mum had been rushed by blue-light ambulance to Newcastle General Hospital, having suffered a seizure of some kind. She was in the intensive care ward. When I arrived the family were all taken into a side room and told to prepare for the worst. It was unlikely Mum would survive the night. Depending on how her vital signs progressed, they would consider switching off life support.

The General held no good memories for me. It was a grey and imposing old building, originally a workhouse. It was here that

Granddad had come in the late 1970s, seriously ill and delu-sional. His daughters had all come to visit and in his confused state he had believed they were his sisters. Having been badly wounded by shrapnel in the trenches in 1916, he'd prayed to see his sisters before he died. Now, sixty years later, he thought his prayer had been answered. To him it was as if he was in a military field hospital as a sixteen-year-old boy. I felt that if he died it would be like his life just hadn't happened. It was very stressful for Mum and her sisters. Fortunately, he eventually pulled through and made a full recovery. He died at home a year or two later.

We stayed through the night at the hospital, two at a time being allowed to see Mum for a short time. Eventually the nurses told us that as she was sedated we might be better off trying to go and get some sleep, as she wouldn't know we were there.

Mum miraculously made it through the night, and within two days, although still unconscious, she was moved to a normal ward.

Steve and I were sitting at either side of her bed when she woke up with a start. She opened her eyes and started to look around. We both stood over her. I spoke first.

'Hello, Mum. Do you know where you are?'

Steve continued, 'You're in hospital, you've had a bit of a funny turn.'

Mum stared at me, and then at Steve. She struggled to speak as she had a tube in her mouth, but she doubled her efforts and said, 'My beautiful boys.'

Only a day or two later, having been told by an ill-informed doctor that Mum might not walk again (he was a bit alarmed when Dad laughed), Mum was on her way back to Matfen Hall.

It was soon announced by the Leonard Cheshire Foundation that Mum's stay at the imposing but in some ways rather sinister hall would come to an end. The charity was selling the building and had in its place taken over a modern care home in Jesmond, only half a mile or so from our office and a mile from my house. There were so many good aspects to this: it was local, and local meant Jesmond, where Mum had lived all her life, except for a few traumatic months of evacuation to Carlisle in the war. The building was airy and light and the bedrooms had French doors that opened on to a lovely central garden. Steve and I furnished Mum's room with a new wardrobe and drawers and hung all of her favourite pictures of us as children and of her grandchildren on the walls.

We so looked forward to Mum coming to this lovely place, despite being very frail and now unable to talk. It was a joyful moment when she arrived. Dad, Steve and I sat with her as she took in her new surroundings. Dad was happy to see her in Jesmond, but he was emotionally drained, and had developed an upsetting habit of talking about Mum in her presence. I'd explained to him that when Andy Pop had been very ill and fallen into a coma he had been completely aware of everything around him in the hospital: he was just unable to respond, as his body had shut down to repair itself. Dad seemed genuinely interested in this and began to behave accordingly, but I often had to remind him. He had aged beyond his time in the last few difficult years.

After Dad and Steve had left I sat with Mum and talked to her about how nice it was to see her come home to Jesmond. I showed her all of the photographs on the walls, taking them down one at a time and holding them for her to see up close. I showed her a photo of Anne, Rachael, Tom and me taken by an ex-girlfriend of Steve's. Mum was really very unwell by now and was fed through a tube, spending her days lying on a pressure-relief mattress with a noisy pump. It was very sad and the worst aspect was that she couldn't say anything or communicate by any means. However, as I put the photo in front of her, she made a huge effort to move her index finger, very slowly, very deliberately, until it was directly over Anne's face. She then turned her head towards me and, with another massive effort, she smiled. In an instant I said, 'Yes, I love her too.'

Mum then fell asleep, the effort to control her hand and face presumably having worn her out.

Visits to see Mum took on a whole new light. I called to see her on my way home from work, which was brilliant: drop in, say hello, talk to her a bit about the day and continue homeward. It was a routine I wanted to last forever.

On Sunday afternoon, 6 November 1994, the day before Dad's birthday, I was shooting a photo story in my house, starring Bob, of Bob and Soo, Ian from Arthur 2 Stroke and a handful of others. The phone rang. It was Dad. He was unable to speak because he was crying so much. I'd only ever seen him cry once before, at the breakfast table when he heard of his father's death when I was six. He tried a few times to get a sentence out. I just said, 'Don't worry, Dad. I know what's happened. I'll come straight down.'

Without a proper explanation I asked Ian if he could take over directing the shoot and handed him my scribbled notes. I ran around the corner to Anne's flat, and as she opened the door I burst into tears and I told her my Mum was dead. I then rushed to see Dad at the home and Anne went to deliver the news to Chris, who was working in the office.

Mum had lived back in Jesmond for just ten days. I can't help thinking that she might have given up the struggle. Thirty years of fighting not just an awful illness, but also society's prejudices and government legislation, would have worn anyone out.

Mum's death caused me some very mixed emotions. I was deeply upset, but also somehow relieved, which in turn caused me troubling feelings of guilt. The Relate counsellor read the news of the death in the paper and rang to offer support in the form of counselling if I felt it would be any use. I took her up on the offer and I'm glad I did. In the sessions she pointed out that my confused feelings were natural: Mum had stopped suffering, so of course it was alright to feel relief. It was only when I saw the situation properly that the feelings of guilt were dissipated. Once again, I can't stress enough how much good counselling did me.

Because Mum had lost her ability to speak in her last few months I felt it was important to make a speech at her funeral, using some of her own words. She'd written a chapter for a book called *Images of Ourselves* in 1981, featuring twelve women, each with a different disability, talking about their own lives and circumstances. I picked a section in which she worried, as all mothers do, that her teenage sons were not helpful, and had no work. She blamed herself, as all mums do, and finished her piece with a sentence that still haunts me: 'How much more could I have achieved, would I have achieved, if I'd not been disabled?'

Things had, of course, changed a lot since the bleak year in which she'd written this and I was able to stand in the church where she'd married Dad and tell the congregation that I was very proud that she'd been able to see her sons grow up, become independent, earn their livings and even become a bit more helpful.

I finished by saying that from now on we should all remember Mum by the person that she was, and not by the illness that she had.

Another loss ... Then a famous win

My relationship with Anne remained fractious and on a lone visit to our relationship counsellor I was told I had to make a decision. If I wasn't convinced I could work things out with Anne then it made no sense for anyone concerned to continue the painful process of continual patching up. I wasn't convinced we could make it work: nothing that was said or done ever stopped the rows. We went to Relate one more time together. Sadly, Anne thought we could keep trying. I had to walk away from the woman and the children who'd brought so much love, friendship and support. It was very hard to do, but in my heart I knew it was the best way. Taking such a painful decision wasn't easy for me. Knowing they were all just around the corner was very hard, and not seeing Rachael and Tom was very difficult as they were so much a part of my life and I knew they would be missing me terribly.

Happily, after a very difficult period of keeping my distance, we began to see each other again as friends. I've always visited the children on Christmas mornings, and for many years I played football with Tom, now a strapping twenty-one-year-old student and keen sportsman. Rachael is a beautiful twenty-two-year-old trainee nurse. They're both lovely, kind people and a credit to their mother.

I was pretty down after the split from Anne. In what I gauged was an attempt to cheer me up, Thorpy invited me to his house one weekend for tea. His sister Julie was visiting. Seven years after a brief spell together after her photo story, we met again. She still looked as beautiful as she had the day I'd first seen her.

She was now living in Leeds, studying medicine. Our first 'date' was at Elland Road to see the Newcastle game, after which Kevin Keegan made his legendary 'I'll love it if we beat them!' outburst about Manchester United live on TV.

When I invited Julie to the game I really had no idea if she'd want to go. I'd bought a pair of tickets to the upcoming game, but I hadn't yet asked any of my regular companions if they wanted one. I was delighted when Julie said she'd love to come. It would be her first ever football match.

As the game approached I didn't bring up the subject of which team she intended to support. As a West Yorkshire lass living in Leeds, with no previous interest in football, I assumed she'd follow her home team. However, also thrown into the mix was her brother living in Newcastle for eight years. This was a very tense game that Newcastle needed to win to remain in with a chance of their first title since 1927. The game had run for what seemed like an eternity, remaining goal-less. Eventually, Keith Gillespie scored, sending our terrace into wild celebrations. Julie leapt from her seat almost before I did. She was black and white. Result.

Julie's peaceful and placid nature seemed very appealing after the madness of the latter stages of my time with Anne. It would be some time before I found she had a hair-trigger temper and a stubborn streak that Cillit Bang couldn't shift in a month of Sundays.

Football became a great bond between us and saw us through some tough times. Whenever things went wrong we'd always have to patch them up before a game. The day Newcastle beat Manchester United 5–0 was probably the happiest day of my life. I was very much in love with Julie and we watched the game together. We each ate a Cadbury's Feast at half time, a chocolate bar that had just been launched and we'd not tried yet. Later we would try and force great victories out of the team by eating Cadbury's Feasts, but not surprisingly this rarely seemed to have a genuine effect on the results.

This famous win was the only game during which I heard no complaints from Waldorf and Statler.

The Russ Abbot incident

One of the first things Julie and I did together, apart from attend football matches, was to go for a curry with Vic Reeves and Bob Mortimer. It happened during the filming of the disastrous *Top Tips* video, which they presented. This had been proposed by a production company and seemed like a great idea. The *Viz* writing team took a trip down to Elstree to see the filming in progress, but were absolutely horrified to see that additional material had been written without our knowledge. Not only were we appalled, but Vic and Bob were not too happy either. Chris and I both queried what was happening with the production company representatives, pointing out that no one from *Viz* was impressed with what they were doing with our work. We were all taken into a side room whereupon an angry row developed over who was in a better position to judge what was happening. The reps pointed out that they'd worked 'in this medium' and we hadn't. I pointed out that a shit joke was still shit, whether on telly or in a magazine. I also pointed out that the public seemed to approve of the way we wrote our comedy, buying it in their millions. The others in our team, always retiring in the advent of aggression, wriggled uncomfortably at the confrontation. I couldn't stop myself and I pushed for an example of what they had done, with comparable success. One of the 'writers' then said, without a shadow of irony, 'We've written for Russ Abbot!'

We left the studio under a cloud. Chris wrote to them, of course, pointing out exactly where he believed they were going wrong. They stuck with the same line of bullshit – they 'knew the medium'. Naturally, the whole project went off at half-cock and was pretty much buried. I don't think hardcore *Viz* fans even knew the *Top Tips* video existed, thankfully enough.

We did all go for a curry though, and afterwards, with a biro, Vic drew portraits of Chris, Dolores, Julie and me. Big night out.

Dine or bathe, Sir?

Rated right up with the best interviews we ever gave – the *London Evening Standard* and *Night Network* – was one we gave to a short-lived magazine called *Comedy Review*, set up by the then nineteen-year-old Danny Wallace.

Our interviewer, Matt Stephenson, arrived at the offices with a photographer and it was decided that we should carry out the interview over lunch. Unfortunately, the question of where we should eat was thrown open to the floor. Chris, in one of his contrary moods, was not keen on anyone's suggestions and we ended up on a wild goose chase, which first took us to a hotel on a traffic junction just off the A19. We arrived at reception and asked for directions to the restaurant.

'Did you want to eat?' asked the receptionist.

'No. We want a bath,' I replied.

She explained, 'The restaurant is closed for food at this time.'

We headed to Whitley Bay for some reason, which, as Stephenson rightly pointed out in his article, was like any British seaside town in April: cold and closed.

After a bizarre round of fruitless attempts to find somewhere to eat, Chris suddenly remembered that he'd arranged for us all to make a visit to a school where our cousin was a dinner lady. He'd forgotten to tell us he'd made the arrangement in the first place, let alone that it was arranged for in ten minutes' time. Remarkably, we happened to be only a few miles away, and off we went to sign a load of autographs for children who were clearly not old enough to read the comic. I reiterate: this day was really quite bizarre.

Eventually, all done at the school, we headed to a deep-pan pizza restaurant only a few hundred yards from the office, having done a seemingly never-ending twenty-plus-mile trip to get there.

Like Phil Morrow and the *Evening Standard* fella before him, Matt Stephenson had a unique idea for carrying out his interview. He talked to us all as a group as we ate, and then, individually, he asked us each to leave the table for a couple of minutes while the others bitched about him as much as they could in the allotted time. The results were fascinating and very funny. Chris went off like a machine gun in everyone's absence, doubling his munitions for me. Thorpy and Graham remained very quiet most of the time, having little in the way of criticism for one another. What I found most interesting was that they criticised Chris for seemingly always having an opposing opinion, of which I was more than aware, but when it came to criticism of me, they actually stuck up for me against Chris's onslaught, which ranged from 'never editing himself when he speaks' to 'wanting to be in showbusiness'. The others actually opposed his negatives with positives, saying I had a lovely house and was very funny. That said, they did have a dig at me for having too many different haircuts.

The interview was fabulous when it was printed, and like the previous two that I've cited, it managed to show quite accurately what it was like to spend a short amount of time with us. Matt's angle focused on us 'just knocking around having a laugh' and being 'regular blokes' despite having made 'loads and loads' of money.

Alan the fish

At *Viz*, sponsorship was never really something we embraced wholeheartedly. Like the dirty world of advertising, it didn't really fit. Sponsors rarely came within a mile of us anyway, although that said we did once get a free teapot each from PG Tips: living the high life, indeed. We engaged in bits and bobs of sponsorship with correctly aligned businesses: ones who either understood *Viz*, or let us carry on regardless. This had always worked nicely for us. The likes of The Rupali sponsored the Letterbocks page, Go! Discs sponsored Billy the Fish, although that had gone horribly wrong during our time at Huntsham Court when a Go! Discs bigwig had phoned up in a strop and tried to put the hammer down about us 'taking the piss in a strip that they were paying for'. First Chris and then Miles had explained that this was how things worked with *Viz*: that was the fun of it; it was all about taking the piss. But he just couldn't see the humour in it and blew his top. We agreed amongst ourselves to just print the piss-take and forget their money. That was *Viz* working at its best.

We did a bit of sponsoring ourselves, becoming the shirt sponsors of the world's most famous non-league football team, Blyth Spartans. We wanted to put 'Drink Beer, Smoke Tabs' on their shirts, but the FA refused to allow this, so the *Viz* logo was settled for. I even played for Blyth on a couple of occasions in charity games, along with Graham, and possibly Chris, I'm not sure. Both games were against Emmerdale. Yes, Emmerdale. I know it's not a real place: it was the cast and crew of the TV show, and they were very good footballers, too. The Blyth manager at the time was John Charlton, son of Jack, and he gave us a team talk before the game.

'Now, remember, this crowd today's come to see the telly stars. They're not a football crowd, they've paid money to a charity to see some lads they watch on telly. Them lads in that dressing room next door, they could spend their Sundays lying in bed, but they haven't, they've come all the way up here to entertain that crowd, and it's all for charity. They might be big stars, they might get paid a fortune for being on telly, but they're getting nothing here today. This is all for charity. I want you to understand that and go out there and show them some respect. Now enjoy yourselves.'

As we headed for the pitch, studs clattering on the dressing room floor, John shouted, 'And another thing, by the way! They didn't come here to fuckin' lose! And neither did we! Now get out there and give them fuckin' hell!'

I loved playing for Blyth. It was a legendary club. Dad took Chris and me to see Spartans play at St James' in 1978 when they reached a fifth-round replay of the FA Cup. Newcastle had been knocked out by Wrexham, and Blyth were drawn away against Wrexham in the next round, managing a remarkable draw. So they brought Wrexham 'home' to St James', their own ground, Croft Park, being far too small. As it turned out, even St James' Park was too small with over 42,000 inside and 10,000 reportedly locked out. Spartans very nearly won, too, but were edged out, losing 2–1. It was a hell of a day, and it left many people in the north east with a great fondness for the club. Graham and his sons have had season tickets at Croft Park for many years.

Surely our best sponsorship deal came when John Brown decided he wanted to sponsor a Newcastle United game. He picked away to Tottenham, as it would be easiest for him to take his London-based staff there. We had a great day out at White Hart Lane, with our guest of honour being Martin Chivers, a Spurs and England legend. The day had two clear highlights: David Ginola's stunning strike in the 1–1 draw, the TV replays of which clearly showed Ginola framed against the *Viz* hoarding, and Martin Chivers, sitting next to me at the meal, asking about the Brown Ale logo on the Newcastle shirts: 'That's strong stuff, mind, isn't it? They call it Journey into Space, don't they?'

We had to select a man of the match, and were told it must be a Spurs player because the club only had access the home team. We sent word around the sponsors' lounge for everyone pick Ruel Fox, who had until recently been a great servant of Newcastle. The most amusing thing about this was that he'd had a pretty poor game and there were rumblings in the crowd at the tannoy announcement. We got to meet Ruel and I presented him with framed piece of my Sid the Sexist artwork, which he assured me he would hang in his toilet, where he kept his *Viz* comics. Nice.

The success of this sponsorship under our belts, we returned the favour the following season, and we happened to pick one of the most amazing games of football I've ever witnessed. We'd wanted to pick Newcastle against Spurs as a return fixture, but it wasn't available, so we settled for Newcastle United versus Leicester City. Chris's daughter, my niece Jamie, aged five, was mascot. Her brother Dale didn't want to go out on the pitch with her. It was a wonderful moment as Rob Lee led her out by the hand and then, during the warm up, the crowd gave her a huge cheer when she scored past a very generous Shaka Hislop.

The game was soon in Newcastle's hands, Robbie Elliott scoring early on. Then in a bizarre turn of events Leicester scored three without reply. Our sponsorship romance appeared to be over – the game had gone from a high to a terrible low very quickly. Then along came Alan Shearer to score a breathtaking hat-trick in the last twelve minutes, his winner in the dying seconds of injury time.

In the scrum-like celebrations following the winner I lost my house keys, but nothing mattered. This was amazing stuff. The *Times* sports section led with full front page devoted to Shearer's remarkable twelve minutes, and opened with the words: 'How fitting that this match was sponsored by *Viz*, the comic that is home to Billy the Fish ...?'

Chris and I both have it framed.

The grouchy young man and the Welshman

From the moment I saw the fifteen-year-old Alex Collier's work, sent to us by his teachers, I was instantly struck, not only by the extremely high standard of his drawings and the very natural quality of his artwork, but also by his ability to construct a story and tell it very well. One of the first things I noticed was that he had fantastic punchlines on his cartoons, and his strips were very complete for such a young lad. They weren't the pitifully drawn half-baked garbage that we were used to dealing with. Terrible child-like contributions arrived at the office on a daily basis and were usually penned by people much older than Alex. His work was drawn and laid out properly, as if done by a professional. Chris was impressed enough to agree with my suggestion that we take Alex on for work experience, despite our previous work experience experiences not being good.

As soon as his work experience was finished I felt it would be important to keep tabs on this young talent. I saw in him the potential to be the future young gun of *Viz*. Alex was keen to come to the office whenever we'd have him, so he began to help out at deadline times. From the moment he arrived it was apparent that he was going to be an easy lad to get on with. He was intelligent and very hard working. By the time he left school we were able to tell him that if a job at *Viz* was what he wanted, there was one waiting for him. If he wanted to go to university, the job would be available on his return. He thought about for about a minute and came to work for us straight away.

From quite early on I felt some responsibility in terms of looking after Alex and mentoring him. We got on very well together. Of all the people who had worked at *Viz* over the years he was the most like me. I didn't stop being impressed by his talents, and to this day it still sickens me how good he is. The big bastard.

We worked closely together on *Viz* and soon effectively became writing partners on the likes of Sid the Sexist. As Geordies we were very familiar with the pub culture, and we both spent time in Newcastle city centre and were able to report accurately on the stereotypes the strip portrays. We would pick each other's brains on Geordie character ideas, with Alex creating his track-suited chavette Tasha Slappa and his rodent-like teenage thief Rat Boy.

Alex's attitude was spot on. He was sufficiently silly and anarchic not only to fit in, but to make me feel less of an extrovert in a room full of introverts. On receiving his first royalty cheque we wandered up to the bank together. I was at the next cashier to Alex when I heard his cashier, presumably preparing to set him up with a pensions advisor or some such clap-trap, ask, 'Do you have any plans for the money?'

Alex replied without delay, 'I'm going to spend it on sweets and prostitutes.'

When I stopped laughing I asked if he minded me using the line the next time I was hit with the same question. He didn't object and I've used it many times since.

Alex told me recently that he'd used the *Viz* interview in *Comedy Review* magazine as 'research' before coming to meet us for his work experience interview. He said it had been a real help because the article had covered our personalities very well. Clever lad.

Around the same time as Alex arriving, Davey Jones relocated to Newcastle and joined us in the office. Davey was the long-time Welsh contributor of all the best and most mentallest things that have ever been in *Viz*, such as Rotating Chin Men, The Vibrating Bum-Faced Goats, Woodlouse School and regulars Roger Irrelevant, Gilbert Ratchet and Tinribs. He is also the only man ever to make me genuinely fall off a seat laughing, which he achieved with There Goes My Knighthood with Donald Sinden, which I saw for the first time in an airport lounge on my return from holiday. I was waiting to change flights at Gatwick, saw the comic in a shop and wanted to see how it looked, as I'd set off as the deadline approached. I was flicking through it and found the strip, was in tears in seconds, and became quite incapable as I read on, not noticing that I was slipping sideways off the seat. I landed on the floor with a jolt, but I still couldn't stop laughing at the image of Donald Sinden trying wank a bee out of the end of his cock in front of the Queen. I do wonder of any of the curious onlookers were aware I was one of the editors of the magazine I was convulsing over, and if so, did they think I was a twat?

Davey took a slightly different role in the writing sessions. When preparing his own cartoons he just made a series of notes rather than a script, and then wrote his final script alone. With Davey being a quiet lad, I took it upon myself to protect him

239

from office ribbings by pasting a giant blow up of an anti-Vietnam demonstration in the 1960s on the wall behind his desk. The protesters were marching against army conscription and were carrying giant placards, encouraging the government not to force the Monkees' frontman to join up: the placards read 'LEAVE DAVY JONES ALONE!'

In the spirit of togetherness in our new workroom, Chris proposed a poetry competition in which all the writers could take part. We each wrote a poem, which had to be devoted to a hideous tea trolley that stood in the office, having been bought months earlier as a comedy gift. The competition would be judged by the girls. When all the entries were presented, Chris was very confident that he would win. He didn't. I won and I pinned my winning entry, 'Golden Trolley of Love', on the notice board with 'WINNER' written all over it. Chris was not well pleased and spent the next few days making references to the unfairness of the judging.

M27 ... Free bacon sandwich

The day Kevin Keegan mysteriously walked out of the Newcastle job in 1998 I was asked on to the BBC News channel to discuss his resignation and later to Channel Five's appalling late-night televised sports phone-in *Under the Moon*, hosted by fat bespectacled presenter Danny Kelly. The show was scheduled to be broadcast from a pub called The Ayresome Park in Middlesbrough, which would be full of members of an official supporters' club. On hearing the shock news from St James', Channel Five invited me down with Micky Davidson and Phil Dangermouse to vocalise Newcastle fans' opinions in light of Keegan's walkout. The filming took place after the pub had closed and the club members welcomed us with open arms into their fold just before closing time. During the remaining minutes that the pub was open, all three of us were pinned to the bar by a drunken Boro fan. On realising we were Newcastle supporters there to discuss Keegan's position, he informed us, 'Now Keveen Keegan. Keveen Keegan. Let me tell youse boys summut ... I work at the froot an' veg maarket in Redcar ... ye see ... now what eet eez, eez, if ya work at the froot an' veg maarket in Redcar ... if ya work nights, right, if ya work nights ... at the froot an' veg maarket in Redcar ... an' I do, right ... ya gerra free bacon sandweech.'

This was just one of those moments from which there's no escape.

He went on, 'Now, the bloke who makes the free bacon sandweeches, y'see he knows, y'see ... he knows ... he knows a few things ... he hears things, y'see ...on the M27 ... think about it, think about it ... did th' tek eez car? ... NO! Did th' tek eez money? ... NO! Think about it ...'

I vaguely understood the M27 reference. Keegan had once been attacked whilst sleeping in his car. Our jovial informative sports correspondent continued, 'Why? Eh? ... Why? ... Think about eet ... Puneeshment beatin'. Y'see? Y'see? And why? ... And I know, cuz of the free bacon sandweeches ... Keveen Keegan is a pee-doh-file! ... puneeshment beatin', y'see."

I honestly don't know why investigative journalists bother when they could just get it all from the man who makes the free bacon sandwiches at Redcar fruit and veg market.

It eventually came to light that our new best friend wasn't with the supporters' club. They thought he was with us and vice versa. He was duly ejected. Surprisingly, none of his revelations proved to be true. Remarkable, when you consider the reputation of his source. The only truth was that the bacon sarnies were free.

Musical drawing boards ... again

Presumably not inspired by the productivity of our trip to Huntsham Court, Chris decided that a good idea would be to relocate to a posh country hotel to write each comic's main body of work. He selected Linden Hall, a hotel in which we'd had a couple of Christmas parties. It was a beautiful location about halfway between Newcastle and Chris's house in Northumberland, so was an ideal compromise for commuting. I got to drive my Mini Cooper S up there, which was lovely, as it's a nice drive from the city and I didn't usually get a chance to drive during the day, except on weekends, which were invariably occupied with work on the house.

As an experiment it was ok: it lasted for a two, maybe three, issues. It was more pleasant than being stuck in an office, but I think on reflection its real purpose might have been Chris trying

241

to find a route back into his enthusiasm about working on the comic.

Chris's fragile temperament came into play quite a lot as the months became years in the new office. One day he left a note attached to my pushbike, explaining that there was no room for it in the office and I would have to chain it in the car park. I wasn't the only person mystified by this bizarre and seemingly random officious memo, as the office was absolutely vast. Andy came to the rescue, allowing me to put it in his room.

By the mid 1990s Chris was hardly drawing any cartoons, having once supplied the majority of stalwart *Viz* strips himself. Even in *Viz*'s infancy he could produce more cartoons than Jim and me put together. When we were on the critical rise to national success his output was astounding, but now his interest in drawing seemed to have waned. He had passed on most of his top characters to be drawn by others: Billy the Fish and Mrs Brady went to Thorpy; Roger Mellie and Biffa Bacon to Graham. I'd also occasionally do Biffa.

Our drawing studio was an extension to the main building, standing on pillars above the side road to the car park. Although it was light and airy, it was exposed to the weather from the front and back, from below and above, making it seriously cold in comparison to the rest of the office space. Our game of musical drawing boards took another spin and we moved our drawing studio into Andy's room, identical in size, but much warmer. Andy took on bigger offices in a vacant suite, right next door.

Our plan was to return to square one. Chris would have his place in the same room as us, rather than in a separate office, and would be more involved in things again. He didn't seem to want to draw any more, but we felt that being in the same room as us his ideas would enhance our work and vice versa, a morale boost being the underlying target.

We moved into our new studio, which despite being only a few yards away was altogether more pleasant. There was a tree just outside our front windows and we were right next to the reception desk, and we took down a partition wall in order to join reception and the studio together. It was a real lift for everyone, being together – or so we thought.

After what seemed like no time at all, in an incident uncannily like the one almost ten years earlier, a joiner arrived

242

unannounced and began to erect a glass and timber partition between our drawing boards and Chris's desk. Our vision of a united *Viz* team was extinguished before it had even caught fire.

Editor edits himself out

His new isolation booth erected, Chris began to arrive later and later in the day, and eventually on some days he wouldn't appear at all, this then advancing into absence for days on end without communication. We all just carried on. We got used to working in the writing sessions without him and before long Chris's only real contributions were written articles. He would also edit the Letterbocks contributions from readers, and the letters page grew and grew in size, seemingly as he lost interest in creating work of his own. This one- or two-page section had now grown to as many as six pages and there was concern amongst the rest of us that the stronger contributions were being spread too thinly amongst some pretty average stuff.

Chris had been in a low state for some time, that had been obvious, but soon it became official. After a prolonged period of absence from work, Dolores broke the news that he was in a state of depression and was unable to face coming in.

I knew what this was like, having gone through it myself a couple of times, and in fact it runs right through the family. Both Steve and Dad had also suffered badly from bouts of depression.

We now faced the challenge of putting the first issue of *Viz* together without contribution from Chris. It was a challenge we all relished. Chris had, due to his low state of wellbeing, been a negative influence in the previous months.

One thing that's guaranteed when spending any length of time with Chris is that negativity will creep in. If he's in a good mood he uses his negativity in his humour; if he's in a bad mood it takes him over and affects those around him badly. Office morale had often suffered at the hands of his apparent will to see the place run like a government department: he seemed to want us to wear sullen faces and he loved creating unnecessary paperwork. I've always thought his time at the DHSS was his model for how an office should be run.

A year or two before we moved into the new studio he'd plastered photocopied notices around the office reading 'Think before you ink. Is that cartoon funny? If it fails, it costs us sales.' This was presumably an assault on someone's work, perhaps everyone's. Rather than discussing whatever issues were arising from the comic's content, as one might expect an editor to do, he posted blunt, indecipherable notices on the walls. No one dared question his reasoning for fear of further negative response. The net result of all this was a drastic drop in office morale.

Facing working without Chris on an issue wasn't really daunting for us, as we'd each worked on *Viz* for at least fifteen years and we'd each done all the jobs involved: writing, drawing, photography and layout. John Brown, however, who had never seen the day-to-day running of the comic, hit the panic button. I assume he must have thought Chris was responsible for all the humour in *Viz*. Quite what he thought the rest of us did, I have no idea, but he genuinely thought *Viz* would disappear without trace without Chris involved. We pointed out that Chris had had little involvement for some time now, but he didn't sway. He had kittens coming out of his arse at a rate of knots.

Even when we completed production of the first issue without Chris, John still wasn't convinced, calling in a high-profile publishing industry 'face' as a consultant to advise us. We ignored his consultant's every word and got on with writing our fart jokes, as usual.

Chris was in theory due to come back to work with us, but as time passed it became clearer and clearer that his heart wasn't in it any more. There was one last attempt at a new start with Chris. We left Crestina House and set up in an office in Milburn House, a beautiful old art nouveau shipping building, built in 1905, on Dean Street in the city centre. We paused for reflection on our last moments in Crestina House, looking around the rooms and remembering all the great times we'd had in them. Graham asked us to stop for a moment and appreciate the quality of the somewhat over-engineered shelf he'd built and fixed to the wall to house a now-redundant waxing machine, used for coating the backs of layout pages with a waxy glue.

'Look at that. I'm proud of that,' he declared happily. 'It's as solid as rock, that is!' he continued as he sat himself on the shelf

244

and began to bounce his stocky frame in a defiant show of the quality of his woodwork. 'Solid as a fuckin' rock.'

As the last word passed his lips, the plaster to which the shelf was fixed suffered a structural collapse. Graham was instantly deposited on the floor, very heavily, in a cloud of plaster dust. He was still sitting partly on his shelf, which was also on the floor, having remained intact – as he said, as solid as a rock

8

Fulchester United At Last

In Milburn House we had windows overlooking the churchyard
of St Nicholas Cathedral. It was really very grand by comparison
with our previous offices. We only had two main rooms, a
drawing studio and a writing room, but there was a small kitchen
and an area between the two that acted as a waiting and sand-
wich-munching room. The city centre was a whole new experience. We'd always been on the edge of town, but away from its
drunkenly erratic heartbeat. In the day it was bustling and bright
and at night it was 'colourful'. It felt good being in the middle of
everything. No matter how much of a placebo it is, it feels like
you're more connected with goings-on.

Chris, having always wanted a city centre office, but never
having had one, didn't come to work with us in Milburn House.
His time on *Viz* was over.

Chris brought his communication skills to the fore for the final
time at *Viz*, as by chance we read a newspaper interview he'd
given, saying he'd left. This was the first any of us had heard. He
was reported in the article as saying that the magazine would
only last another year. Eleven years later, it is still selling in
numbers to grab headlines.

After Chris's departure became official we had to go through a
very long-winded, costly and painful process to have the contract
for creating *Viz* rewritten to name those of us who were now in
sole charge of content. A compromise is said to be a situation in
which both sides are equally dissatisfied. I only hope all parties
were as dissatisfied as me. I suspect all the lawyers weren't.

The next couple of years were a breath of fresh air. We really did have a new start this time around. Sheila and Susan left us after many years of great service and Stevie now stepped into an up-rated job uniting parts of both their posts. A new person was sought to take over Sheila's magazine layout duties, and we pushed the boat out and found someone who was not only literate in digital layout, but was also a professional designer. Wayne Gamble, like Sheila before him, was taken on mainly on his character traits. He was a young, skinny, no-nonsense York-shireman with a passion for football and comedy and the look of a heroin-addicted car thief. He was easygoing and understood the ethic of *Viz* very well, thus getting a good grip of what was required of him straight away.

A few issues into work without Chris and we found a whole new life in the office: new building, new location, new staff and a whole new freedom from written chastisement for unsatisfactory bicycle location or tatty poke-holes in ringbound filing systems.

Working with Alex and Davey was great for me. Although I get on well with Graham and Thorpy and we're friends, they're family men and they spent any spare time they had with their children. Davey, Alex and I were child free and fond of a night out. Davey would drink with Alex and me if he was about in town, but Alex and I spent a lot of time together and became close friends. He took a flat just a few hundred yards from the office – an amazing attic apartment in the Northern Goldsmiths building on Westgate Road. Many a mental night out would begin or end there.

Alex had been a great fan of live comedy all his life and before coming to *Viz* he'd volunteered as a runner at the old Newcastle Comedy Festival, based at the Hyena, formerly The Jewish Mother, scene of the Kidney Machine and Silver-Tongued Cavalier Incidents. He was well connected there and threw both his eighteenth and twenty-first parties at the venue. The latter was a night he'll never forget.

Leaving the club, he decided pop back home before venturing to a late bar. Already mortal drunk, he approached the pedestrian crossing lights at Gallowgate. As a fairly athletic and lanky young man, he decided to take a short cut and vault the kerbside fence. As he leapt, he fell awkwardly, breaking his left wrist. On realising he was lying prone in the road, he got up and ran to the opposite barrier, leaping over that, too. Once again, he landed awkwardly, breaking his right wrist. He was so drunk he didn't feel the pain and continued to enjoy his night out.

The next day, with a deadline approaching, he walked into the office with both of his lower arms in plaster. On the upside, his right one wasn't as bad and the pot was removable, so he was able to struggle on with work. Also, the waitress in the café we went to for lunch, on seeing he had both his hands in plaster, offered to wank him off. He didn't accept the offer.

Murphy's law

In the spring of 1999 *Viz* received an invitation from the legendary Kilkenny Cat Laughs Comedy Festival in Ireland to supply *Viz* artwork for an exhibition in a pub the festival had acquired. We were also invited, so Davey, Stevie and I packed our toothbrushes.

It was my first visit to Ireland and I absolutely loved every minute of it. When we got to Kilkenny both the hospitality and the comedy were brilliant. I cannot recommend the Cat Laughs enough. I met some upcoming comics, including Peter Kay and Johnny Vegas, and I was also delighted to meet Graham Linehan and Pauline McLynn. Graham was one of the writers of *Father Ted* and Pauline played Mrs Doyle. Graham's writing partner on *Father Ted*, Arthur Mathews, was a one-time contributor to *Viz* in the mid 1980s, writing a piece called 'How to Improve Your Golf After the Bomb'. At around the same time a cartoon called 'Jelly Head', about a young girl whose brain had been replaced with a lime jelly, was printed. It was the work of a young man called Charlie Higson, who most of you will know from his brilliant work on *The Fast Show*, amongst others.

Every building in the whole town seemed to be alive with comedy and after the day's entertainment there was live music in our hotel. The house band were old Irish pros and they made an announcement as they got started that anyone with any musical abilities was welcome to join them on stage. It was a proper Irish knees-up. I'd recently played the piano at my friends Bondy and Emma's wedding. I'd not been playing long, and their wedding reception was what's known in northern clubs as a 'go as you please' – everyone being welcome to get up and perform – so it wasn't like I was Dame Kiri Te Kanawa singing for Prince Charles and Her Royal Highness Lady Princess Diana Spencer of Hearts. It hadn't been a pressure gig. It occurred to me that now would be another great opportunity to display my new-found skills, so I told the band I'd like to play and sing 'Love Me Tender', as I'd done at the wedding.

There was a bit of a waiting list, with lots of people wanting to get up and perform before me, so I had to hang around for over an hour, and the standard was pretty high. Then my time came. The band's leader announced, 'And now Simon's going to take things down a little bit, a change of pace, a great love song – ladies and gentlemen, Simon singing "Love Me Tender".'

It suddenly dawned on me that the pressure was on. He'd given me a huge build-up. I placed my hands on the keyboard and was horrified to discover the keys weren't weighted. I'd only ever played weighted keys and these lightweight plastic things felt all wrong. I soldiered on and went to place my hands down to make the first chord. As I looked at the keyboard I couldn't work out where to put my fingers. I took stock for a moment. I was sure it was just nerves. I looked again and for the second time I didn't seem to know how to form the chord. Some of the positions were there, but some of my fingers were lost. I braved it and played what I thought was the opening chord of the introduction. I sounded fucking atrocious. I apologised into the mic, saying I'd be on line any moment. I tried again, another comedy chord, then the next time I got it right, but three chords in I hit another stinker. I apologised again and pushed on, this time getting almost to the vocals before a fuck up. I was succeeding by degrees and continued delivering the occasional apology until I'd manage to play the entire introduction to an acceptable standard. I then suddenly realised I had to sing. In a rush to get my mouth to the mic, I sang the worst bum note you could imagine. I began the song all over again. This time I proceeded well enough to get as far as the third line of vocals before forgetting the words. I stopped playing and took a breath, and as I did so I suddenly had a vision flash before my eyes: I saw my own hands in front of me and they were repeatedly passing Murphy's beer tokens to numerous bar staff at different venues.

It dawned on me that this vision was formed of many genuine moments from my day. I'd been given a number of free beer tokens, as had Stevie, who doesn't drink, so I'd had hers as well. I'd been on the piss all day long and for some reason I hadn't noticed. It certainly explained the piano-playing issues.

I looked at the keyboard for a moment and said 'Fuck it' into the mic. I began playing 'Molly Malone', a traditional Irish song, and the band all joined in, but it wasn't long before I fucked up totally and it all fell apart. I then started to bash out a twelve-bar blues. The band joined in again, but predictably enough, it all went to pot. I left the stage in shame, but not before I apologised to the crowd and the band, announcing over the PA that I was 'obviously fuckin' pissed'.

This Kilkenny Piano Fiasco is a story that by rights should have me waking in a cold sweat to this day. I can only bring myself to tell it here and laugh about it because I made it my mission to redeem myself the next night, which I did, if I say so myself, in some style. Firstly, I stayed well away from the drink, and secondly, I steered well clear of the piano. I had to get back on the horse, though, so I went for a much safer option: I assured the band I was sober and asked them to simply jam a funk beat, over which I would rap. I explained that all they needed to do was change whatever they were playing when I signalled a chorus, and as long as the tempo was the same, I could cope. I sang the 'Geordie Rap', a song I'd performed many times. On this occasion, free of drink, I got all the words right and the band were magnificent. The crowd danced, I got a huge round of applause, and I could safely proceed with the rest of my life, the piano incident buried.

The Wheel of Fart Tunes

In 1999 *Viz* celebrated its twentieth birthday and we put a big exhibition together to mark it, showing in both London and Newcastle. In our now-vacant offices at Crestina House, Steve, utilising his animatronics skills, created the exhibits for the show. The theme was interaction and the exhibits were built to look and work like old-fashioned penny arcade machines.

There was the Johnny Fartpants Wheel of Fart Tunes, in which, under a life-sized model of Johnny, visitors spun a segmented wheel, each division representing a country. When the wheel stopped, Johnny farted the national anthem of the selected country.

The Sid the Sexist I Speak Your Tits Machine was, not surprisingly, based on a 'speak your weight' machine. The visitor stood on the 'scales' and a full-sized Sid made groping gestures with his hands, then made a vocal announcement passing judgement on the breasts of the person.

There was a ride-on vibrating Bum-Faced Goat, like the Noddy cars found in supermarket doorways. This one didn't actually work, and Steve built it to look like it had gone horribly wrong, the mechanics all hanging out of a badly burnt machine, which appeared to have exploded, complete with a CIS-style masking-tape outline of a child's body. The effect was completed by the exhibit being fenced off with police cordon tape.

On first seeing the goat piece, John Brown panicked and asked someone to clear it all up. 'My God! What has happened here?' John is always good value for an unintentional laugh.

There was also a town model of Fulchester on which visitors pressed buttons and, for instance, Eight Ace's second home, Mr Patel's shop, would light up.

The exhibition was a great success and at the Newcastle event the buffet was supplied by Abdul Latif, Lord of Harpole, and guest of honour was Rod Griffiths, who had inspired the creation of Roger Mellie.

During the exhibition's time in London we had an invite to appear on *The Big Breakfast*. As young Alex was more media friendly than Thorpy, Graham or Davey, i.e. he speaks a lot and is animated, it was decided he would come on the show with me. We were collected from The Groucho at some frankly fucking stupid hour, having to be at the studio for around 5am.

We were shown into a dressing room and two researchers went through the questions we'd be asked. The questions were pretty predictable, which was annoying in itself, but then they showed us our answers. That's right: our *answers*. They said the answers were just put in the script to make things easier, and if we liked we could say anything we pleased. They then stressed that

251

'anything' didn't include swearing, and this was something that was taken very seriously. They went on to mention that Mohamed Al-Fayed had said 'shit' the previous week, which had in itself then hit the fan. They bombarded us with repeated insistences that we mustn't swear until I was ready to punch one of them. I was getting very annoyed at being treated like a child.

We sat watching Richard Bacon doing his outside broadcast from some cold and grey miserable-looking street somewhere, surrounded by unfeasibly cheerful families preparing for their working days of repetition and drudgery.

I felt awful. Very often Alex and I would have only just been going to bed at this time. Here we were, trying to get psyched up to be articulate and sell, sell, *sell* our exhibition. I hated breakfast telly, its incessant, unwarranted cheerfulness being wrong on so many levels.

One of the researchers reappeared with a footnote about our interview. We mustn't wear any branded clothing. Broadcasting regulations. She pointed at my sweatshirt's Fred Perry logo.

'You aren't going to be wearing that, are you? Have you got anything else?'

The rudeness of many London-based people who work in television has always got my goat, and this was no exception. I said that I'd be wearing another shirt for the show. It had a small Ben Sherman tag on it, but I could cover that with my *Big Breakfast* name tag. Agreement was reached. She left again.

As we sat watching Bacon interviewing people I noticed he was wearing an identical top to the one I had on: a Fred Perry sweatshirt. I couldn't believe it after the fuss they'd made about mine. Then, speaking to him from the studio, Liza Tarbuck said, 'Ooh you've got that same shirt on again today. You'll have to tell them to get you a new one!'

My blood was boiling. Obviously, the 'celebs' had very different rules from us, seemingly not controlled by 'broadcasting regulations'.

Minutes later we were in the middle of our interview, live on air, at around 7.30 in the bloody morning. Johnny Vaughn, a big *Viz* fan, asked Alex a question about legal problems revolving around the first character he'd done for *Viz*. In replying, Alex almost accidentally slipped out the name of the sportswear giant

252

that had claimed he'd cost them £30,000 of sales. I threw my hand across his mouth and declared, 'I think our lawyer just browned his trousers.'

Tarbuck and Vaughn looked at me, aghast. They seemed unable to respond.

'Don't worry,' I said, 'at least I didn't say "shit". Your researchers were just telling me that Mohamed Al-Fayed said "shit" last week. And another thing I've done right is I've covered up the Ben Sherman logo on my shirt: earlier I'd been wearing the same Fred Perry that Richard Bacon's got on. Mind, I see you're wearing Ralph Lauren – I've noticed you always wear the Ralph Lauren logo.'

The studio went into a blind panic. The show went to ads. We were hastily 'escorted' to our dressing room, in which we were locked, until a taxi came to take us away. We sat feeling pretty miserable about the whole experience. It wasn't until we got talking with the taxi driver as we got back into central London that I realised what I'd done.

'Naaah,' he said, 'that's just what you *want* to have of done, mate. The bloke off *Viz* swearing and kicking a few arses. That's what you want, mate.'

Normally, I'd associate cabbies with talking utter shit, but on this occasion I was refreshed by the imparted wisdom.

Dawn of the porn

As *Viz* moved into the new millennium, John Brown decided to sell our publishing contract to a new company. John was now working mainly on 'contract' publishing – the sort of magazines that no one actually buys, like in-house store magazines for Ikea. I personally thought it was sad that John, who'd really pushed *Viz* in the early years of JBP, was letting the deal go elsewhere, but he thought it was time for a younger company with a fresher outlook to come in and give the publishing side of *Viz* a boost. So along came I Feel Good Limited.

At this time there was an unfortunate misunderstanding in the press. Someone read on the stock exchange that JBP had sold the rights to publish *Viz* and two other titles to IFG, and this was misconstrued by the reporter as meaning that Chris and I had sold

253

Viz. It wasn't the first time this had happened – we were also reported as selling *Viz* to Richard Branston when a distribution contract changed hands years earlier. About twice a week, in pubs and in public generally, I have to field questions about why I decided to sell *Viz*. Of course, with lazy reporters using the internet for their research, and so many stories having been printed based on the original misunderstanding, it's become a self-perpetuating urban myth.

Unfortunately, the shot in the arm that was given to *Viz* by the new company seemed mainly to involve them getting fuckwits to tell us that our objection to pornography adverts was unreasonable, saying it would not affect anyone's perception of the product. I explained that in twenty-one years of working on *Viz* the only person I listened to on judgements of that magnitude was me, and every sinew in my body knew it was wrong for *Viz* to carry porn ads. They then started to say it was 'fine' for *Viz* to carry ads for the *Sunday Sport*, which obviously it wasn't.

They sent a hugely uncharismatic man called Mike Dash to see us once a quarter or so. He would sit in the writing room and read out the gloomy sales figures, detailing just how many sales we'd lost in particular types of retailing, and what the projected additional loss of sales would be at certain points if the trend were to continue. He did all of this whilst eating egg sandwiches. The vision of gloomy sales predictions emitted in a monotone by a mouth smeared with egg mayonnaise is an image I'll have trouble ever erasing from my consciousness.

Mike's great move in the world of publishing was to write a book on tulips. On hearing about this I told him I wasn't aware he was a plant lover. He explained that he wasn't – he'd just noticed that tulips were one of the most popular flowers, gardening books sold well, and there was not currently a book about tulips in print. He'd written a book on a subject that wasn't close to his heart simply because he'd spotted a gap in the market.

It seemed that Mike's reasons for being in publishing and mine were poles apart.

Huw had married Sandra, a beautiful girl from Belgrade who we both knew through Anne. It was lovely that two of my good friends had got together and I visited them most days on my way home from work.

One afternoon Huw had picked up a copy of *Viz* for the first time in a couple of years. He was very annoyed about the porn ads and went into a lecture about its integrity being affected. I was already more than aware of the problem, but hearing what sounded like my very own words coming from a friend I had so much respect for was close to being the final straw.

With this and the egg sandwich nightmares hanging over me, I longed for the days of the public school twat.

Trouble brewing

Despite the gloomy predictions of the vibrant young Mike Dash, we still managed to produce some of the best work *Viz* has ever printed. *Viz* might not have been new anymore, and existed in a world quite different from the one it was born in, but it was still as funny as fuck.

I took a photo for a spoof ad in the cathedral yard. It showed two tramps sitting shivering on a park bench, wrapped in clothes stuffed with newspaper. In the foreground of the image was a third tramp, happily skipping past, carrying a can of Special Brew, a warm orange glow surrounded his body, like in the old Ready Brek adverts on TV. The caption read 'Central Heating for Tramps'.

We had a very good relationship with Caroline, the *Viz* libel lawyer, and I phoned her and asked if she was giving clearance for the ad.

'Oh, yes, no problem,' she assured me.

'Are you sure about that?' I asked.

'Yes, yes,' she said. 'Let's face it, Simon, Carlsberg Special Brew could hardly deny that their core drinker is a tramp.'

I was delighted, not only with her giving the clearance for what I thought was one of my funniest pieces of work, but also for the assuring and entertaining words of a trained legal professional that I knew I could tell people about for years to come.

However, the story doesn't end there. About a fortnight later I took a call from a lawyer whose company represented Carlsberg. He regretted to inform me that an action was being prepared against us as a result of us publishing the Special Brew ad. My heart sank. Caroline had seemed so confident, and her words had already become one of my favourite pub anecdotes.

255

The lawyer on the phone continued, 'Well Mr Donald, I will tell you, off the record, that as far as I'm concerned, and I have mentioned this to the team putting this case together, in my opinion this is an action which is doomed to failure.'

I felt a certain amount of relief. I probed a little. 'If we're off the record, could you say why you think that?'

'Well, let's face it, Mr Donald,' he continued. 'Carlsberg Special Brew could hardly deny that their core drinker is a tramp.'

I nearly dropped the phone. When I eventually hung up I was laughing that much that it must have been five minutes before I could manage to compose myself and tell everyone in the office what had happened. We didn't hear from them again.

The birth of Bingo

Alex and I began to hang around with a DJ called Catboy, real name Simon Smedley. He first came to our attention when he began to appear on Metro Radio in the middle of the night. He clearly had a bit of a free reign, as like those DJs on the Metro swing shift before him he knew there was only the night staff at Greggs listening. He did a hilariously simple feature called 'The Swearing Milkman', and it immediately grabbed our attention. He had a knack for comedy and a personality that made for good radio. After we'd befriended this slightly mad, very sharp-witted Yorkshireman, we discovered he'd got into radio when one of his friends bumped into a producer in a club one night. The producer was pulling his hair out, as one of his DJs had walked out unexpectedly. Catboy's friend introduced Catboy as a top DJ who happened to be looking for a new station.

Catboy started to grab quite a bit of attention at Metro and he was soon asked to fill in for the legendary Alan Robson on the Night Owls programme. He became quite nervous about the prospect of being on air and none of Robson's callers wanting to ring him. He was waking up with nightmares about having to talk for three hours without any callers, so he asked if Alex and I would ring in and just chat, so he knew he would at least get some phone-in action.

As soon as he made the suggestion I knew what to do. As early as 1983 I'd been doing a character piece at parties based on something Phil Dangermouse had once said. We were travelling

256

to a caravan park near York on a coach and he noticed the tourists sitting behind us were quietly discussing our Geordie accents. Phil seamlessly cranked up the accent and began to ask me if I thought trains could go faster than busses because they had more wheels. In 1988 I once phoned Night Owls' Alan Robson while in character. I didn't have a name for the character then, I was just Simon from Heaton on air, but with the help of an insider manning the phones we seemingly convinced Alan that I really was of monumentally limited intelligence.

With Catboy's turn at the Night Owls controls the chance came to develop the 'Why do trains go faster?' character. I called the show from the *Viz* office as we worked late one night. I scribbled down a few topics to talk about and waited to be put on air. Julie and I had just got a dog from the rescue centre in Benton and we'd called him Bingo. Needing to think of a character name in a hurry, I came up with Bingo from Benton.

Over the course of two weeks Bingo called the show a number of times, creating outrage with some listeners who believed his ignorant and twisted drunken philosophy and carefree tales of domestic abuse and animal cruelty to be real. Others called to say he was the funniest thing they'd ever heard. He was the Marmite of Metro Radio.

Weller I never

Angie Jenkison had progressed from hairdressing to the music industry, a path she had taken through styling the hair of the likes of Phil Lynott of Thin Lizzy. She worked her way up the job ladder in recording studios, eventually working for Sanctuary Records, before moving into music management. During her time in studios, Paul Weller began to use one of her rehearsal spaces. Much of his material after launching his solo career, at the beginning of the 1990s, was first played here. Angie became friends with Weller and on many occasions offered me the chance to meet him. I really didn't feel comfortable with this idea, and I politely turned her offers down. I also turned down other offers from her to meet other heroes of mine, most notably John Entwistle.

My inexplicable lack of willingness to meet my heroes at this time tumbled down on me the day I was called by Wayne from

Viz, who told me that he had just heard of John Entwistle's sudden death. I contacted Angie immediately by text message, offering my condolences, not realising that I was the one to bring her the news of the death of her friend and my hero.

John Entwistle's death was tragic, and it brought upon me a realisation that I was wasting opportunities in my own life. The opportunity I had my hands to meet this delightfully eccentric man had passed me by, and that brought on a serious realisation in me that life is too short to waste such chances. I made a vow to myself that from that moment on that I would never turn down a chance to meet one of my heroes. In thinking about it I realised that, regardless of how awkward any potential meeting may be, I had to throw away any insecurities, suspicions and concerns about it all being a bit too 'showbiz' and put aside any of my friends' feelings of jealousy. I knew I'd also have to toughen myself up to accusations of namedropping. I didn't want to lose another chance to meet somebody special to me.

I used to pay for my tickets to see Paul Weller at the City Hall and the Ice Rink at Whitley Bay. Now I decided to take Angie up on her offers of free guest passes, with the added incentive, as if one was needed, of an after-show backstage party. I had already bought tickets to see Weller at Newcastle Arena in 2002. Angie had been in touch asking, as she often did, if I was going to come and meet Paul after the gig. For the first time, I accepted the offer. At the end of the show Julie and I had to meet Angie in order to be escorted back stage. I assumed that what would happen would be something like this: we would be led to a room somewhere where there would be dozens of people. Paul Weller might be visible somewhere, chatting to all and sundry, maybe mingling, if you will, and if we were lucky we may get a brief introduction and a shake of the hand. I couldn't believe what actually did happen. When Angie knocked on the door, instead of the burly security guard, suited Newcastle Arena employee or roadie dressed in three-quarter-length shorts and boots I had been expecting, it was actually Paul Weller himself that answered. He greeted Angie with a hug and a kiss, then looked at me and said, 'You must be Simon. I've been looking forward to meeting you. I've heard a lot about you.'

That thing happened in my head, like that Steven Spielberg focus trick where everything seems to suddenly go down a tunnel without actually moving at tall.

He continued, 'Then you must be Julie? Come in, come in!'

He beckoned us into the room. There was nobody inside except Paul and the rest of his band.

'Let me get you all a drink, what would you like?'

He attended to Angie first, and then Julie.

'Simon. What can I get you? Do you want a beer?'

He gestured towards some plastic crates filled with cans of Red Stripe and ice, which sat on the floor underneath a table, on top of which were sandwiches, crisps, fruit and so on.

'Red Stripe, is that okay? Would you like a glass with that?'

I couldn't believe what I was witnessing. Small gestures like this go a hell of a long way. Just being polite for, instance, being attentive, showing an interest in people: these things mean so much in an industry where losing your grip on reality seems to be the accepted norm. It was instantly apparent that Paul was a very down-to-earth bloke.

He pulled out a packet of Benson & Hedges, which he opened and offered to me. 'You wanna fag?'

I declined, but thanked him for the offer.

I didn't know which was harder to believe: the fact that I was here at all, or the fact that he was being so kind.

'So, you're Angie's cousin?' he asked.

This was news to me. Although Angie and I had sat next to one another at school, no mention of us being cousins had ever arisen. Paul's question did bring to mind an awkward moment a few years earlier when Angie had told me that Paul Weller was her cousin. I had wondered at the time why she had never mentioned this back in Mr Dixon's art class.

This moment aside, the conversation with Paul was comfortable: he made it that way. Our chat quickly came around to John Otway and his recent chart success, brought about by a well-organised and shameless publicity campaign, fuelled by both Otway's own desire to have a second hit and by the fervent support of his remarkable hardcore fans. (Having scored a minor hit at Christmas in 1977, and having toured persistently ever since, John planned to have a hit on his fiftieth birthday. With the help of his insanely loyal following, he began a close-to-military

259

campaign to make his dream come true. Part of this involved getting a thousand of his fans singing as a choir on the B side of the single, recorded at Abbey Road. To the amazement of all involved, he reached chart position nine on the afternoon of his half century celebration.)

Paul asked many questions about John, including whether he still played with Wild Willy Barrett. I was curious about Weller's familiarity with him, so I asked, 'Do you know Otway?'

He replied, 'Oh yes. We used to support him with The Jam.'

I realised immediately that both had been Polydor artists at the time of Otway's first hit 'Cor Baby, That's Really Free' in 1977, the year in which The Jam were beginning to make waves.

Otway's hit had fatally being paired with the truly fantastic 'Beware of the Flowers 'Cause I'm Sure They're Going to Get You Yeah', which was supposed to be the follow-up single. The record company had somehow accidentally pressed it on the B-side, a mistake Otway claims, probably rightly, in his autobiography *Cor Baby That's Really Me*, did irreparable damage to his career.

Weller and I talked for a while about what a decent bloke John Otway is, Paul saying he hadn't seen him for many years. He asked me if I would pass on my regards the next time I saw him.

The conversation continued in a very friendly and relaxed fashion until suddenly, after a short pause, Weller exclaimed, 'Here. You once called me a cunt in *Viz*.'

I was genuinely taken aback. I couldn't for the life of me think why we'd called him a cunt. It was many weeks later when I realised what he must have been referring to. *Viz* had for a few months run a section on the letters page called Celebrity Cunt Hunt, in which readers accused celebrities of being cunts after meeting them in some random circumstance. I seemed to remember a reader was speaking to Weller while he was having a piss somewhere, and Paul had told him to fuck off. This would seem not to be the behaviour of a cunt, but more the behaviour of somebody who doesn't like people trying to strike up a conversation with him when he's trying to drain his spuds.

The spiky issue of whether or not I was guilty of calling Paul a cunt soon passed, we said our goodbyes and left him, dressed in an all-white parka, standing at the compound gates at the back of

Newcastle Arena, signing autographs for adoring, but no longer teenage, fans.

My overriding feeling was that Paul Weller was a remarkably likeable man who seemed to have time for everybody. I've heard a lot of second-hand rumours about rudeness, arrogance and so on, but as far as I can tell these accusations are either made by the press or are about him being rude to the press. I don't find it difficult to draw reasonable conclusions about this. If the press don't get what they want from somebody they will invariably shoot him or her down. Paul is not in the business of giving the press what they want, unless it happens to be what he wants to give. He is, and always has been, his own man.

The second time I met Weller was almost a year later, at Newcastle City Hall. After seeing one of the best performances I've ever seen from him, I was shown backstage and walked through the double doors into the main changing room. The room was full of people drinking, chatting, engaged in general party mingledge. I immediately saw Steve Cradock and began having a rabbit on with him. After a few seconds a can of Red Stripe appeared in front of my face. My eyes followed the arm that was holding it, only to see that it was Paul Weller himself. He had not only been good enough to fetch me a drink the instant he laid eyes on me, but had remembered my drink of choice from a year earlier. I'm told the band call him Memory Man.

Top trumped

In the office one day I took an unexpected call from Andy Wilman, ex-*Auto Express* and *Top Gear* magazine, for which in the first year of its life in the early 1990s I'd done a page of freelance cartoons for each issue. Andy had moved into the TV side of the *Top Gear* brand and was about to re-launch the show, which had mysteriously been axed despite being BBC2's most-watched programme. He asked if I'd be interested in a screen test for the revamped show, which was quite a surprise. I'm certainly a lover of cars and of driving, but I'm not a lover of Clarkson's politics, so the last thing I wanted was to appear to be a yes man for him. I went and did the screen test, for the experience, mainly. It was good fun, but I didn't say what they wanted to hear, and that was that. I wasn't going to compromise who I am in order to fit a show's remit – that's not me. The driving and presenting would have been incredible fun, but I couldn't have done all that chummy–matey agreement and staged banter.

I was told that in the auditions I finished in the top three, which by my reckoning puts me only a fanny hair's breadth from a rocket-propelled near-death experience.

I swear on this book

We'd been working on the *Profanisaurus* for some time now. This started life as 'Sweary Mary's Swearing Dictionary' on *Viz*'s original website and was an interactive section in which visitors could contribute their own swearwords and definitions. It hadn't been properly thought out and all contributions were published online without being vetted. The results were horrendous, the error was quickly spotted and it was taken down, but the seed was planted for a swearing dictionary. The project was renamed *Roger's Profanisaurus* as a nod to *Roget's Thesaurus*, but combining profanity and thesaurus to create a 'clever' new word, and of course tying Roget to Roger Mellie, who swears a lot.

The initial Profanisauri were cover-mounts on regular issues of the comic before being combined and enlarged in a single paperback volume. This was such as success that a hardback was proposed and a deal was struck with Macmillan, a proper right-big publishing house. I had the joyful task of designing the dust jacket for the book, and it really was a lovely job to undertake. The main image was a photograph of a typewriter on Roger Mellie's desk, with the book title on the sheet of paper in it. The front and back of the book's jacket would be comparatively clean, and the areas wrapped inside would reveal darker items amongst the clutter around Roger's typewriter: whisky, overflowing ashtray, hardcore pornographic playing cards and so on. The keys of the typewriter on the front of the jacket spelled out 'BOLLOCKS' and the gold-scripted type where the manufacturer's name should appear read 'The Ultimate SWEARING DICTIONARY'. There were bullet points under the book's title, written out by the typewriter, that claimed:

- The definitive reference volume of English obscenities
- Over 4,000 coarse and offensive words and phrases
- Ideal for use in the home, office and schoolroom
- Contains words like fuck and cunt

The word 'fuck' was half obscured by the typewriter ribbon, on which the word 'cunt' could be found by keen-eyed readers.

Having completed my design, I sent it off to IFG, who wanted to see it before it went to Macmillan. A young publishing genius rang me to say that he loved the cover, but there was one thing missing from it: 'It needs a sticker to advise of explicit content.'

I replied, 'Are you fucking joking?'

He assured me not.

I continued, 'It's a swearing dictionary.'

He was unmoved. 'I know, but it's to advise about the content. Everyone does it nowadays.'

I was getting annoyed. 'You want to put a warning on the front of a swearing dictionary to alert potential buyers that it contains swearing?'

'Yes,' he said. 'We think it'll sell more with a warning on the front.'

'What, you mean to the people who miss the words "The Ultimate SWEARING DICTIONARY" and "Over 4,000 coarse and offensive words and phrases"?'

Believe it or not, this matter had to be referred to his seniors before the idea was thrown away. For fuck's sake.

A Vegas wedding

The phone rang in the office one day and the unmistakable voice of Johnny Vegas was on the other end. I'd not seen or heard from him since the day I met him at Kilkenny three years earlier,

'Si, d'yu want to buy me weddin' photos for a quid?'

I didn't have to think about it much.

'Erm ... Yes. Is there a catch?'

'No. It's just that I could sell 'em to the papers or the magazines for money, but I think that'd be wrong, don't you?'

So the deal was struck in an instant. He duly sent us his pictures and they were printed in a cut-out-and-make celebrity wedding attendance kit. Johnny later ribbed me on many occasions, saying he'd never got his money, which is true, but he joked that we should go to the papers over it and claim that we'd settled out of court for 80p.

I was shocked to read in the *News of the Screws* after his divorce that his ex, Kitty, said his decision to sell their wedding photos to us was 'The first worrying sign of trying to control his new wife.' She went on to say, 'And I didn't get my share: he still owes me the 50p!'

I guess she doesn't know, it but she's actually owed 40p by me.

I played at St James' Park

My old friend Ciro from Beer Davies, the company that did PR for *Viz* in the comic's heyday, was involved in the organisation of annual charity football tournaments that took place at major football stadiums around England, known as the Music Industry Soccer Sixes.

In early spring 2003 Ciro got in touch to ask if I'd play in the next round, at St James' Park. I was stunned. He also asked if I could hook him up with any north-east celebrities who might also want to play. Newcastle being Newcastle, finding people who wanted to play on the pitch at St James' certainly wouldn't be a problem. Finding people who classified as 'celebrities' would be another matter altogether.

My first port of call was comedian Gavin Webster, an absolutely tremendous Geordie comedian who'd played football at a competitive level until comparatively recently, and, of course, was as keen as me to get on to that pitch. The only genuine 'celebrity' I could get for him was the bloke who plays the vicar in *Emmerdale*, a gentle and unassuming man who had never played football in his life. The poor cunt ended up on a team with Frank McAvennie, who spent the whole afternoon screaming abuse at him.

We arrived at St James' Park. It was surreal. Out of the blue, we were about to play a game of football on the actual pitch at St James' Park. Not just a kickabout, either, but a competitive game.

Gavin and I were directed to a kit room and told we were to play with an up-and-coming band called The Darkness. Everyone on the Soccer Sixes admin team seemed to have heard of them, but neither of us had. We were only introduced to the band when we walked on to the pitch for the warm-up. Straight away it was apparent that, amongst the ex-professional footballers, the shiny, well-groomed *Hollyoaks* stars and the page-three models with spray-on tans and inflatable tits, these boys didn't fit in. They were, in the main, a motley bunch of skinny, long-haired misfits, and, alarmingly, were smoking tabs on the pitch.

It wasn't long before we realised they were a down-to-earth, football-loving group of lads. They introduced themselves as Justin, Dan, Frankie and Terry. Ed, the drummer, didn't play football, but he was along, with a few others, to offer support from the stands. Terry was their driver, or so it said in the programme. A year later I discovered he didn't actually work with the band at all: he was just a friend, a civil servant apparently, who happened to be a good goalkeeper.

Apart from The Darkness and their goalkeeper Terry, the only person on our team, besides me and Gavin, was a young actor by the name of Marcus Patrick. We were told that Marcus was a regular in the aforementioned masturbation-joke teenage soap opera *Hollyoaks*. Master Patrick walked out on us to join Ralf Little's team before any of us had even kicked a ball.

The experience of appearing on the pitch at St James' was one of those events in life that are simply too difficult to take in at the time. I think it's not possible to be at all prepared for something as unique as fulfilling a lifelong ambition, something you never believed would come true.

The tournament itself didn't leave a truly indelible mark on my memory, the highpoint being a game against Blue. They were a boy band with a serious reputation in football tournaments, and it has to be said that they tore a strip off us in the game, but Justin's celebration after scoring our consolation goal was something to be witnessed. He stripped to the waist, revealing for the first time his skinny, tattooed torso, and waved his shirt around his head, helicopter fashion, as he ran the length of the touchline in front of a Gallowgate End packed with Blue fans. His exuberance was received by the previously delirious teenagers in total silence.

Having been knocked out in our quarter-final game, Gavin and I met with the rest of the team in the green room, a large hospitality suite in the main stand, overlooking the pitch. The room was a throng of B-list celebrities and their hangers on.

We sat and joined The Darkness lads and their girlfriends at a big table. They had all travelled from Lowestoft in a transit van, and were returning to East Anglia immediately after having a drink with us, as they couldn't afford to stay in a hotel in Newcastle. That's a round trip, in good driving conditions, without stops or hold-ups, of just under twelve hours. Around us the glamour models, soap actors, pop stars and media types all buzzed around one another like flies round shit. Without exception none of them buzzed past our table, and we found ourselves completely ignored by all and sundry. That suited me just fine.

The Ginger Song

The furthest I've travelled to see Newcastle play is Belgrade. When the draw was made for a Champions League game pitting Newcastle against Partizan Belgrade the chance was on to go and stay with (Hugh's wife) Sandra's family for a few days and attend the game. Her family are Red Star fans, Red Star being Partizan's arch rivals, and the teams are based only a few yards from each other in the centre of the city.

Sandra's brother Zoran and I went to the game together. With his sister being married to a Geordie and Partizan being his club's great rival, it was a perfect game for us both to enjoy.

I flew to Belgrade and was welcomed into the family's communist-era high-rise like I was part of the family. It was fascinating to see a city that had been popular with tourists only years earlier now trying to rebuild itself after a hugely destructive conflict. The scars of the war were visible in the city centre where areas of unrepaired bomb damage were very tangible reminders of how recent the war had been. It wasn't a pretty sight and no doubt the wounds of these recent troubles will take a long time to heal.

In Eastern Europe there is a huge passion for fervent support at football games and this is especially true with the younger men. There's a great tradition for all the fans to turn up long before the game and sing the club's songs for hours on the terraces, creating a fabulous atmosphere by the time the game kicks off. It's absolutely breathtaking. I think a page could be taken out of the

266

Eastern European book in order to rebuild the atmosphere in English stadiums. As well as the more obvious passion killer of the all-seater stadium – the seats – the excessive use of the modern high-quality PA systems to pump out loud music right up to the kick-off prevents fans from building their own atmosphere with songs and chants. Once the game begins the fans are on a mission to try and create a cauldron of support from a cold start.

Zoran and I walked the streets of the city to the ground feeling unbelievably conspicuous. We were the only two fair-haired people anywhere on the streets, his red and mine a mix of blonde and red. With the very unusual exception of Zoran, everyone in Belgrade has hair ranging from extremely dark brown to jet black. They also have olive skin, and we both have fair, freckled skin. We really stuck out like sore thumbs. By the time we got into our section of the traditional concrete terracing the entire ground was packed with Partizan fans, all in mid song and chant frenzy. It was a balmy night and as we walked out on to the steps I saw the ground was an open bowl with no roofing anywhere. The sides of our small section where they met the fenced-off areas of home supporters were lined with single files of police. The atmosphere was fantastic, but there was one thing missing – Newcastle fans. We were, quite literally, the only fans in the whole away section. Our arrival caused quite a stir amongst the home support, and as we took up a position sitting right in the middle of the terracing they were all chanting and waving pointed fingers at us. I had no idea what they were singing, but it wasn't difficult to guess. 'Your football team is not as good as ours and our team will score more goals and your mother sucks cocks in hell' ... something along those lines. I made a point of ignoring them and began to roll a cigarette. Zoran was clearly a bit edgy about it, so I engaged him in casual conversation as a diversion. After all, there was nothing we could do. I smiled and waved at them.

My tickets for the game had been bought through Newcastle's box office and the plan was that all fans would go to the game using their inclusive package deal, including hotel and travel. As I was staying with friends in Belgrade, I had made all my own arrangements, so Zoran and I were the only Newcastle fans not with the official party, who, shortly before kickoff, streamed on to the terrace around us. It turned out the Serbian police had

267

escorted them from the airport to their hotel and then refused to allow them to leave, intending to escort them to the game and back without allowing them to go anywhere of their own accord. The fans considered this to be an infringement of their civil liberties and they made a call to the British Consulate. In a stunning piece of diplomacy the Consul told them to bring their bus round to the consulate. He proceeded to entertain them all afternoon on his spacious lawn, which had football goals on it. They played football with his children in the sunshine, food and drinks were provided and everyone came out of the deal more than satisfied: the fans, the Consul and the police. They were then bussed to the ground and before the match began they had just enough time to tell me and Zoran what we'd missed.

Speaking about the game many years later, Sandra asked if the match I was describing was the one at which the fans had sung the 'ginger song'. I had had no idea what she meant. It turned out that Zoran and I had been on the receiving end of 20,000 fans chanting 'Gingers!' at us. He'd thought it better not to tell me.

Coincidentally, as I write, I've just heard of the death of another ginger and great supporter of Newcastle: he sat with Zoran and me on the terracing in Belgrade and told us the whole consulate story. Bryan Williams, RIP.

9

What Do You Do After Twenty-Four Years Of Fart Jokes?

My memories of deciding to leave *Viz*, and then actually going through with it, are a little hazy. I don't remember who I first spoke to about the idea, but I do remember Alex approaching me quietly one day and asking if the rumour he'd heard was true. On hearing it was, he told me that he too had been having similar ideas. We then began to discuss the possibility of setting up together in a business devoted to the other projects we'd both longed to be involved with, but were prevented from indulging ourselves in due to our regular commitment to *Viz* deadlines. It seems strange to say it now, but I don't actually remember announcing my intention to leave, and consequently I have no particular recollection of anyone's reaction. That said, I know there were no adverse reactions, and I think everyone had always been aware that for years I'd had my eye on other types of work, especially television.

Once the subject was broached, the prospect of staying on, continuing to work on *Viz* in the knowledge that we were both about to leave, seemed unattractive as a proposition. After another discussion Alex and I decided to leave with immediate effect. The Christmas issue of 2003 was the last we would work on together, and the last on which I would be a member of the editorial team. I did plan to continue working as a contributor, as Alex has done in all the years since, but once I'd committed to a career outside of *Viz*, I've never felt the temptation to sit down and draw a cartoon again.

So I'd left, after twenty-four years. What would I do? To take our experience of writing comedy together on *Viz*, and to put it into different mediums, we wasted no time in setting up Blissna, a writing partnership, to work on TV, stage and radio projects. The name Blissna? At the time we named *Viz*, many British comics' names were based on slang words for good: *Beano*, *Topper*, *Whizzer*, *Dandy* ... Alex and I thought that, had we known this in 1979, we may well have chosen a Geordie slang word for good as a title. The word 'blissna' is a Geordie 'charva' word meaning 'excellent, good, enjoyable, of a high standard'. It's taken from the word 'bliss' with the charva nasal suffix 'na', often used to complement any word that doesn't finish on a sufficiently harsh note, e.g. 'That's purely fuckin' blissna, that!'

Alex used his great connections in the world of stand-up comedy to see if he could find us an agent, particularly for TV and radio work. He spoke to Off the Kerb Productions, who represent many of Britain's top comedians. We arranged to meet Off the Kerb's Joe Norris at a hotel in Manchester, where, without further ado, he offered to represent us. We spent the drive back to Newcastle from the north west discussing if there could be any reason why we shouldn't go with Off the Kerb, and concluded that, had we been given a choice of all the top agents in the country, Off the Kerb would actually have been our first choice, so the deal was done. The Blissna office was set up in my study at home, and Alex began to arrive on a daily basis as we set about establishing ourselves.

Back in around 1999, in order to speak about the history of *Viz*, Alex and I were invited to Dublin by a small literary group. We made the trip, taking with us two or three overhead projector slides of various milestone *Viz* covers, and presented a rather shabby but nevertheless successful lecture. At the foundation of Blissna we decided to see if we could turn this talk into a show suitable for the Edinburgh Festival. With a decent amount of development and a good number of digital slides, we created a three-part show. In the first part I told the story of the comic's beginnings; in the second Alex told how he came to us at just fifteen and became involved in various legal wrangles shortly afterwards; and in the final section together we told the funniest anecdotes of our careers working on *Viz*. We called it *Swearing is Both Big and Clever* and it showed at The Pleasance in Edinburgh in the summer of 2004. Although we only performed two dates, the show was a great success, and we were astonished at the number of comedians that came to see us. The back two rows comprised almost entirely of amazing comedy names: Stewart Lee, Adam Bloom and the truly legendary Barry Cryer to name just quarter of a dozen. We later toured the show, the best gig of all probably being the Newcastle Comedy Festival, at which Abdul Latif, Lord of Harpole, dressed in his ceremonial robes, appeared on stage to introduce us. This was such a success that we went to The Rupali Restaurant, 6 Bigg Market, Newcastle upon Tyne, NE1 1UW, and filmed Mr Latif doing his introduction, which we used on video at the start of the show for the rest of the tour.

Our first venture into TV was a tremendous success. *The Regionnaires* was a comedy panel show, based on local knowledge and broadcast by Tyne Tees, specifically aimed at the residents of the area that Tyne Tees was transmitted to. Our mission in producing this programme was to prove the value of regional TV in light of the competition from satellite and cable. I felt that with more and more TV stations appearing left right and centre, it seemed most didn't have a valid reason for existing. There were exceptions to this: The History Channel and National Geographic for example, or music stations, even shopping channels – all were specialists, and could justify their existence as such. Many, however, seemed only to exist to broadcast endless worthless repeats and to sell advertising to an ever more thinly spread audience. My idea was to show that regional TV, i.e. ITV's regional network, could produce entertainment programmes that appealed specifically to their own areas. We all know that comedians have material that they can storm with at home, but due to the specific local references, or dialect used, can never work anywhere else, but it's every bit as valid (if not more so) than a piece that can appeal to the whole nation. So, a quiz based on regional knowledge would surely open doors for entertainers to use their locality-specific stuff.

We put together our proposal and arranged to meet with Tyne Tees. We were so convinced of the validity of our idea that in order to entice the decision makers we offered to make a series for expenses only. They were bowled over by the idea, contracts were drawn up through Off the Kerb and Alex and I set about writing the programme. Our first port of call was Gavin Webster, also looked after by Off the Kerb, as our first choice as a team captain. We also shared our first choice for the other team captain, Catboy, who was by now Metro Radio's breakfast show DJ. Both agreed to appear and it was also agreed that I would be the quizmaster.

Tyne Tees provided us with in-house staff, including series producer Sheilagh Mattheson, who I was already familiar with, as years earlier, during her days as a Tyne Tees newsreader, Steve had made her up with prosthetic make-up for a Halloween item. She was great to work with, though she found our methods a little strange, as did everyone at TTTV, but she embraced them and really enjoyed working on our show.

Alex and I put together the format of the quiz's rounds, one of which featured Arthur 2 Stroke as our roving reporter. Phil had always been a great success in his TV work and we knew we could use him to great effect on the streets of the north east, interviewing members of the public. His round was called 'Reeg-On the Road' and in each show he would visit two towns, where he would ask a question of a number of passers-by, and in the studio the panellists had to guess the number of correct answers given. For example, in Bedlington he showed people four pictures of dogs and they had to identify which was the Bedlington terrier, the teams guessing how many got it right. Phil's interaction with the public was a delight, as it had been since he interviewed the old lady on Northumberland Street on the *Viz* Christmas present video in 1988.

Alex and I had used Phil in a similar role on a radio programme we were offered at Century Radio on Friday nights in the early noughties. He had recorded his first vox pops and we'd recorded our jingles, and as the first show approached negotiations over payment finally got underway. When we were offered £80 between us for a five-hour programme we decided not to proceed.

It took us four months to put *The Regionnaires* together, with hours and hours of endless research. Alex proved to be absolutely invaluable when it came to writing my pieces to camera and the questions themselves. His work was of a ridiculously high standard.

We brought Steve in to animate our title sequence, which was based around a cartoon Alex had drawn of Catboy, Gavin and me arriving at the studio, but taking a detour into the pub next door, while Mike Neville was mobbed by a gaggle of screaming girls. We called in Archie Brown to make the music for the title sequence and the round introductions. Everybody's work on the show was fantastic and Phil was joined on his sections by a young director and editor called Emma McKinney, who, like all the Tyne Tees staff we worked with, proved to be dedicated to our cause and was a delight to work with.

We recorded all six programmes over three days in Studio 5 of Tyne Tees, the very room where *The Tube* was made and where The Jam made their last TV appearance: a place steeped in history. As the time approached I became nervous at the thought of using an autocue for the first time. In the weeks leading to the recording dates, the Tyne Tees staff allowed me to visit during quiet periods and practise by reading the day's news. In the end, the autocue turned out to be a doddle, my nervousness in reading from it resulted in my speech being slower, precise and clear, and the professionals in the studio who had worked there for many years all said that I had behaved like an old pro.

Unlike the likes of *A Question of Sport*, *Have I Got News for You* and *Never Mind the Buzzcocks*, we were seriously restricted by budget. This resulted in a very limited amount of time per show in the studio in order to avoid the editing of the studio footage, a very time-consuming and therefore costly process. The 'big' shows take as much as three hours to record a thirty-minute show, but we had to record ours as if live, only three minutes being edited out, mainly just 'umms' and 'aahs'. Also restricted by budget and regulations was the amount of promotion and advertising we were afforded – this was effectively zero. We would have no trailers, no adverts, no press coverage ... the only promotion of the show on Tyne Tees itself would be a studio interview with me on the local news on the night of the first broadcast.

While waiting to be interviewed by Mike Neville, the man himself sat in the next make-up chair to me and joked to the girl who was applying powder to his face that we had 'ribbed his dental work in *Viz*', speaking the words through the very dental work to which he referred.

To be fair, Mike Neville was a great sport and gave his permission to be featured in the animated title sequence of the show, despite the fact that we were being rather cheeky in it.

Staff at Tyne Tees informed us that the target viewing figures for a show broadcast at 11.30pm on a Friday night was seven to twelve per cent of all TV viewers in the region, including those watching satellite and cable. When the figures came in we were astonished, as were all the people who'd worked on the show – we had achieved a figure of twenty-three per cent, almost twice the top target figure. This was surely proof positive that what we were doing worked. The next show's figure dropped to twelve per cent, the high end of the target, and then rose steadily to the end of the series, achieving twenty per cent on the final show. The initial peak, drop and steady rise was presumably due to the first programme's promotion on the news, but without advertising we knew that the gradual rise could only be down to word of mouth, the show steadily finding its proper audience.

I shan't delve into the politics of what happened next, except to say that despite the show's amazing success it wasn't recommissioned. Not long afterwards Tyne Tees' studios were sold off and the station itself moved into a nondescript business park in Gateshead. The studio buildings have now been demolished, but perhaps even sadder was the flattening of the Egypt Cottage, the pub that stood in the middle of the studio site. A pub by that name had stood on the same site for centuries.

It's sad to think that had we approached TTTV only a year or two earlier and brought *The Regionnaires* to the TV-watching public before the process to wind down the station had begun, I think we really could have done very something significant and proven the worth of regional entertainment shows. Needless to say, no one who worked on the show was happy that we didn't get another series. The means by which we were informed left an awful lot to be desired. It's no consolation that our historical mark in the story of Tyne Tees is that we made the last ever studio audience programme there.

One day Alex broke the rather unexpected news that he had booked himself a spot as a stand-up comedian. If you're unfamiliar with the way comedy clubs work, as a rule there are four or five acts on the bill. There is a compère, an opening act and a closing act, and one or two middle acts. The middle act is the spot where new acts are tried out, or established acts may try new material. In smaller clubs you're always guaranteed to get one or two unpaid acts on in this slot. These are known as 'open spots'.

Alex had arranged himself an open spot at the Chillingham Arms in Heaton. Comedy nights there witnessed some genuinely bizarre acts, something that's sadly lacking in most comedy clubs nowadays. Alex had decided to throw himself in at the deep end. He was quite nervous about telling me he was going to perform, but the biggest shock came when he asked my permission to use one of my anecdotes. I didn't know what he meant. He explained that telling stories is a trait for which I have something of a reputation.

He hoped to use a story that I had recently told him about Bingo (the dog), which went something like this. The dog found a young couple 'having the sexy times' in the local woods. In the darkness I thought that he had found a dead body, and the newspaper headlines flashed across my mind: 'MURDERED GIRL FOUND BY DOG WALKER.' It turned out to be a semi-naked couple in the throes of passion, who had frozen like statues upon the arrival of a big dog, a big excited dog. Bingo was always very keen crotch sniffer, and on this occasion his route to the area of the body for which he had an almost morbid fascination was not barred in the usual way by clothing, so, enjoying the freedoms there provided, he tucked his nose as far into the girl's behind as his cold, wiry Greyhound racing muzzle would allow. As I got closer and my eyes became accustomed to the light I saw that I wasn't looking at one body, but two, and the whole picture suddenly came crashing down on me. Obviously I had to call the dog off. I shouted 'Bingo!', and instantly regretted giving my dog a name which, when shouted, is more commonly associated with an exclamation of joy in a victorious moment.

I gave Alex permission, of course, and he did pretty well out of the story, using it regularly over the next few months as he developed his stand-up routine. The pivotal part of this story, though, is that on realising that Alex could get up on stage as a stand-up comic and tell my anecdotes, so could I. It really was a Eureka moment. For some reason I'd never seen these true-life funny stories as having any potential for the stage, but on thinking about it I realised they were a perfect first step for my creation of a routine. Spurred on by Alex's success, I booked myself an open spot at the same venue.

My act that night consisted mainly of anecdotes based around true-life observations of incidents, some of which inspired my work in *Viz*. They were quite extreme in parts and were very well received, but easily the greatest satisfaction all round came when I finished on my Bingo from Benton stories. I had simply tagged a couple of these on at the end of the act, telling stories about Bingo as if he were a real character that I met occasionally on the street. Because of the radio success of Bingo during Catboy's time standing in for Alan Robson, I'd guessed it would be popular. It was very easy for me to slip into the voice, as I had done it so many times before.

It's easy looking back now to ask why I didn't simply appear dressed as the character straight away, but I felt very strongly at the time that I wanted to be myself on stage and only go into voices occasionally to make the stories more fun. My act has developed an awful lot since then, and although life has taken me on a less than straightforward journey, I've never looked back. Getting up on stage at the Chillingham Arms in 2005 was the best career move of my life. Not that I've made many career moves.

In those early days of stand-up I felt that my future as an act would be as a raconteur, telling almost entirely true stories, manipulated only to increase the effect of their delivery. I would edit, move and exaggerate different parts of them to make sure they flowed and finished with a bang.

The first material I wrote specifically for my stand-up routine was a series of mother-in-law jokes. I used to play up the fact that I was new to stand-up and I based a lot of jokes around this, the premise being that as somebody new to comedy I didn't really understand how humour worked. I certainly did pretty well in those early gigs, but I was, of course, a beginner, and my sets suffered from a lack of cohesion.

The rest of the comedians on the circuit were extremely supportive, and I learned a lot from their advice. I was always conscious that I had come into their world from outside, and my experience in writing comedy, albeit long and very successful, may not have any value in this totally separate world. I realised I was entering a profession in which it is easy to fall very hard and very quickly, and I knew only too well there was no place for complacency. But I relished the challenge.

The local promoters, most of whom were comedians themselves, quickly embraced me. Steffen Peddie was one such promoter, from whom an embrace is probably worth avoiding – he's an ex-professional wrestler. I'm not saying he's a big lad, but instead of reading his weight, his bathroom scales sing, 'Who ate all the pies?'

Steffen was one of a succession of local comics who ran a gig in Sunderland at a pub called The Royalty. It was called Mack'em Laff, and along with the Chillingham's Laughing Horse it was to be a foundation stone of my move into stand-up.

I felt so strongly that I was doing the right thing that in order to fulfil a commitment to a show at The Royalty I turned down an offer to sit at Paul Weller's table at the Brits when he received his outstanding achievement award. I look back now and can't work out what the fuck I was thinking. I felt that I needed to show the comedians and promoters that I was serious; that I wasn't just waltzing in and out of their profession for the fun of it. When I think about it, I guess it was a good statement to make. However, I really wish I'd been at the Brits. The upside was that I wrote a piece of stand-up specially for the occasion, all about the fact that I'd turned down the opportunity to stand on this stage, in a pub in Sunderland, in front of fewer than twenty people, when I could have been out on the piss with one of my lifetime heroes. I listened back to a tape of that show recently and it still made me laugh, so maybe I did do the right thing. The people in the room that night certainly appreciated the effort. Sadly, gigs at The Royalty recently came to an end. I have great memories of that room.

Alex and I worked on many more projects under the Blissna banner, including writing for some national TV shows, TV and radio scripts with comedians, plus sitcom proposals that may still come to fruition at some point. One of these we are particularly proud of was presented to Channel Five. We'd written a treatment about one man who for farcical reasons needed to pretend at work to be gay, doing so in a flamboyant and camp fashion, and whose colleague was actually gay, but whose behaviour was effectively straight. The commissioning editor of the station, Graham Smith, asked if either of us were gay. When we said we weren't he informed us that he envisaged trouble ahead with us writing for a gay character. I assume that this would also leave us unable to write anything for female characters, children, people taller than ourselves, or anyone who didn't like the same flavour of crisps. For fuck's sake.

One of my favourite memories of our time working from my house was a day on which Alex hadn't turned up for work. It was a hot and sunny mid-morning and I'd just taken Bingo (the dog) for a walk. As I turned the corner into my street, Alex appeared, driving his car in the opposite direction. As he stopped at the junction, his open window was directly opposite Bingo and me. He was carrying a passenger who I didn't recognise and, despite my closeness, he didn't appear to see me. At the top of my voice, straight into the open window of the car from only two or three yards away, I shouted, 'Wanker!'

As I approached my front door I began to think what a miserable bastard he was, having not only not laughed at my hilarious prank, but having not even acknowledged my presence. And who was this person he was carrying in his car? Someone so important that he was prepared to behave as if he didn't know me?

As I went to put the key in the door the penny dropped. Alex had told me he wasn't coming in. In fact, it was quite a big deal: he was sitting his driving test.

I rang him shortly afterwards to apologise and he simply bawled, 'You bastard!' down the phone.

He'd failed, although he did later admit that he'd already done more than enough to fail before the drive-by shouting.

I scored past Neville Southall at Goodison Park

A year after the Soccer Sixes at St James' Park I was invited to play again with The Darkness, but this time it was a very different situation. In the month immediately after the band had travelled in their Transit to Newcastle, they'd scored their first chart success. By the time the Soccer Six tournament came to Everton they were the hottest property in the UK charts.

Julie and I were invited to stay at a hotel in Liverpool the night before the event. A night out was arranged with the players, and all our expenses were paid for by The Darkness. We were presented with specially made orange and black kits with flames on them, and then driven to the stadium in a coach. On arrival, the coach was escorted by mounted police through hoards of screaming girls. This was as close to seeing what it was like to be in The Beatles as I was ever going to get.

The contrast between the tournaments in 2003 and 2004 couldn't have been greater. We were the lepers of St James', but now everyone wanted a piece of us. Even *Newsround* wanted to interview me – I suspect they thought I was in the band.

We also had an abundance of playing staff this time around – six players and five subs, and all of them pretty serious players. We had John Aldridge as our ex-pro, a privilege denied us the previous year, and others included Harvey from So Solid Crew and Ralf Little, both very good footballers. Our team picture from St James' took pride of place on the cover of the programme, and both Steve McManaman and Robbie Fowler were drafted in as our 'coaching staff'.

We were widely accepted as favourites for the competition, and we pretty much cruised through the opposition. Team tactics were the order of the day and we used all of our best players to put each game beyond doubt before sending the lesser players on to finish off the job.

I was introduced as a sub when we were 4–0 up against Goldie Lookin' Chain in the quarter final. I was flying up the wing when a sliding tackle came in and felled me in full flight. I landed awkwardly on my shoulder and neck and I think I must have blacked out for a moment. I awoke in the arms of the Everton physio.

'Did I get a free kick?' I asked.

'He won the ball, mate. But you've got a throw in.'

I was about to be substituted when I signalled to the bench that I could play on. In pretty bad pain and with my left shoulder not wanting to move at all, I carried on. Spurred on by the resulting adrenalin rush, soon afterwards I picked up the ball in my right-back position and charged on. I was approaching the halfway mark and no one closed me down, so pushed my run on as far as I could. Eventually, a defender came to cover me, and as he did so I looked up and saw a good opening to the right of him. I could see about two feet of goal clearly, so I put my head down and put as much leather through the ball as I could muster. The shot, a low drive, or daisycutter, absolutely flew.

Neville Southall was the Welsh international keeper for many years and won the league title with Everton in 1985. He's a legend amongst goalkeepers, although, to be fair, he's not skipped too many breakfasts in recent times. He saw the shot late and dived at full stretch, his despairing hand just missing the ball, which smacked the inside of the post and, seemingly in slow motion, spun along the goal line, hit him on his sizeable arse and was deflected into the net.

The next thing I knew, Harvey had picked me up and was carrying me aloft, the whole team congratulating me on my stretcher-case-to-goal-hero turnaround.

In the final we played a team that had amongst its number a certain Marcus Patrick, the very man who'd abandoned us at St James' for a more fashionable outfit. We thumped them. Sweet revenge. Crowned Soccer Six Champions, we retired to our hotel for a party. It was a truly marvellous experience.

Silver Jubilee

A year after Alex and I left *Viz* the comic celebrated its twenty-fifth anniversary. This was marked with two books and a party. Chris launched his autobiography, *Rude Kids*, and at the same time the official history of *Viz*, *25 Years of Viz: Silver Plated Jubilee*, was written by well-respected comedy biographer William Cook. He interviewed everyone from the bands that played at The Gosforth Hotel to Brian from the Kard Bar to John Brown and all the artists and writers from all the years of production. Unfortunately, due to some confusion over train

280

arrangements, he wasn't able to speak to Jim face to face. His book was a fantastic piece of work and gave a voice to many of the people who had contributed so much to *Viz* without ever standing in the spotlight. I think the only downside to that book is that the artwork section of it was put together from work donated for use in the project by the artists themselves, the net result being a very small amount from Chris and nothing at all from Jim. I felt that was a real oversight, the two of them having not only forged the beginnings of *Viz* itself, but their undoubted natural talent for producing simple and yet extremely stylish cartoons was a massive part of both the comic's identity and success.

I know little about Chris's autobiography. I didn't read it at the time and I made a conscious decision not to when I began work on my own book. I felt I would be happier writing my own story without having been influenced by his. I hear regularly from *Viz* fans that it's a great read, although most of them then go on to thank me for writing it. I hear from others that it focuses very much on the business side of things, which doesn't surprise me – that's the way he's built.

The anniversary party was put on at the Café de Paris in Soho, arranged by IFG Ltd, the publishers of the comic at the time. They had an idea that a 'celebrity party' would be a great idea, but unfortunately there wasn't a huge amount of irony involved. I arrived and had the pleasure of meeting proper real-life nutty professor Colin Pillinger and Ross Noble, to name a couple of the worthy guests to be found enjoying the entertainment: all-in wrestling and ukulele music (both selected by the *Viz* creators, not the publisher).

As I wondered about saying hello to various people I was stopped by a woman I recognised to be Jodie Marsh.

'Thanks!' she said, smiling.

'Sorry, thanks for what?' I replied.

'For the party!'

'Oh, it's not my party,' I explained. 'It's been arranged by the publisher. I'm a guest here too.'

I couldn't believe my luck when her next sentence was, 'If it was your party, what would you have done differently?'

'I wouldn't have invited you,' was my instant reply, of which I'm still proud.

An eavesdropping journalist wrote the story up in a tabloid the next day. The journo stopped short of mentioning that I was friendly to her afterwards. I've never enjoyed reading a tabloid paper quite so much.

Hungover Stuntmen

As Alex and I were writing in my home studio one day a CD was posted through the letterbox of my front door. It was a home-recorded disc accompanied by a handwritten note, which read something along the lines of, 'Hello. We are Hungover Stunt-men, a band living at the opposite end of your street. Please listen to our CD and play it to all your rich and influential friends in the world of showbusiness. If you don't like it, consider it a gift of a free coaster. Yours, Oxy (and Tino, Jamesy and Iain).'

I told Alex about the CD as I put it on a shelf in the studio. It was to sit there for many weeks. I was eventually having a tidy and prepared to throw it out. Having spent many years seeing all the cartoons sent by readers to *Viz*, and indeed having listened to so many entry attempts to the *Viz* Top Ten, a music chart in which the highest-bribe bidder was openly given top spot, I was only too aware of the often dreadful quality of the majority of unsolicited contributions. As I held the CD over the bin it occurred to me that I might bump into one of these lads on the street and it would be embarrassing it they asked what I'd thought of it, so I decided to listen to a couple of tracks before binning it. Alex said, in all seriousness, 'You never know, they might be something special.'

Within two tracks I was on the phone to Angie Jenkison, the only person I knew in the management end of the music industry. I said I thought I'd found something special. I told her all about the band and she was very interested. I posted the disc off to her and the rest, as they say, is history. Well, not quite. This became the story of me becoming manager to a young band who were supremely talented, devoted and smart, had some great breaks, had some awful downfalls, had some amazing times, landed a record deal, played some huge gigs … and then sadly faded away.

To be honest, I just don't have the time or the remit to write the whole story of my four years on the road with the Stuntmen. I think there's a whole book in that in itself, but I'm going to try and give an account here of the real highs and lows that left me and these young men as inseparable friends.

Angie quickly became the band's manager and soon afterwards asked me to become her eyes and ears in Newcastle by becoming co-manager. It wasn't something I really wanted to do, getting into the music industry, but the boys were so talented I just felt I had to help them out.

Their music was really rather unexpected – well-constructed, catchy songs, some with clever and challenging lyrics, and they could all play, but the most noticeable quality that put them above and beyond any other band I could name was their vocal harmonies. They could all sing and they put their talents together to make a sum greater than the individual parts. They looked good too, dressing and cutting their hair in a style something like The Beatles circa 1966. Oxy was the group's drummer and a very talented and outspoken entertainer; Martin 'Tino' was guitarist and took lead vocal in most songs; James 'Jamesy', later 'Jimmy', also played guitar and took lead vocal for a couple of songs, notably the show stealer 'One Reason' with which they closed their act; Iain was an awesome bass player, like John Entwistle in the early 1960s. He wanted to wear his hair straight, despite his natural curls, and consequently spent much time attending to his locks. Martin later stepped down to start a family and was replaced by Stu, a very talented and chiselled young guitarist who had known Oxy from teenage years. All of the lads had a tremendous sense of humour.

Angie was quickly on the case, sorting out some great contacts for the boys, and they were soon recording demos in a London studio with Mark Wallace, previously known for his work with The La's. She then played these demos to Paul Weller, who personally invited the lads to support him at Newcastle Arena.

The Arena gig was amazing. On reflection, it possibly gave the lads a lift a bit too early, but it was a hell of an experience for all of us, either way. The lads had to start their set soon after the doors opened, but this wasn't a problem. With no seating on the floor area there was a rush to take up positions right at the front, so they played to a throng of appreciative Weller fans. Having been given the job of introducing them on to the stage, I stood in the wings and watched with Steve Cradock, Weller's guitarist, who also plays with Ocean Colour Scene, and he liked what he saw. He later told me he fancied recording the lads as he wanted to try his hand at production with a guitar band.

Angie set up a couple of days at a studio with Steve and the Stuntmen in London and he produced three tracks for them. Steve visited the band and played on stage with them at a lovely gig at a pub called Mr Lynch in Jesmond. On his visit he came to my house and played my piano, a fact of which I was very proud. The boys later supported Ocean Colour Scene at Newcastle Carling Academy and Steve played my Rickenbacker guitar during the sound check, a fact of which I'm even more proud.

The next of Angie's connections to be utilised was her friendship with fellow Geordie Andy Taylor, a kind, eccentric and generous man, brilliant guitarist and founder member of one of my least favourite bands of all time, Duran Duran. He later had great success with Robert Palmer in Power Station. Andy was setting up a studio at his home in Ibiza and was looking to test out the facilities by recording a band there. An offer was made that if the Stuntmen could pay their own airfares out to Ibiza, Andy would put them up and record some more demos with them.

Angie was also looking after a band called Electric City, including Andy's son (also called Andy) and featuring James Taylor, son of Duran's Roger Taylor, and Dan Laithwaite, nephew of Simon Le Bon. She eventually decided to take them into a management deal with another company and the Stuntmen decided to stay with me, so I became Hungover Stuntmen's full-time manager. Alex had decided to move into animation and went off to Sunderland University to become an even more talented bastard.

So for me and the Stuntmen, here began many months of seemingly constant trips to Ibiza, recording demos and playing gigs, as well as shooting video and eventually recording a whole album. During this time the band played Ibiza Rocks twice, headlining it once, and became the first resident band at the Ibiza Rocks Hotel, where on that particular trip we initially stayed until burglaries and the insane behaviour of the residents sent us packing to live in a nearby apartment instead.

Recording at Andy's studio was idyllic in many respects, not least because of the isolated rural location and the constant sunshine. The accommodation shared a courtyard with Andy's home and we spent many long hours in the company of his lovely wife Tracey and their children Andy, Bethany, Georgie and eleven-year-old, Izzy, the youngest and most talkative.

A day of recording would usually involve everyone rising around 10am, breakfast would be served by the pool, during which studio engineer and ex-racing champion Henry would arrive across country on a deafening lunatic of a motorbike with slick tyres. We'd then take the sun, swim, lark around and play acoustic guitars until noon, at which point we'd wander up to the studio, just around the corner from the courtyard, and the day's work would begin. During the recording sessions trays of tea would be ferried back and forth and we'd have nostalgic conversations with Andy about life in the north east before breaking for an evening meal, also served by the pool, and then back to work until midnight, the day finishing with guitars and a few drinks by the pool until the early hours.

On one occasion in Andy's kitchen we were all drinking tea and telling stories of childhoods in the north east to Henry, who was slightly alarmed at some of the tales of street fights and sex behind skips, and after a while he went out to make a call. During his time out of the room, the subject of air guns came up. On his return, not having heard the all-important words 'air gun' mentioned, he walked in just in time to hear Oxy exclaim, 'Si! Tell Henry about that time you shot that kid in the head!'

I obliged. 'I thought I'd shoot the football at his feet! It would be hilarious! Caught him in the head! Ha! Ha! ... He spun round and fell like a stone! Ha! Ha!'

Everyone else in the room, already familiar with the story, burst out laughing. Henry sat, ashen-faced and silent. Only when the story ended did he try to force out a limp 'Wow.'

Only then did the penny drop with the rest of us that he was clearly upset by our callous disregard for human life. His relief was tangible when we all started shouting, 'Air gun, man, Henry!'

'Shit! A BB gun? Just a BB gun? Jesus! Now that makes sense! I thought you guys were, like, totally insane!'

Life in Ibiza certainly beat sitting in a city centre office churning out repetitive drawings. But arena gigs with musical legends and album sessions in the glorious sunshine of the Balearics were the high points of four years, most of them spent touring the deepest shitholes of the United Kingdom. There follows some of the highs and lows.

Not long after playing Newcastle Arena to close to ten thousand people, the band was booked to play at a Newcastle nightclub on a Monday evening. Mondays are traditionally when a lot of students come out to take advantage of the cheap drink deals as, unlike proper people, they don't have to get out of bed on a Tuesday. The promoter was keen to inform us that he had the market nailed and the venue would be rammed with young people. We went ahead with the gig, despite the fact that the band and entourage outnumbered the audience of eight. I would console the band on such occasions that it was free practice time.

The music industry is riddled with chancers, and promoters are often the worst. Good promoters are well worth their salt, but far too many people call themselves promoters without considering the task of promotion to be any part of their job description. Some even try to get the bands to sell tickets themselves and if they're not all sold the band will be charged for them. It's a horrible business.

In the years of touring we played at some of the most famous little rock 'n' roll venues Britain has ever had, but the experiences were sometimes not as legendary as the buildings themselves. For example, we did a couple of gigs at north London's famous Hope and Anchor in a room that saw many punk groups of the 1970s cut their teeth. It continues as a permanent music venue to this day. The sound check was challenging, to say the least. The Stuntmen always needed good on-stage sound: the tight harmonies they sang while playing meant they each needed to hear everyone else's vocal, and their own, as well as all the instruments, so all this had to be mixed properly in their on-stage monitors. As anyone who's ever been in a band will know, that's quite a challenge for a venue's sound person to cope with in the fifteen minutes or so available to set up the sound for each band. Monitoring was particularly difficult to achieve for Oxy, as the sound of his drum kit around him pretty much drowned everything out, so he really needed a good, powerful monitor.

The 'stage' at the Hope and Anchor was a tiny corner of the low-ceilinged basement room, with no riser at all. As the boys stepped up for their sound check Oxy noticed there was no monitor beside the drum kit.

'There's no monitor!?' he shouted to the sound man, who looked like he'd died three weeks earlier.

'It's on the wall!' was the reply. 'We put it there to save floor space!'

Sure enough, there it was, mounted at forty-five degrees, facing down at Oxy.

'Excellent. Thanks!' Ox shouted back.

As everyone began to play Oxy complained that there was no sound at all coming from his monitor.

'Yeah. It doesn't work.'

The rest of the sound check was a debacle. The three working monitors were clearly knackered and couldn't produce any sound worth hearing. After the shambolic level tests were completed the soundman confided in us, 'What we tend to find with these particular monitors is, unless you're Aretha Franklin, you'll not get a lot of sound back out of them.'

Casting my eyes around the tiny, dark, dingy room with its function-free drum monitor, overpowering smell of stale beer, BO and farts, with a capacity of fifty or maybe fewer, I asked, 'Does she play here often?'

All he could manage to give me back was an embarrassed smile.

Probably the funniest road trip in all the years was to Brighton to play at the Great Escape Festival. For some reason this weekend seemed to generate an abundance of funny stories. En route to the gig we walked across a huge green just off the sea front where some young lads were playing football. Their ball shot wide of their jumper goalposts and ended up about twenty yards from us, and fifty or more from their goalkeeper. I jogged over and as I approached the ball, immediately before I launched it back towards him, I shouted, 'On your clems!'

This was an expression we'd taken to shouting when playing 'One Bounce', a keepy-up football game we invented in the front street where we lived and which we played outside venues in downtime on the road. In One Bounce, 'On your clems!' was an instruction to control the ball with your testicles, and was used in truth only to put off an opponent as he received a difficult pass.

The young lad, about twelve years old, ran towards where he anticipated my huge booted pass would land. His run and the trajectory angle of the ball coincided such that he ran at full pace into the descending ball, which went between his flailing arms and caught him full in the bollocks, flooring him instantaneously. Angie was with us, and she stood, baffled, as me and the band all reeled around her, barely able to stay on our feet for laughing.

'What's funny about that?' she demanded.

None of us were able to answer.

We attended an 'industry drinks party' at a hotel later that night. Angie, who could often be quite stern with the band and wasn't renowned for practical jokes, made a most welcome and unexpected announcement to me, Martin, James and Oxy.

'You see that bloke over there? He's the editor of a top music magazine.'

'Right,' I replied, expecting we were about to be asked to introduce ourselves.

'He's gay. I'm going to introduce him to Iain, but first I'm going to tell him that Iain's gay.'

With this she walked off determinedly.

What happened next was verging on a *Two Ronnies* sketch. We all stood nearby and watched the introduction take place. The innocent look on Iain's face was a delight and the trick worked beautifully. The gay man began to engage the boyishly good-looking Iain in a very long conversation, no doubt Iain seeing in his mind's eye his band on the front cover of the magazine. As the conversation continued we made our way around the room, telling everyone we spoke to what was happening. Before long almost every single person at the party was secretly watching poor Iain as he was unknowingly courted. Before long the editor was touching Iain's hair and asking where he had it done, and

Iain now had seven drinks lined up on the table, all bought for him by the friendly magazine editor.

Eventually I was telling a total stranger what was happening and recommended he follow events, like everyone else in the room. He calmly told me he was the magazine editor's assistant. Funnily enough, the band was never featured in the magazine, but my god we got some laughs out of it.

We stayed at Angie's in London the next night and we all sat outside, recounting our Brighton adventure. Iain was last to come outside and there wasn't a seat left for him. He sat on a box with only the top of his face visible over the garden table. As the story of the gay encounter came up we all rolled with laughter, Iain's sad eyes peering pathetically up over the table.

We played a number of fantastic gigs at The Cavern in Liverpool. On one occasion we were drinking coffee in a nearby pub and a very, and I mean *very*, drunken man approached us for a 'chat'. He informed us that he was supposed to have gone straight home from work for his tea, but instead he'd stayed out to enjoy himself. However, in order to avoid his wife's wrath, he'd come up with a brilliant plan. He produced a Liverpool Slavery Museum leaflet from his pocket.

'Foggin' look a' tha' meeyte.'

'Sorry, I'm not following you,' I said. I didn't see how the leaflet could save him from his wife's anger at him not coming home for tea.

'See, I'm supozzed to cum home for me tea, right. But, right, but, I've come out on the foggin' piss, la'. See? I'll show her this, see ...' – he waved the leaflet – 'I'll tell 'er thass where I've been.'

I could see two errors in his plan. Firstly, I suspected that leaflets advertising the museum are probably not on display at the museum itself, and the second point I put to him directly.

'Do you think they've got a bar in the Slavery Museum?'

This seemed to throw him.

'You see,' I continued, 'even if she believes you've heroically forfeited your meal to learn about the injustices and suffering of the past, I suspect she may still notice that you're pissed.'

He wandered off, looking confused.

The band was asked to play a Love Music Hate Racism gig, also in Liverpool. It was a good cause and it paid quite well, so I agreed to it. Bizarrely, it turned out that the gig wasn't actually in Liverpool city centre, but was in a very rough neighbourhood, which will remain nameless for various reasons that will become apparent.

Confused as the sat-nav guided us through a desolate area of 1950s local authority housing, much of it boarded up, we spotted the club. It looked more like a prison camp. A ten-foot-high security fence surrounded the building itself, its car park a separate high-security compound with its fence topped with plastic-bag-strewn razor wire. All the windows in the club had been boarded up with steel plates. We were sure this was the wrong place, but a passer-by assured us this unwelcoming scare-box was our destination. I pulled the van into the compound and we hesitantly entered the foyer on foot. As we did so, the first thing I noticed was a trail of dried blood across the tiled floor between the bar door and the exit. As we walked in a tiny yet fearsome woman was ejecting some underage track-suited youths for underage use of the slot machines. There were notices everywhere warning the clientele that using and selling drugs on the premises was strictly forbidden.

Even more bizarre was the fact that everything about the gig was brilliantly arranged, bar the venue itself. The sound team were an organised, efficient, high-end independent body, second to none we'd ever worked with. We later worked with the same team at Ibiza Rocks. There was a Norwegian band on the bill who were all students at the Liverpool music school founded by Paul McCartney. After sound checking they locked themselves in their van in the vehicle compound and remained there, terrified.

Inside the building, in which there was no natural light, the audience comprised of nothing more than a rag-tag bunch of regulars. It pretty much resembled that bar full of ropey aliens in *Star Wars*, but dingier and more scary. The only saving grace of this frankly terrifying experience was that we all got on very well with the regulars, who loved the band. Leaving was the best bit, though.

I think everyone associated with the band would doubtless agree that the worst gig of all was in County Durham. The band always went down very well in a big local town called Stanley, and a Sunderland-based promoter pointed out that the band had never played in Bishop Auckland, another big Durham town. He said he could get us a gig there and it seemed like a good idea, so I went ahead with it. Unfortunately, as we approached Bishop Auckland, the sat-nav just kept telling us to keep going. Miles later we arrived at a dismal-looking ex-pit village that comprised of one street of houses, facing each other across the main road. In the middle of this modest row of terraced housing were *four* pubs. It turned out the promoter had booked us to play in one of the four pubs in Coundon, a village in the middle of nowhere, not in Bishop Auckland itself, but within the Bishop Auckland postcode area.

The pub was tiny and clearly not a proper music venue. The room the band was to play in would only hold about thirty at capacity. We decided just to get on with it and set up the equipment.

When the punters began to filter in, the real bombshell dropped: coincidentally, there had been two funerals in Coundon on that day, and of the four pubs available in the tiny village, they'd both decided to bring their wakes to the one where the band was playing.

It's difficult to sum up in words the sheer awkwardness of what followed, the band kicking into their loud, high-energy guitar riffs and thunderous drum patterns to two devastated-looking groups of bereaved pit villagers, dressed entirely in black.

The gig was like nothing I've ever known, representatives of each bereaved family constantly approaching me and members of the band, asking for songs to be dedicated to the memory of their lost loved ones. This happened so many times that the boys ran out of suitable songs and ended up dedicating one called 'Love is Suicide'.

After the show finished, Oxy had to fight off the advances of a tired and emotional female mourner who offered to wank him off up a back lane. Happy days.

One of the strangest moments in my time with the band came on a night off. Me and the lads had been invited by Angie to watch *The Mighty Boosh* stage show in Wimbledon, and in the crowd with us were Paul Weller and The Dogs, the Stuntmen having shared the bill with both at Newcastle Arena and later at Newcastle City Hall. After the show we all went to a little gathering in a room in the theatre with a balcony overlooking the front street. Angie, Weller, Tino, Oxy and I all stood on the balcony discussing the Boosh show. Somehow the conversation came around to football, and for some reason Tino decided that now, in front of Paul Weller, would be a good time to tell me that he, Oxy and Iain were Sunderland fans. I was astounded. For some reason it had never occurred to me that lads living in Newcastle could possibly support Sunderland. All the evidence had been there, though: I'd just not seen it. Perhaps I was thrown by the fact James was a mad Newcastle fan and worked at St James' Park. Oxy was originally from Sunderland, Tino's family were from South Shields and Iain came from County Durham. The strangest thing was they'd kept it from me, fearing I would stop managing the band if I found out.

Weller, a Woking supporter and not a huge fan of football, was baffled by the cacophony that followed the announcement, Angie, also a Newcastle fan, having waded in too. Paul interjected to establish what was going on and it wasn't long before we were all laughing as I began to remember the times Oxy and Tino had turned down my invites to come and see Newcastle at St James'. They did, though, accept an invite to watch a game on my TV at home, and I now remembered that they sat with miserable faces as all my other mates and I jumped and cheered when the goals flew in. Apparently, they'd considered it a sensible career move to behave like wartime double agents and sit through an enemy victory without flinching. That thought still makes me laugh.

I genuinely loved my time with the band, and they will all be lifelong friends. The day they decided to throw in the towel was very sad for all of us. The circumstances leading to that decision were a hideous series of unfortunate events, each of which we could have survived if they'd happened over a period of time, but as a combined assault things just tipped us all over the edge. I still feel guilty that I couldn't realise their dreams of the success they deserved.

Logical to the last

The day I arrived at the Ibiza Rocks Hotel with the Stuntmen in the summer of 2008 I got an email from Steve. He'd been ill for about eighteen months with flu-like symptoms and had been losing weight steadily. He was dating a doctor, Kath, at the time and neither she nor her medical friends, or more importantly Steve's own doctor and various specialists, could work out what he was suffering from.

His email said there was good news and bad news. The good news was that his doctors now knew what was wrong with him. The bad news was that it was cancer.

It was cancer of the kidney, notoriously difficult to diagnose due to the other, unaffected, kidney taking over the function of the diseased one. He would have further tests to establish if other organs were affected, especially his bones, which would take two weeks or so.

The next two weeks in Ibiza were tough. I couldn't stop thinking about Steve and what he was going through, but although darker possibilities were difficult to ignore, the thought was always there that he could have a kidney removed and live a completely normal life.

Two weeks later I was on the balcony of our apartment in Ibiza and my phone rang. It was Steve. He told me the cancer was not in his bones, but it was in both his lungs, and therefore his condition was terminal.

Steve tried to console me, telling me that terminal didn't necessarily mean soon – he may still live for years. He was trying to make me feel better; he could tell how upset I was. Now I was feeling guilty for making him have to think about my feelings when he'd just been told he was going to die.

I asked if he wanted me to come home, but he said we'd only sit staring at the walls, and there wasn't anything I could do to help him practically. I spluttered that I loved him. I guess I hung up, as the rest is a blur. I ended up in Iain's arms, crying like a baby.

Steve had moved into my house a couple of years earlier, so I was returning home knowing we'd be living together through whatever happened next. It was very hard coming home to see my big brother, my inspiration, my friend, in many ways my hero, knowing that he was going to die.

I prefer not to go into too much detail about what happened in the following weeks and months, but soon after I returned home Steve went into hospital to have his affected kidney removed. It wasn't long before he was home again, recovering from the operation. I would be his carer during his recuperation.

Soon he was able to take a walk to the local shops on his own for an ice cream and things seemed to be on the up. His consultant planned, in the event of the operation being a success, to put Steve on a relatively new cancer drug, which had a very promising record. He told us one man in a similar situation was continuing to live a normal life seven years on. Sadly, this wasn't to be the way for Steve.

He was soon admitted to Newcastle General with lung problems and spent a difficult few weeks in there before coming home noticeably less well than when he'd gone in. It was clear that I was now his full-time carer.

I had to tell the Stuntmen I wasn't able to help them anymore. This was a really horrible time, I felt so bad letting the boys down, but they knew I couldn't do anything else but care for Steve. Around this time the band's record distribution company, the biggest independent in the UK, went bust, and then what I had believed was a confirmed tour with a major artist fell through. Everything had conspired against the band all at once. James was offered a job that would give him security and a decent wage and that was that. Goodnight Vienna.

I wasn't able to think about that too much. All that was on my mind night and day was Steve. We soon got into a routine that wasn't too bad: he'd get himself up and come downstairs, I'd make his breakfast, and he'd then have a sleep in an armchair. In the evening we'd watch a film of his choice together, a habit that had started when he was in hospital. Every day I'd taken in a DVD player and two pairs of headphones and we'd escaped from it all in one of his favourite films.

His condition went downhill rapidly. He soon had to have his bedroom moved downstairs and the Macmillan nurses arranged for daily help. It wasn't long before he wasn't able to stay awake long enough to sit through a whole film. It was just too sad.

I got the chance to discuss many things with Steve that we'd never have talked about if it weren't for his condition. I told him how much he meant to me and how I'd always admired his independence and the way he'd created his own success from his dream of working in films. I'm glad I got to tell him those things. Preparing for bed became more difficult as the days passed, as Steve's Asperger's tendencies became more and more dominant. Everything had to be lined up exactly in its place and then checked and double checked time and again. One night, once he was finally satisfied that all in the room was where it belonged, I took hold of him around his now-feeble body and hugged him. He began to cry and said, 'I'm no good at this.'

I said, 'Shut up. You don't have to be good at it. Just do it.'

He held me and we wept.

The next day he began to tell me about the music he'd like at his funeral. It wasn't a conversation we ever completed, but he let me know the album, not surprisingly a film soundtrack – *O Brother Where Art Thou?* We'd watched it together only days earlier.

Steve had a discussion with his Macmillan nurse and decided he wanted to die in St Oswald's, a local hospice that he'd been having day visits to for a few weeks. When I said he could stay at home if he wanted, he said the house was my home, not his. I told him I wanted it to be his home, but he chose the hospice, saying, rather typically, 'I see no reason why I should live out the last days of my life in this particular building.'

I felt that maybe he wanted to protect me from his death, to not have it happen in my house. He always looked out for me.

He was now drifting in and out of consciousness and Chris, Dolores, Dale and Thea joined me at his hospice bedside. With Chris holding one of his hands and me the other, he died peacefully.

The time from the phone call in Ibiza to Steve's funeral was under than five months – the toughest five months I've ever lived through.

Chris and I both spoke at Steve's funeral and his favourite poem from childhood, 'If' by Rudyard Kipling, was read by the

295

Humanist minister. It was very sad to see Dad, looking elderly and frail after a stroke, attending his own son's funeral, especially when he'd been through so much with Mum.

As he lay dying, Steve wrote his own epitaph, saying to Chris, 'I'm ready to go now. I feel I've done enough, created enough. That's me.'

I'm very proud that he was my brother.

From page to stage

It was while Steve was still alive that I made my decision to make a serious go of the stand-up. Things had come apart with the band, and I knew that Steve was dying. These two things combined had a profound effect on me, and without realising, I set about an evaluation of my life. It was time to pursue something with which to prove myself, something I knew I was good at, something I really enjoyed. The three-year break, the emotional rollercoaster of both the band's demise and Steve's illness all contributed to me seeing a comeback in a different light. I wanted to go on stage as my character creations. It now felt like a completely natural open doorway through which I was very happy to stride. I called Steffen Peddie and asked if he could give me an open spot to perform as Bingo from Benton, and he kindly obliged. I have Steffen to thank for finally tipping the balance in my mind in favour of becoming a character comedian. Almost every promoter I worked for in my early months suggested I do it, but it was Steffen who was most insistent.

Fortunately, I was still in possession of the foam rubber belly and man-tits that I'd made, with the help from Steve, for the Sunday for Sammy show in 2002, when I appeared as Sid the Sexist. It was perfect for Bingo. There was a character of mine in *Viz* called Big Fucking Dave who had the name DAVE tattooed in reverse on his forehead. This was inspired by two separate incidents, one being when I saw a man in a scrapyard in Shieldfield with the name STEVE tattooed on his forehead. It looked like he'd done it himself, and the E at the end was approximately half the size of the S at the beginning. The other was a tattoo seen on a teenager's forehead in Gosforth in the 1970s, which read PUNK, the N being the wrong way round. Clever lad. Bingo being very stupid, I felt it was only right that he too should have a DIY mirror-writing tattoo.

So the look I chose for Bingo was that of an ageing hooligan. I completed the outfit with an outdated England shirt, a nylon bomber jacket and a small woollen hat that I used to scrape back my hair and give the appearance of a cropped haircut. I assembled a lot of my previously used Bingo material both from the radio and from my early stand-up gigs when Bingo was a character I talked about.

Everything was ready, Bingo was ready to come to life, but there was one problem for which I was not prepared. Mid-afternoon on the day of the gig, alone in the house, I tried out all of the material for timing. It came to exactly seven minutes in total. I had told Steffen I would be doing fifteen. I needed seven more minutes and I had no material.

What happened next was one of the best things I've done in my career. I remembered something I'd once tried at The Royalty, something I'd really enjoyed and the crowd had laughed at heartily, but it needed work – a lot more work. I'd wanted for some time to do a piece about market research. It's always good to write about things that you hate. The venom spurs you on and on to create more and more biting jokes.

In 2005 or so I'd written a piece in which I asked members of the audience market research questions from a clipboard. It worked really well, although it was underdeveloped. I told the audience the promoter wanted to buy advertising and the ad agency insisted that before placing adverts he should run one of their market research questionnaires in order to best place the commercials with the right target group. I ended up just writing jokes like, 'How do you feel the comedians were presented? Answer where 1 is equal to "They were so smart you could have cut bacon on the creases in their trousers" and where 5 is equal to "They were minging. They were a total bunch of Harold Ramps."' It was funny, but there was no logic in why the questions were funny – that part was missing.

Faced with having to produce an extra seven minutes of material, I was instantly drawn back to this market research idea. I read through my original notes and tried to think of an additional angle. For some reason, unknown to me to this day, I came up with the idea of the survey having been written by charvas. It struck me straight away as being a very funny idea, but there was no explanation of why charvas would ask market research questions. I came up with the idea of a development grant of some kind having been exploited by charvas in order to get money for tack, large plastic bottles of cider, sportswear and so on. But this would have been too complex.

I started writing the questions. I knew that I could write funny questions in the style of charvas, and that was how the piece would work. All I was looking for was something that tied it all up, leaving a regular market research worker asking the outrageous questions. My Eureka moment was so simple – a market research company has been asked by the council to find what's important to the kids who hang around on street corners in order to find them a useful place in society. Their decision has been to allow the kids themselves to pose the questions. The kids have then simply given a load of cheek back, which the researchers have written down verbatim. It sounds like a complicated premise, but the beauty would lie in a mission statement, explaining all of the above in politically correct language. I would read the statement as a contractual obligation at the beginning of the questionnaire.

All I needed now was a new character to deliver the questions to the crowd. I knew that a market research dogsbody was needed, and it had to be somebody uninteresting, not at all clever and somewhat disinterested in what he was doing. I tried going through some voices to see if anything created a character in my mind. I was frankly pretty desperate as the clock was ticking down. I tried doing a voice that I'd used many times just to get laughs out of my friends. It was meant to be a gay hairdresser, an understated camp Geordie, who most importantly was quite particular and careful about delivering his words. I tried reading some of the mission statement and questions in the voice and it worked. I think what rubberstamped my decision to go ahead with it was I could get into the voice, and stay in it, compared to something I'd have to create on the spot. I practised a bit, trying to tone down the campness, but stick with the slightly effeminate, careful pronunciation. This was really the key to the development of the character, which wasn't to begin until after I'd established that the piece worked.

298

So I had my character, I had my routine, but I didn't have a name. I remembered meeting a woman in the bar after a TV shoot who'd asked what I did for a living. When I told her that I worked as a stand-up comedian she told me that she'd never heard of me and then asked me to tell her some jokes. I told her I didn't do jokes as such and gave her a couple of short samples of my routines instead. She was utterly unimpressed. Being rather obviously drunk, she then asked me what my name was again. I was getting rather tired of this, knowing that she was probably never going to understand my humour, and certainly not in this situation.

'Jimmy Shit,' I replied.

She laughed hysterically for quite some time. That tickled me and I always remembered it. I like the idea of a character having a funny name and Jimmy Shit seemed sufficiently stupid that it would work. However, I decided that Jimmy sounded too cool a name for my market researcher.

I love using British men's names in comedy. They can add such a lovely dimension. To work its magic in comedy a British name has simply not to fit a cowboy or a rock star or a Holly-wood actor, or anyone remotely dynamic – it has to be just a British bloke's name, like Colin. Brian in *The Life of Brian* is a great example of an unheroic name being asked to write cheques it cannot cash. *Monty Python* always got great mileage out of names.

Putting my great British name theory into practice, Jimmy became Barry and Shit was given the suffix 'house'. Barry Shithouse was born, to be renamed Barry Twyford a few months later after my agent pointed out that it may make promoting shows difficult on radio, television etc. I only agreed to make the change when I realised I could get an additional joke out of it, inventing the story that Barry's parents both had names of lavatory manufacturers, Twyford and Armitage, and that conse-quently his nickname at school was Barry Shithouse. This added another layer of depth to the character's back story.

The time from the moment I realised I was seven minutes short for my fifteen-minute open spot to the moment I set off to the gig was just over two hours. The seven minutes of material I wrote in those two short hours form the backbone of my act to this day, and represent probably my greatest moment of creation since Sid the Sexist.

Since I've taken to stand-up I've never felt that anything I've done in my life before has been so challenging, so rewarding, and, strangely enough, so easy. It just seems that this is what I was meant to do.

Making people laugh seems to be what I'm good at. It's always been that way. Laughter seems to be the thing that feeds my ego and my imagination. Once I start making the laughs happen in a room, I want more. If the laughs don't come, I feel very disappointed, so I push on, I know I have to work – I have to work on my delivery, I have to work on my writing, and that keeps me hungry, keeps me hungry to do more work. The more rewarding the work is, the more I enjoy it, and the more of it I want to do. If it still doesn't work, that just doubles my effort to succeed.

Stand-up is, without a doubt, the first thing that I have been able to devote myself to in a way that absolutely suits my personality. It suits the way I live, the way I seem to be naturally. I've always been a night person; I'm never any good in the mornings. I always work best after dark. The comedy life really suits me. I love the travelling. I love being somewhere different, seeing different people, working with different people, different crowds, in different towns, different neighbourhoods.

I never really enjoyed working in an office. For me, the most uninspiring part of my career was sitting down with the rest of the *Viz* team to write stuff. For some reason, that just didn't ever make me happy. I didn't like the restriction of being stuck in a room. With stand-up comedy, finding an idea never seems to be as much of a challenge as it always was with the cartoons. There are just so many more hoops to jump through when you're working on a cartoon – you come up with an idea, you suggest it to the other people you're working with, and then, if it passes that occasionally torturous test, you have to have faith that the reader will also find the idea funny. Not only do you have to have faith in your reader, but you must also do a sufficiently good job of translating it from the idea in your head, to the spoken word in the office, to the written words of the script, to the drawn images and written words on the printed page, and through all this hope that somehow the reader sees the same picture as the one you initially had in your head.

In simple terms, with stand-up you just write a joke and then tell it.

After Steve's death I was free to go on the road and try my act out at clubs all around the UK. Now I was establishing myself as character comedian. I met a couple of promoters from the north east, John Smith and Dan Willis. They were setting up some comedy nights in Newcastle and the surrounding area and they gave me free reign to do a different character at each of their shows over a period of five months. This was fantastic for my reputation in my hometown and also through John I met a comic called Maff Brown, who, as well as doing his own comedy, promoted clubs in the south. Maff was looking to share an hour at the Edinburgh Fringe, a last-minute arrangement, and asked if I'd come on board. I was delighted to oblige and we hastily set up a show in which Maff would behave as if he was the compère and I was a number of different acts. It wasn't particularly well planned, but for both of us it was great groundwork, as we planned to do one-man shows in the following year, 2010. I managed to arrange sharing a flat with Gavin Webster, and my first full Edinburgh run was set up.

Once at the Fringe gig offers came in thick and fast from showcase venues, where acts perform a bit of their show in order to attract in punters. Edinburgh 2009 also saw me as a semi-finalist in So You Think You're Funny?, a competition I'd been talked into entering by John Smith and had accidentally suc-ceeded at. This was it – life as a stand-up comic. All was going according to plan.

The day of the So You Think You're Funny? gig I got a call from Chris saying that Dad had taken ill at his care home and had been taken into hospital with pneumonia. I told him I'd get down as soon as possible, but maybe not until the next day, due to the big competition that night. I went off to do a showcase and when I came out of it I had a text message. The doctors were saying Dad had taken a turn for the worse and I should make haste if I wanted to see him. I went straight to the railway station and found there wasn't a train to Newcastle for more than an hour. As

301

I sat on the platform alone, I received a text. Dad had died as I waited for the train.

I blame myself for not going straight away when I got the first call, but who isn't wise with hindsight? I rang fellow comic Ava Vidal, who was nearby and came straight to comfort me as I sat on a station bench, making a little puddle of tears at my feet. I didn't know what to do with myself. I realised I had no reason to go home. I was too late. My brother had his family with him, so I thought I might as well stay and do my show, and that's exactly what I did.

Unfortunately, despite the organisers being aware of my circumstances, they sent me on first – always the most difficult spot in a night of many acts. Fred MacAulay was compère and had a nightmare with the crowd, who were all being cooked in a stifling room. I went on, did my seven minutes, got my laughs and that was that. I didn't win, I knew I wouldn't: no one under thirty ever wins these things. I'm glad I did it, though, as it gives me confidence. If I could face that gig, what gig can't I face?

Dad's death was very sad, but having seen Mum's and then Steve's passings I couldn't help but see it in a more positive light. Dad was eighty-two, much older, I'm sure, than the life expectancy in the slums of Shieldfield where he was born in the 1920s. He'd realised his life's ambition to live in the affluent neighbourhood where he'd delivered milk as a boy, and he'd brought three very creative and independent boys into the world through a loving relationship. As one of the leading authorities on the history of Newcastle, he'd become a published author, and his photographic collection is treasured by the City Library. He had a good life.

I'd called in to see him on my way to Edinburgh, only for a few minutes, but it was one of the most important visits I've ever made. I miss him very much.

London calling

Shortly before going to the Fringe in 2009 I sold my house in Newcastle, having made the decision to move to London. Lots of my friends struggled with the idea of me selling a house into which I'd put eighteen years of my life. For me it was less of a

302

problem, as the house had never worked out for me like it was supposed to. In my mind I'd seen myself living with Anne and her children, but that was never to happen.

I lived with Julie there for a while, but that wasn't a good experience – she wasn't really happy in her life. She'd not been happy since taking up her first post as a junior doctor. She wasn't ever able to talk to me about any of her problems, instead taking to 'retail therapy', filling every single room in the house with purchases, most of which she never touched after the day she bought them. It became such a serious problem that I told her I could take no more. She couldn't change her ways, and with regret I told her I no longer wanted to live with her. That was a very sad episode and a few months later, neither of us having found anyone else, I went back to her. We didn't live together again, but off and on we continued to see each other. Our relationship had been crumbling for years on end, but the challenge of Steve's illness really brought an unpleasant end to it. My troubles with Julie are something I've avoided writing about. I guess I don't want to drag her through it all in public. It's a shame in a way, as it's resulted in me not really writing about the good times either. Communication was always a problem for us and I suppose that's why we could never sort things out. No talking means no compromise and no compromise means no solution. It's a very sad story, as we were once so happy together.

I had many reasons for the London move, not least the fact I'd wanted to live there since I was seventeen. I also wanted to escape from what had happened with Steve, and indeed with Julie.

Moving to London is doubtless the most exciting thing I've done in my life. Having spent forty-five years rooted to Newcastle, I felt like an eighteen year old who was just starting college. Not that I know what that feels like. I think it's a pretty decent guess, though.

I see many places where I spent time with Steve. I remember how happy and successful he was here. He had an amazing career long before *Viz* ever earned a living for his younger brothers. He had a car and a credit card at a time when my bank wouldn't even give me a cheque guarantee card. The first time I ever saw a credit card used was in a restaurant in Hampstead.

303

Steve took it out and the waitress brought a mechanical device to the table that made the customer a carbon copy of the transaction paperwork. I had never witnessed such a thing. It was amazing.

I remember him telling me at the time that he was earning £50 a day, a sum, he informed me, that was his basic pay, but the film he was working on, probably *Little Shop of Horrors* or possibly *Labyrinth*, was running so far over time that his basic eight-hour day was usually increased, often to as much as sixteen hours, and all the extra hours paid double time. So that meant he was earning as much as £150 a day. This was at a time when I was earning £40 a week from Enterprise Allowance with a few extra quid coming in from freelance cartoons and much less from *Viz*, so I would guess in a good week I can't have been making more than £60 or £70. Not only was Steve earning a prince's ransom, but he had an amazing job too, working for Jim Henson. I remember going down to see him one time and we went and ate a café in Hampstead. It was sunny and it was the first time I'd ever eaten outdoors at a café. It was an adventure. It was a beautiful neighbourhood and was somehow tranquil, despite being busy. Connie Booth arrived and sat at a table next to us. As she was behind me, Steve discreetly pointed her out, advising me not to turn and stare.

That's a great memory for me, my brother enjoying the high life in London, and I've always associated London with good times, success and sunshine, everything being a bit different, more cosmopolitan. London is still my favourite place outside of Newcastle. I'm very much a man of the place I come from, but I'm not happy with the predictable stereotyping of Geordies. However, I don't mind the fact people see us as being unusual. As my friend John Smith says in his stand-up act, 'As soon as people hear the accent they assume you're drunk, aggressive, involved in domestic violence ... sexist ... racist ... homophobic ... but friendly.' The fun of that joke being that the friendliness overrides all the other traits, no matter how awful they are. I do like where I come from, and where I come from seems to like me too. People in Newcastle tell me I've never changed and that I should be proud of that. I watched the service for Sir Bobby Robson at Durham Cathedral, and from what people said about their respect for Bobby, keeping your feet on the ground certainly seems to be a trait that people appreciate.

I was recently told by a drunken man at a party, 'Simon, ye knaa what I like about ye? ... Ye never forget where you're from.'

I said, 'Jesmond.'

He said, 'Naah. Heaton.'

10

A New Chapter, And Not A Good One

A totally unexpected turn of events unfolded in the run-up to Christmas of 2009 that left me unable to write anything, or even think about writing anything, for over a month. I seem to be unintentionally beating around the bush here: I'm not even sure myself how much of this is an attempt to create dramatic effect and how much is to avoid writing down the facts.

On Friday 27 November 2009, completely out of the blue, I was diagnosed with multiple sclerosis.

I was approached earlier in the year by a TV production company who proposed the making of a TV film about stem cell research into the condition. They had been pointed in my direction by the MS Society, who apparently have me on their books as a 'celebrity' with a connection to MS. Multiple sclerosis was, of course, the illness with which Mum suffered, and I have over the years been involved in a number of fundraising projects for them, not least of all the sale of many pieces of my original *Viz* artwork.

The TV crew had received funding from the Wellcome Trust to produce a film documenting the current situation in research and treatment for MS sufferers. They wanted to create a film that was adventurous and fun as well as interesting and factual. They had first approached Colin Pillinger, the real-life nutty professor behind the Beagle 2 mission, in which a bunch of eccentric British dads in a shed managed to successfully send a rocket to Mars. OK, if you know the story, it didn't do what it was supposed to do when it got there, but after all, heroic failure is the speciality of the great British eccentric.

Colin had agreed to work on the show, having himself been diagnosed with MS five years earlier. The plan was to have Colin and me as its co-presenters, travelling around and investigating everything happening in the world of MS research and treatment. The team were keen that we should use animation to liven up the show, not only giving it a fun and edgy look and feel, but also allowing us to go on adventures in the world of science that reality wouldn't allow. We would be able to look into Colin's work by visiting Mars together, and then journey around Colin's nervous system in order to see exactly what multiple sclerosis is and why it was giving him his symptoms. We could also use this method to investigate potential treatments and look at the possible improvements the future might hold for sufferers.

Shortly after we began filming it became apparent that Colin wasn't able to commit as much time to the project as I could, so I became the main presenter with Colin becoming effectively a special guest.

Soon after work began I was asked if I was prepared to go through the neurological tests given to people suspected of suffering from the condition, and also if I would undergo an MRI scan of my brain. The idea of this was to show viewers how specialists look for and diagnose MS. I had to sign a disclaimer saying that I understood that the neurologist might actually diagnose a neurological condition as a result of these tests. The disclaimer was, of course, routine procedure, and although no part of me truly believes that anyone involved knew or even suspected I was a sufferer, my mind seems to naturally develop every possible conspiracy scenario, which I then have to eradicate by means of common sense.

I look back now to the time when I was approached to become involved in the show and I remember the subject of the tests being mentioned. I knew that this was the chance to put my mind at rest about things that had been troubling me for some time. For the previous few months I had been suffering from pins and needles in my fingers, and occasionally in my toes. This wasn't anything new – after a nasty fall at Goodison Park when I was playing in the Music Industry Soccer Sixes I had felt this effect very strongly every time I moved my chin towards my chest.

This lasted for six months or maybe even a year, the feeling becoming less and less strong as time moved on. I never considered it necessary to visit a doctor, as those that I knew, including Julie, seemed unconcerned, all thinking a nerve had been trapped or damaged by the fall. As the problem faded with time I was happy that their thoughts seemed to make perfect sense.

So it turns out I've had MS at least since I was as young as twenty-one and probably even younger. I've been through many more tests now, and it appears that I have signs of the condition both in my brain and my spinal cord.

It's not the best news I've ever received, but on the up side I don't have any symptoms beyond the occasional pins and needles episode. I do have some other symptoms that may or may not be caused by the MS – occasional days of inexplicable fatigue, pains in my feet and stiff muscles, especially in my shoulders and down the right side of my spine. These are all things I've suffered with for years, but have always been explained by over work or poor posture.

In a way I'm very lucky that through the documentary I ended up being diagnosed by the country's top specialists. My consultant has classified the condition as benign, so I'm pretty much in the lowest category of MS sufferer. I just have to keep my fingers crossed that things stay that way.

I'd planned to finish this book on a high note about my rising career as a comedian, but I was accidentally diagnosed with an incurable neurological condition and that somewhat pissed in the pint of my cheerful book conclusion.

The truth is, however, my career in stand-up is going better than I had planned and, most importantly, I'm loving every minute of it. My attitude to the MS has been very pragmatic: I see that in reality there is only here and now, and here and now I feel fine and I'm happy, so I'm ok with it. I suppose that having seen what Mum, Steve and Dad went through I'm not counting my blessings.

And Finally ... Jesus. Did This Really Happen?

Most people's dreams of meeting their idols are never realised. I consider myself extremely lucky to have met so many of my boyhood heroes. My work on *Viz* has brought me, through many different avenues, into contact with some of the people I looked up to as a child. My meetings with all of these people have been, without exception, very positive. I'm aware that often meetings with one's heroes can be a terrible disappointment, so in that respect I'm doubly lucky.

I've decided to finish with a chapter made up of some of my happiest memories of meeting some of the legends who shaped my world.

I was a guest at SuperMac's birthday party

I was lucky enough to have SuperMac, Malcolm MacDonald, my childhood football hero, appear as a team member on *The Regionnaires*. Having truly ridden the highs and lows of fame and fortune, Malcolm, a Londoner, had returned to Tyneside, a place where he is still regarded as an absolute legend. From difficult times struggling with alcohol he had pulled himself up by his bootstraps and become a well-respected radio presenter.

Malcolm and his wife Carol have since become friends to both me and Chris and Dolores and we were all honoured to be guests at his sixtieth birthday party. I was invited by the master of ceremonies to make a speech. I stood and told Malcolm and his guests the story of the divot from his boot that I carried as a boy.

(In around 1974 I went to see a game at St James' with Dad and Chris. I positioned myself right at the front of the terrace, where the ground was even lower than the pitch. SuperMac was involved in a challenge right in front of me and a divot with his stud holes through it landed on the track. Excitedly, I grabbed it and put it in my pocket. I took it home and Steve gave me a plastic Petrie dish to keep it in. I wrote the words 'SuperMac's divot' and the date on it and stuck the lid down with Sellotape. I took it to every game until the end of the season, then put it in my wardrobe during the summer. When I went to take it out, the divot had turned to dust. Bitterly disappointed, I threw it away.)

It was wonderful to see him laughing so heartily. I'm very proud to call SuperMac a friend.

I drank with The Clash and The Sex Pistols

I was in The Groucho Club in 2002 or so, presumably on some publicity-based visit or other. I was drinking in the bar and after a while I headed for the toilet. As I reached out to open the door, someone opened it from the other side. I immediately recognised the face that appeared as being Mick Jones from The Clash. I thought to myself, 'Shit. This is Mick Jones from The Clash.'

Before I could even open my mouth to speak, he pointed at me and said, 'Paul Whicker the Tall Vicar!'

I was stunned. Mick Jones knew who I was. He knew I was from *Viz* and he was clearly a fan. I was a bit too taken aback to say much, but I did manage, 'Mick Jones out of the Clash!'

Considering I was gobsmacked, it wasn't a bad thing to blurt in the circumstances.

Shortly afterwards I spotted Paul Simonon, also of The Clash, drinking in another room. I couldn't resist the temptation and I approached him.

'Hello, Paul? Nice to meet you. I'm a big fan, mate. Sorry, I don't normally approach people like this, but I just bumped into Mick Jones and the chance of talking to two of my heroes in one night was too much to miss.'

He smiled at me. 'You're the guy from *Viz*, aren't you?'

'Jesus. Yes, Simon. You know who I am too? So did Mick. Listen, let me get out of your hair, I just wanted to thank you for all the music that I've loved for so long. It was the soundtrack of my youth.'

He smiled again. 'Yeah. Mine too.'

If you could bottle a moment like that you'd be the richest person alive. He went on to thank me for *Viz* and we had a lovely conversation about what we were up to.

One amazing coincidence: two very genuine blokes.

I was lucky enough to meet Glen Matlock and Paul Cook from The Sex Pistols at The Rhythm Factory in the east end of London. The Stuntmen were on the same bill as Glen's outfit The Philistines. I said hello to Cooky and shook his hand, and he wasn't too polite, but is that what you want from The Pistols? Glen, on the other hand, was lovely – a bright and engaging man who complimented me on my clothes and informed me that my jacket was made of Bedford Cord. I've met him again a couple of times and he was an absolute gent. By the way, if you're the kind of person from the punk generation who thinks Matlock is a bit of a joke, just remember he wrote 'Pretty Vacant'. Talented *and* a gent.

Lemmy gave me the finger

In 1981 I saw Motorhead at Newcastle City Hall, when their popularity on the punk scene had been boosted by their association with The Damned. It was common practice in the early years of *Viz* for us to hand comics to any touring bands we went to see, so after the show I waited with the autograph hunters to go backstage and hand over some copies. To my enormous surprise, when I gave one to Lemmy he said, 'Thanks. Yeah I know this comic, I like it. I like the vicar best, Paul Whicker is it?'

Many years later, around 2003 or so, Angie was visiting Newcastle and she told me she was going out for a drink with Lemmy, who was playing in town that night. Alex and I went along and met Angie and the Lemster in the bar of the Vermont Hotel. After some polite conversation, Lemmy, still a *Viz* fan, turned to Alex and me and asked, 'Do you boys like to gamble?'

The obvious answer, which occurred to both of us at the time, although neither of us was brave enough to say it, was 'Gambling's for fools, but that's the way I like it baby, I don't wanna to live forever.'

What we actually both mumbled was 'Naah ... not really.'

Lemmy then declared that he wanted to go and 'look at chicks' – he wanted to go to a strip club. We had to phone a friend to find out where there was one. Until very recently there hadn't been any Newcastle, hence the old adage 'You can't sell it in a city where you can get it for nowt.'

We walked up Dean Street to drop him off at Blue Velvet and as we walked a drunken group of stag-nighters passed in the opposite direction. One did a giant double-take and declared excitedly to his friend, 'Hey! It's Lemmy!'

His friend, even more drunk than him, replied, 'Lemmy who?'

I later bumped into Lemmy again in a club in London. He invited me to join him for a drink and I told him I'd recently read an interview with him. I told him that it read very well for three reasons. He's had a very interesting life, from his beginnings in a beat group who came very close to massive success, and then his progress through Hawkwind and the bizarre happenings along the way. This was all fascinating. Then, as he's an eloquent man, he tells his stories well without overblowing them. Finally, he doesn't pretend to be anything he's not. Honesty in that respect is a fantastic quality in any performer: you can't be found out or exposed if you're honest.

Lemmy sat back and contemplated my observations for a moment. He then held out his right hand, offering me his crooked little finger. We had a little finger shake. I was being shown the highest respect by one of the world's most infamous dirty rock 'n' rollers. Nice.

I sang on the same bill as Joe Cocker

In 1987, as part of Tyne Tees TV's celebrations of the success of *The Roxy*, its short-lived successor to *The Tube*, I was offered the chance to sing the legendary Tyneside piss-up song The Geordie Rap on stage at Newcastle's Jewish Mother club in front of, amongst others, the performers from the show. Joe Cocker was on that night and remarkably he agreed to perform 'With a Little Help From My Friends' at the same aftershow party.

Unfortunately, through a combination of nerves and drink, I managed to forget a couple of lines in the song, but it went down pretty well. I was then introduced to Ben Elton, who I annoyed by repeatedly butting with the peak of my cap as I tried to shout in his ear.

I didn't get a chance to talk to Joe Cocker, but performing on the same bill as him is something of a feather in the cap of my swollen ego.

I was later told, by a reliable source, that Cocker had been persuaded to sing the song by less-than-honourable means and was very angry about it, which has taken the gloss off the memory for me slightly.

Van Morrison was nice to me

For many years I'd been a huge fan of Van Morrison and when I met Anne it turned out this was something we had in common. We began to go and see him play wherever we could. In the mid 1990s we took a trip to watch him in Birmingham and as we returned to our hotel we noticed the man himself sitting in a car outside. Ann was tempted to ask him for his autograph. I warned her that his reputation as a temperamental man preceded him, but I told her she should take her opportunity and not get too upset if it were to backfire. She approached the car and he wound down his window. She asked if he'd sign her ticket and he very politely obliged. As we walked away, Ann said to me, 'Ooh. Do you think I should have got a photo with him?'

I said, 'Well, you've already taken your risk and you've come away on top. Why not quit while you're ahead?'

She began to dilly and dally. I said, 'Listen, he can see you flapping from where he's sitting. Make a decision. Standing here in a quandary will only make matters worse for you both.'

She made her decision and I flinched as she tapped on his car window. The next thing I knew he was climbing out of the car and standing next to her, happily posing for the shot. I took the photo and he politely wished us a good night. Neither of us could believe how nice he'd been.

313

We returned to our room and then decided on a nightcap. We went down to the bar and to our surprise there was Van and his band and crew all sitting there. We opted to be polite and took seats in a corner away from them. We had a quiet drink or two and then headed for the door. As we did so, Van got up from his seat and hurriedly caught us up. He shook us both by the hand, saying, 'Goodnight, now. Safe home. Goodnight.'

Like with Paul Weller, I now wonder how much truth there is in what you read about the man. If it's true that he is fractious at times, I was lucky enough to get him on a day when he couldn't have been kinder. Now I even forgive him the duet with Cliff.

I played for Newcastle United

My old friend Andy Storey, at whose house I used to see *Watch with Mother* and who'd got us all chased out of Mark Toney's by a chef with meat cleaver for saying 'Waaaaaah!', now works in TV. In 2007 he was working on a live show for Sky TV in which Premier League clubs entered teams in a tournament at the David Beckham Academy in London, each team comprising of ex-pros, celebrities and fans. Andy asked if I'd be interested in being one of the celebrity Newcastle United players. He didn't have to wait for an answer.

It was great fun, each team raising money for local charities. Ours was St Oswald's Hospice. Little did I know at the time that just over a year later Steve would be a patient there.

Our team was made up of ex-Newcastle stars Kevin Carr, Warren Barton, John Beresford and Rob Lee. The celebs were me, Anthony Hutton and Jonathan Edwards. The fans were called Dean Russo, Rob Hedley and Dougie Grant.

Hutton was a very good player, as was Dougie Grant, who'd been an amateur player all his adult life. He was a striker for Shildon Town in County Durham and had scored for them in a cup tie on *Match of the Day* in 1988. Jonathan Edwards was kack.

We were favourites for the tournament and our first game was against Middlesbrough. It was to be a north-east derby played out in London. It was a very tight game and we battled back from being behind to draw 3–3. Our goal scorers, remarkably, were Hutton and Grant, Dougie getting two.

The tie went to penalty kicks and, true to form, we lost, Warren Barton skying his kick and seeing us out at the first time of asking. Boro went on to win the trophy and we were left to wonder what could have been.

It was a day out I'll never forget. The players were great to us, especially Kevin Carr, who was very supportive and gave me some great defensive coaching. I made good friends with Dougie Grant and he invited me to play in his testimonial at Shildon, which we won.

I really can't believe the opportunities I've had in football. It's been very good to me, especially considering I'm at best an average player.

Paul Weller bought me a pint

Having already met Paul and become quite friendly with him, I was delighted to be involved in organising a very special event on Tyneside in which he and many other great names made appearances. Through her music industry connections, Angie had been working for some time with the Teenage Cancer Trust, a charity founded to build special units at NHS hospitals to give teenage cancer sufferers a chance to have an environment of their own. The idea is to keep teenagers out of children's wards, in which they can be looked after alongside children as young as newborns, and also to keep them out of general wards for cancer treatment, in which they can be treated alongside the very elderly. Figures show teenagers have better recovery rates in wards designed for their needs. Roger Daltrey is the patron of the charity and Angie has helped him to organise the TCT's annual Royal Albert Hall shows for many years. In 2005, I was invited to join a committee made up of some of the real greats of the north east, including the brilliant and hilarious filmmaker Geoff Wonfor, who has awards dropping out of his knicker drawer, and Ray Laidlaw, drummer with folk rock legends Lindisfarne and now also a filmmaker. The purpose of the committee was to put on a show on Tyneside to raise funds for a new TCT unit at the proposed Great North Hospital.

Over the following year we put a show together combining the best of the UK's live music and stand-up comedy at The Sage in

Gateshead. The event also saw The Sage's second venue host a night of music by local talent.

To celebrate to combination of bands and stand-up, the event was named BandStand and the line up was stunning: Paul Weller, Ross Noble, Jools Holland, Johnny Vegas, Stewart Lee and Ava Vidal, with a backing band made up of some of the best musicians the north east's ever produced. To top it all I was offered the chance to compère the event, which I accepted at hand-biting speed. It was a stunning night, really something special.

Many great things happened at BandStand. Geoff filmed it all for a DVD and with two days to go he decided to replace all his professional cameramen with teenage patients from the Newcastle TCT ward. The teenagers were involved left right and centre and one of them, Melissa Cavanagh, stole the show. She sang a version of the ballad 'Strong Enough' that brought the audience to their feet.

I was delighted to introduce Weller on to the stage, which really was quite an honour for me. I'd collected him and Steve Cradock and their partners from the Central Station that day, and en route to the venue Paul asked me for a tour of any *Get Carter* locations, and I duly obliged. It was surreal. The highlight of the whole event for me, though, was at the after-show party. I stood next to Paul at the bar, waiting to be served.

Paul turned to me and said, 'Can I buy you a pint, Simon?'

I said, 'Have you not got a pink star on your pass? You should get free drinks if you've got one of them.'

Quite calmly and in a matter-of-fact way he explained, 'I want to buy you a pint.'

It was such a simple gesture, but it meant the world to me.

I can't mention BandStand or TCT without sparing a thought for those who were involved that day who are no longer with us. My thoughts are with their families and friends.

I made Roger Daltrey a cup of tea

Angie was married last year and amongst the guests were legends 'whispering' Bob Harris and 'screamy' Roger Daltrey. The reception took place in a wonderful castle belonging to a frightfully eccentric friend of hers. It was a fabulous affair and I acted as master of ceremonies for the speeches. I made a few cheeky jokes and introduced all the speakers, after which the dancing began and Roger got up on stage with the band and performed 'Substitute'. Not the sort of turn you get at your average wedding.

After his performance, I bumped into Roger in the kitchen. He was looking for a cup of tea. I made him one. He had it black, not too strong.

That's right. I made Roger Daltrey a cup of tea. Me. I did it. It really happened.

I scored a goal for Pelé

During Catboy's time as the breakfast show DJ at Metro Radio he was involved in something of a scoop for the station, which he was generous enough to involve me in. Pelé was visiting Newcastle to publicise an exhibition of photographs of him at the city's Hutton Gallery. On the morning of the event Catboy interviewed the great man in the penthouse of 55 Degrees North, the luxury apartment block which had, twenty-five years earlier, been the Department of Employment offices at which me, Chris, Steve and Dad had all signed on.

Catboy hatched a brilliant plan to get me introduced to Pelé. During the interview he would have his photo taken with him, and he'd then email me the photo, which I would then interpret as a cartoon. That night, when Pelé turned up at the exhibition, I'd be there to present the artwork to him. It was brilliant.

The plan was absolutely perfect. I'm no caricaturist, but this was as much about the gesture and presenting him with a specially made gift as it was about how much it would look like him.

I worked on the drawing for several hours before setting off for the gallery. The room was rammed with people, but before long I managed to find Catboy, who straight away took me over to a particularly thronged corner. We waited patiently and

317

eventually he managed to step up to the great man, who was somewhat smaller than I'd imagined, and introduced me. Pelé smiled warmly. Catboy explained that I was cartoonist, at which point I produced the artwork and showed it to him. I explained it was a gift and he smiled even more broadly. He thanked me very much and we all posed for a photograph together.

My experience with meeting so many of my heroes had taught me that sometimes it's best not to hang around too long and allow the conversation to dry up. Often the best thing is to get in, have your moment and leave on a high. With this in mind, I decided to let Pelé get on with meeting the masses of people who were clearly waiting to be introduced. I said, 'It's been a pleasure to meet you. I'll leave you to get on with your exhibition.'

As an afterthought, on realising where I was going, I declared, 'I'm off to play football.'

I saw Pelé's face light up immediately. He'd spotted an opportunity to give me something back. Like that famous photo from 1970 with Bobby Moore, he put his hand around the back of my head and looked me directly in the eyes. He spoke slowly and clearly. 'Score one for me.'

His smile turned to a laugh, his eyes filled with boyish fun. My knees trembled. I couldn't believe it.

It must be so easy for him to give people moments like that, but I could see in his eyes he wasn't just going through the motions – it was something he clearly loved doing.

As I was leaving Sir Bobby Robson arrived and decided to make an impromptu speech, welcoming Pelé to Newcastle. In the crowded gallery he decided on the spur of the moment to stand on a chair in order to be seen and heard. I ended up holding the chair for him as climbed on to it. His speech heaped praise on Pelé for his achievements and highlighted just what a legend he is, not just in football, but as one of the most famous people who has ever lived.

I walked out of that building with my head in the clouds. In one night I'd met two of the most talented and gentlest men the football world has ever seen.

It was a Tuesday night and I was going to play my regular six-a-side game at North Shields. When I arrived at the pitch I was still buzzing. I made the foolish mistake of immediately announcing to everyone that Pelé had told me to score one for him. It put so much pressure on me it was ridiculous. I was at sixes and sevens for the first twenty minutes or so of the game.

The goalkeeper of the opposing team was Andy Inman, who coincidentally had also been at the exhibition. He'd bought a photo and also met Pelé.

It took me nearly the whole game, but I did score one – a toe-poke under the keeper at the near post. I lay on my back and looked up at the sky, trying to take in what had happened. As I lay there I heard Andy's voice.

'We're never going to hear the fucking end of this.'

My sincere thanks to my boyhood heroes SuperMac and Michael Palin, to comedy gods Stewart Lee, Ross Noble, Charlie Higson, Vic Reeves, all-round good eggs Huw and Sandra Evans, Alex Collier, Jurate Geciate, Tamatha Weisser, Angie Jenkison, Andrew Barnden, Phil Dangermouse, Paul Smith, Pat Evans, Ava Vidal, Sally Gill, my whole family and all my friends for their help and support. To anyone I've forgotten, I apologise unreservedly. Special thanks to Paul Weller for his quote about James Whale being a fat fuck.